Lix 4
1891

THE ALPINE CLUB GUIDE-BOOKS AND MAPS.

THE ALPINE GUIDE.
By JOHN BALL, M.R.I.A.

Post 8vo. with Maps and other Illustrations :—
THE EASTERN ALPS, 10s. 6d.
CENTRAL ALPS, including all the Oberland District, 7s. 6d.
WESTERN ALPS, including Mont Blanc, Monte Rosa, Zermatt, &c. 6s. 6d.

THE ALPINE CLUB MAP
OF
SWITZERLAND AND ADJACENT COUNTRIES

Engraved on the Scale of 4 Miles to the Inch.

Constructed under the superintendence of the ALPINE CLUB, and Edited by
R. C. NICHOLS, F.S.A.

Complete in Four Sheets Coloured, in Portfolio, price 42s. or mounted in a Case, 52s. 6d.
Each Sheet may be had separately, price 12s. or mounted in a Case, 15s.
The MAP may also be had Uncoloured, complete in Portfolio, price 34s.
(The Sheets are not sold separately Uncoloured.)

THE ENLARGED
ALPINE CLUB MAP
OF THE
SWISS AND ITALIAN ALPS,

On the Scale of Three English Statute Miles to One Inch.
In Eight Sheets, price Eighteenpence per Sheet.
Each Sheet sold separately.

SHEET 1—Includes the country lying between the Jura Mountains and the Lakes of Geneva and Neuchâtel.
 ,, 2—Has Interlachen in the centre, and extends to Brieg and Bern.
 ,, 3—Includes Andermatt and the St. Gothard Pass, Dissentis and the Lukmanier Pass, the Splügen Pass and Chiavenna.
 ,, 4—Includes Davos Platz, Pontresina and the Upper Engadine, the Stelvio and Ortler Spitze.
 ,, 5—Includes Geneva and Mont Blanc.
 ,, 6—Has Zermatt in the centre, and extends to Sion, Aosta, and the Simplon.
 ,, 7—Includes the Lakes of Maggio, Lugano, and Como.
 ,, 8—Includes Bergamo, the Lake of Iseo, Sondrio, and the Adamello.

The Complete Map, fully coloured, price £1 ; or, mounted to fold in case, £1. 10s.

London: LONGMANS, GREEN, & CO.

BOOKS OF TRAVEL AND ADVENTURE.

A VOYAGE IN THE 'SUNBEAM,' our Home on the Ocean for Eleven Months. By Lady BRASSEY. With Map and numerous Wood Engravings.

Library Edition, 8vo. 21s.	School Edition, fcp. 2s.
Cabinet Edition, crown 8vo. 7s. 6d.	Popular Edition, 4to. 6d.

SUNSHINE AND STORM IN THE EAST; or, Cruises to Cyprus and Constantinople. By Lady BRASSEY. With 2 Maps and 114 Illustrations engraved on Wood.

Library Edition, 8vo. 21s.	Cabinet Edition, crown 8vo. 7s. 6d.

IN THE TRADES, THE TROPICS, AND THE 'ROARING FORTIES'; or, Fourteen Thousand Miles in the *Sunbeam* in 1883. By Lady BRASSEY. With nearly 250 Illustrations engraved on Wood from drawings by R. T. PRITCHETT, and 8 Maps and Charts.

Édition de Luxe, 1 vol. imperial 8vo. price Three Guineas and a Half (*only 250 copies printed*).

Library Edition, 1 vol. 8vo. price One Guinea.

RANCH NOTES IN KANSAS, COLORADO, THE INDIAN TERRITORY, AND NORTHERN TEXAS. By REGINALD ALDRIDGE. Crown 8vo. with 4 Illustrations on Wood by G. PEARSON. Crown 8vo. 5s.

EIGHT YEARS IN CEYLON. By Sir SAMUEL W. BAKER, M.A. Crown 8vo. Woodcuts. 5s.

THE RIFLE AND THE HOUND IN CEYLON. By Sir SAMUEL W. BAKER, M.A. Crown 8vo. Woodcuts. 5s.

SOME IMPRESSIONS OF THE UNITED STATES. By E. A. FREEMAN, D.C.L. Crown 8vo. 6s.

SAN REMO, Climatically and Medically considered. By ARTHUR HILL HASSALL, M.D. With 30 Illustrations. Crown 8vo. 5s.

WINTERING IN THE RIVIERA. With Notes of Travel in Italy and France, and Practical Hints to Travellers. By W. MILLER. With 12 Illustrations. Post 8vo. 7s. 6d.

THREE IN NORWAY. By Two OF THEM. With a Map and 59 Illustrations on Wood from Sketches by the Authors. Crown 8vo. 6s.

ACROSS THE PAMPAS AND THE ANDES: being an Account of an Exploring and Surveying Expedition across the Continent of South America. By ROBERT CRAWFORD, M.A., Professor of Civil Engineering in the University of Dublin. With a Map and Illustrations. Crown 8vo. 7s. 6d.

London: LONGMANS, GREEN, & CO.

THE MARITIME ALPS

AND THEIR SEABOARD

LONDON : PRINTED BY
SPOTTISWOODE AND CO., NEW-STREET SQUARE
AND PARLIAMENT STREET

Frontispiece.

ST. MARTIN DE LANTOSQUE.
BY H.R.H. THE COMTE DE CASERTA.

Frontispiece.

ST. MARTIN DE LANTOSQUE.
BY H.I.H. THE COMTE DE CASERTA.

THE MARITIME ALPS

AND THEIR SEABOARD

BY THE

AUTHOR OF 'VERA' 'BLUE ROSES' &c.

WITH ILLUSTRATIONS

LONDON
LONGMANS, GREEN, AND CO.
1885

All rights reserved

DEDICATED

BY PERMISSION
TO
HER ROYAL HIGHNESS THE COMTESSE DE PARIS.

À SON ALTESSE ROYALE

MARIE-ISABELLE, COMTESSE DE PARIS.

Madame,

Vous avez daigné m'accorder la permission, tout en parcourant les champs et les plages de la Provence et en feuilletant mes livres, de penser à vous et aux enfants que vous conduisez chaque printemps jouir du soleil de ce pays enchanteur.

Je viens vous offrir ces quelques pages. Permettez-moi, en les déposant entre vos mains royales, de vous exprimer mes vœux qu'ici au moins ne s'épanouissent pour vous que les roses sans épines.

J'ai l'honneur, Madame, d'être, avec un très profond respect,

de votre Altesse Royale
la servante la plus dévouée,

L'AUTEUR.

Villa Rey, Cannes:
1884.

CONTENTS.

CHAPTER		PAGE
I.	INTRODUCTION	1
II.	FROM THE MOUNTAINS TO THE SEA	15
III.	THE PEOPLE	30
IV.	CORN, WINE, AND OIL	55
V.	ON THE FARMS	70
VI.	GRASSE	82
VII.	VENCE	101
VIII.	THE TRUTH ABOUT THE MAN IN THE IRON MASK	122
IX.	ST. HONORAT	142
X.	THE MONASTERY ON THE LÉRINS	158
XI.	NICE	178
XII.	THROUGH THE COUNTY OF NICE	195
XIII.	ST. PAUL-DU-VAR	203

CONTENTS.

CHAPTER		PAGE
XIV.	VILLENEUVE-LOUBET	222
XV.	JEANNE DE PROVENCE, QUEEN OF NAPLES	236
XVI.	THE TEMPLARS IN MARITIME PROVENCE	251
XVII.	OF SOME NOBLE FAMILIES	266
XVIII.	THE GRIMALDI OF MONACO	289
XIX.	TWO FRENCH ADMIRALS	302
XX.	CANNES AS IT WAS	317
XXI.	NAPOLEON AT CANNES	327
XXII.	OFF THE BEATEN TRACK	338
	1. LAGHET	338
	2. THE CASTLE OF BEAUREGARD	343
	3. A CELTO-LIGURIAN CAMP	351
	4. VILLA NEVADA	354
	5. NOTRE DAME DE GAROUBE	362
XXIII.	MENTONE	367
INDEX		381

ILLUSTRATIONS.

FULL-PAGE WOODCUTS.

ST. MARTIN-DE-LANTOSQUE	*Frontispiece*
(From a photograph by H.R.H. the Comte de Caserta)	
IN THE FOREST OF THE ESTERELS . . .	*To face p.* 26
(From a photograph by Frith of Reigate)	
THE FARM	,, 76
THE CROISETTE	,, 122
THE FORT AND PRISONS OF STE. MARGUÈRITE .	,, 124
(From a photograph by Frith of Reigate)	
IN THE CASTLE OF ST. HONORAT . . .	,, 162
THE GATE OF ST.-PAUL-DU-VAR . . .	,, 212
(From a photograph by W. Cotesworth)	
IN AN OLD HOUSE	,, 216
(From a photograph by W. Cotesworth)	
A STREET IN COGOLIN	,, 293
(By M. François Vincent)	
ST. CLAUDE DU CANNET	,, 322
(By Miss Helen Hawkins Dempster)	
SUNSET AT CANNES	,, 324
(By F. S. de Wessilow)	

ILLUSTRATIONS.

WEST CANNES	*To face p.*	332
(*By Mrs. John Surtees*)		
MEISSONIER AT ANTIBES	,,	365
(*By Meissonier*)		
LA ROQUEBRUNE	,,	371
(*By Signor Corelli*)		

WOODCUTS IN TEXT.

	PAGE
THE AMPHITHEATRE OF FRÉJUS	1
DRAWING THE NET	38
(*From a sketch done for this book by the late Hon. Henry Graves*)	
CABRIS, AND 'LOU CABRES'	96
(*From a sketch done for this book by the late Hon. Henry Graves*)	
GOURDON ON THE LOUP	111
(*By Miss Louisa Denison*)	
THE CLOISTERS OF ST. HONORAT	142
THE CASTLE ON ST. HONORAT	158
ROMAN BRIDGE OF CANNES	182
ST.-PAUL-DU-VAR	203
(*By the Author*)	
VILLENEUVE-LOUBET	222
ARABS AT WORK	234
MOUGINS	242
(*By Mrs. Norwich Duff*)	
THE CASTLE OF CALIAN	348
(*By Mr. James Harris, H.B.M. Consul at Nice*)	
VILLA NEVADA	354
(*By Admiral Sir Spencer Robinson, K.C.B.*)	
A VISTA AT MONTFLEURI	356
CORSICA FROM MENTONE	379
(*By E. B. Crawley Bovey*)	

RUINS OF FRÉJUS.

THE MARITIME ALPS.

CHAPTER I.

INTRODUCTION.

'When, however, I look over the hints and memorandums I have taken down for the purpose, my heart almost fails me at finding how my idle humour has led me aside from the great objects studied by every regular traveller who would make a book.'—WASHINGTON IRVING.

THE carriages on the Paris, Lyons, and Mediterranean Railway are generally crowded, and the one in which we recently found ourselves was no exception to this unpleasant rule. Many persons were already on their way to the Riviera, on different errands of business, health, or pleasure, and we were not fortunate in our company. Two French *entrepreneurs* talked incessantly, and ate with their clasp-knives frequently. They discussed with great animation the operations of the Société-Foncière-Lyonnaise in Nice and Cannes, and all along a coast where fabulous prices have recently been asked and given for land in the neighbourhood of the cities of the seaboard. Their conversation succeeded in interesting a speculator of the feminine gender, a cross, old, Russian lady, who, with her shabby companion, was bound for Monte Carlo. This quartett accordingly discussed gambling in all its branches, direct and indirect. In the further corner of the carriage there lolled an olive-faced man who had a ticket for Grasse. He smelt of garlic, though he 'travelled in pomatums'; but as he was silent, he did not add to the excitement of the disputants. Great was our relief when the train stopped at Carnoulles. There is a junction at that point for Aix, and the line of the Durance, and we took in a French gentleman and his daughter. We had a previous and very pleasant acquaintance with this person, whom I shall call the Comte de Thibaut, and were glad to find that he was on his way to Cannes for the winter. His son was on board the 'Colbert': one of the ironclads about to be sent to Golfe Jouan for the winter manœuvres, and his daughter was delighted as each station diminished the distance between herself and Roger. She had never seen the big ships yet, she said, but *cette coquine de marine* would no longer, she hoped, be able to rob her wholly of an only brother. M. de Thibaut said that he had only that morning left his château, where the vintage had been fine, and where vats of new wine were fermenting under the terrace. He spoke of his home with pleasure, and I knew that those lands had been held by the Thibauts for generations—in fact, since a daughter of the Chancellor of Navarre brought them with her as a dowry. In all France and Navarre there was therefore no nobler blood than that which flowed in the veins of Mademoiselle Estefanette. She was a pretty and lively girl, who might possibly in due time develop all the graces and all the worldliness of the modern *Parisienne*, but who in the meantime was simple, intelligent, and ready to be pleased. She had lived chiefly in Paris, but last year she had gone with her father to Baden, and she had even seen London. One of her friends—one of the best of her friends, she assured me, looking wise over her own discrimination—was married to the naval *attaché* there. But a visit to them had not satisfied Estefanette. What she most ardently wished to do was to travel in Scotland, 'that charming country which *Valter* Scott has made so interesting to us all.' I smiled, and after expressing myself flattered by her appreciation of his genius, I said to M. de Thibaut,—

'What a pity that no French author has done for France what Scott has certainly done for us at home!'

'There is nothing of very great note,' he replied, 'nothing that has made its mark out of France, but as regards southern France, you will find a good deal of local colour in the sketches of Dumas, in "Misé Brun," in the "Auberge des Adrets," and in "Numa Roumestan": they are also good as works of art. The same might be said of the "Cadet de Colobrières," and even of the "Tamaris" of George Sand. It describes that Provence *inédite* (if I may so term it) which lies between Toulon, Hyères, Pierrefeu, St. Tropèz, and the

Bay of Grimaud. I admit that it is not a tale which, like a novel of Scott's, could be put into every hand, while the little work of Elisée Reclus is too technically a guide-book to be appreciated except by persons who travel, and who in travelling prefer their itinerary to be written in French.'

'Most of the books you name are unknown to the English. France itself is really unknown to us. We forget its history, and consider the country flat, though it certainly contains more ruins and mountains than are required in a search after the picturesque. Furthermore I must add that Englishwomen are advised not to read French novels, and that they are convinced that there is no French poetry. The result of all this is that, of the thousands who yearly betake themselves to the Riviera, few know or care much about the country.'

'I must say,' cried Estefanette, 'that the history of Provence is very far away.'

'That depends on the point at which you begin,' replied her father: 'if by the past you mean Lord Brougham's visit to Cannes, or Prosper Mérimée's sketches there, or the death of the Grand-Duc Héritier at Nice, or the holiday of the Queen of England in a châlet at Mentone, it seems to me to be recent enough even for a big, little girl like you. Even the landing of Napoleon at Golfe Jouan is as a thing of yesterday to your elders.'

'Impossible: you are now laughing at me.'

'Not the least in the world. I have myself spoken with four persons who can remember every incident of it most distinctly, and of those four only one (the excellent mayor of Cannes, M. Reybaud) is now dead. I am sorry, *petite*, that you can never hear him describe, as I have done, the cross preoccupation of Napoleon as he sat by the bivouac fire.'

'At least, you will admit that Francis the First is a very old story.'

'Certainly; yet when you have seen Villeneuve-Loubet, where the King lived for three weeks, where he met the Pope and where he would not meet the Emperor, I hope that you may begin to take an interest even in that old story. This country has a past, an old civilisation—what do I say? it has had many civilisations.'

'You mean,' I said, 'her Greek and Carthaginian colonists, and her Roman conquerors.'

'Or perhaps,' cried Estefanette, 'her best conquerors, her saints and martyrs. I mean to go and see the Lérins. You will take me, father?'

'Yes, *petite*, for those constitute part of the past of thy native land.' And then turning to me, M. de Thibaut added, 'What do you say of the cave-men whose bones are in the caverns of Mentone and Sospello; of the inscriptions in the department to eighteen Roman emperors and to twenty-one Roman divinities; of the *Aves* said by the boatmen of Napoule to the Diana of their shore; of the altar of Venus in the plain of Laval; of the battle-field of Otho and Vitellius; of the storehouses at Auribeau and Napoule; of the Golden Gate at Fréjus, and of the great Aurelian road which ran not many hundred feet from the line that we now follow?'

'I doubt,' I replied, 'if I could interest a dozen people in these topics.'

M. de Thibaut gave his shoulders a shrug.

'But why?' asked Estefanette.

'Because people will answer, just as you did a little while ago, that these are such very old stories: because the English prefer to meet English people and to read English books, and to talk of their ailments, hotel bills, and lawn-tennis parties, to say nothing of their charities, picnics, and quarrels.'

Estefanette laughed. 'Is it true,' she asked, 'that the two colonies, the French and the English, see very little of each other?'

'Every year less, as far as Cannes is concerned. The French do not need strangers, and the English do not readily make themselves ties in a foreign land. They seem numerous enough to depend on themselves. But if they cannot get over their two great stumbling-blocks, a foreign language and a different Church, they have at least admitted to their sympathies the insects and the flowers.'

'You are much better gardeners than we are,' said M. de Thibaut, 'for *nothing* will make a Provençal tidy in his work, or methodical in his care of anything.'

'I hear that the English go out with butterfly-nets,' said Estefanette; 'I shall do so too.'

'Yes, and we take an interest in sea-anemones, in trap-door spiders, in the praying Mantis, and the burying beetle.'

'Those creatures, besides the notice with which you honour them, are so typical that they deserve all the respect I can show them,' said M. de Thibaut, laughing.

'Why, father?'

'At Nice and Monte Carlo I dare say there are not many persons as devout as the praying Mantis; no: that poor little creature often prays alone; but at Cannes we shall meet with many specimens of the gentleman with the trap-door; excellent persons, who shut out all strange impressions and new ideas.'

'You are satirical, M. le Comte.'

'Not at all; for let me ask you, do we not all do with the past what the beetle does: *bury* it?'

At this moment the train stopped at Fréjus.

It is the residence of the Bishop of Fréjus-and-Toulon, but it is none the less a forlorn and deserted place, where the waves have receded nearly a mile from the port of the Cæsars, and where the broken aqueducts may be seen stretching away through the bean-fields and the weedy drills of corn.

'How dismal it looks!' I exclaimed.

'Yes, here indeed a whole civilisation is buried; here is a past that can never live again. The harbour is dried up, the sailors have departed, so that to think of the fleet of Actium rocking where these vines and lettuces grow seems like a fable. And no one cares about its past, unless it be some canon of that melancholy little cathedral who may have a taste for archæology. All that the present landowner asks is that the Foncière should take a fancy to his lettuce-bed, and buy it of him, at sixty francs a mètre. This suburb of Saint Raphael has a certain success as a bathing-place, but as it catches a contagious sadness from Fréjus I must say that it does not attract me.'

'Alphonse Karr can generally make me in love

with any beach that he describes, but were I condemned to live on this side of the Esterels I think I should fix upon Valescure, and bargain that its pines should not all be cut down by people who build what is called a " health resort." It is the first thing that they set themselves to do, and the most silly, since an invalid can have few better neighbours than a pine tree.'

'I wonder,' said Estefanette, 'what the Romans of whom you spoke would think if they could see this coast all dotted with white houses, and the sea ploughed by ironclads?'

'Some of the old traders had a very fair aptitude for gain,' replied her father. 'Commerce creates adventure, and Narbonne was once as full of Jews as Marseilles is now full of foreign merchants.'

After shooting through a tunnel we found ourselves in the forest of the Esterels..

'If,' said M. de Thibaut, 'you are in search of an historic site or theme, there is the Tour Drammont,[1] where they say that Jeanne, who was Countess of Provence as well as Queen of Naples, spent her last night in Provence.'

'You mean Jeanne with the four husbands?' cried Estefanette.

'Well, it appears that our liege lady of Provence, besides being a droll mixture of wit and wickedness, of devotion and indecorum, was also a woman of much experience as far as matrimony was concerned. She was however near the end of her

[1] Or d'Armont.

experiences when she fled to the Tour Drammont, and took ship from Agay.'

'To go and be smothered at Naples,' added Estefanette, as she looked at the shell of the castle where Jeanne sheltered herself from the wrath of her barons.

The wild scenery of the short mountain range of the Esterels never looked more beautiful than at this moment. The purple heath was in flower, and the arbutus displayed both the scarlet of its berries and the beauty of its pale, wax-like flowers. Against the dusky, red rocks of this little roadstead of Agay broke the translucent waves, and down every little valley there hurried a rill, making the solitary places glad with its tinkle, or washing the myrtles to a brighter green.

'The forest is beautiful to-day,' I cried, 'not sombre or solitary, but yet more fit for the flying feet of some mountain nymph than for the robber bands of Gaspard de Besse, or for the march of a guilty queen.'

'The ancients thought so too. They dedicated the whole region to Diana, the huntress sister of Apollo, and this forest had its especial nymph, its *Oreade*, the fairy Estrella.'

'Oh! I should like to see her,' cried Estefanette.

'I do not know that she ever appeared to little maidens like you. She bestowed fertility on mothers, but especially favoured the noble sex. Yet woe betide the shepherd who met and kissed her in some fold of the hills!'

'Ah: what did she do to him? turn into a wolf, and eat him?'

'No, she did nothing to him, but after kissing her

he ceased to behave like other people. He went mad. He had made himself her victim: in fact, there are people one knows who have met and kissed Estrella—lives fatally devoted to one idea.'

We were silent, till as the train ran past the mouths of the Siagne, and the wooded hills of the Tanneron came in sight, M. de Thibaut sat back in the carriage, and repeated to himself De Musset's lines :—

> Regrettez-vous le temps, où le ciel sur la terre,
> Marchait et respirait dans un peuple de dieux ;
> Où Vénus-Astarte, fille de l'onde amère,
> Secouait, vierge encore, les larmes de sa mère
> Et fécondait le monde en tordant ses cheveux ;
> Où, du nord au midi, sur la création
> Hercule promenait l'éternelle justice,
> Sous son manteau sanglant, taillé dans un lion ;
> Où les Sylvains moqueurs, dans l'écorce des chênes,
> Avec les rameaux verts se balançaient au vent,
> Et sifflaient dans l'écho le chant du passant ;
> Où tout était divin, jusqu'aux douleurs humaines ;
> Où le monde adorait ce qu'il tue aujourd'hui ;
> Où quatre mille dieux n'avaient pas un athée ?

* * * * * *

A few days later, when recalling this conversation, I said to myself, 'I will try to interest visitors in this beautiful country: in the history of the Maritime Alps and their seaboard. Such a book will certainly bore some people; but then they need not do more than look at the pictures. Others, on the contrary, may be pleased to find that there is really something to know. They will then set to work for themselves, and in looking around them will find the famous "sermons in stones, and good in everything."'

For some invalids on this coast the present must

perforce be colourless: days of tedium succeeding to nights of pain. Perhaps these pages may please them —may people the sick-room with brave men and fair women, or perfume it with the breath of the hill-flowers. There are also spirits cruelly in want of rest, and of the soothing to be derived from a complete change of scene. Will they go out with me to the river or the beach? or can I tempt them to give an hour of thought to a past which is not their own? It may not be their own in one sense, but in another sense how real is our possession of the past! Does there not rise from it a strange hum of dead voices, telling how others before us have toiled all the night, and taken nothing? Patience is the great lesson of history, for history convinces us of the slow growth of truth, and of the rejection, by prejudice, of much that ought ere now to have become the heirlooms of the world. Error only is longlived, and so far is the race from being adjudged to the swift that the strong powers of *ennui*, mediocrity, and envy often make us despair of progress in a world where grace, catholicity, and generosity leave but little mark on the shifting sands of society. Here under our feet many old civilisations lie buried. They can never come again in their good or in their evil, because 'tongues' cease, and because manners also die, like men. Some of the new developments are good, yet the past has its charms, and this Provençal past will prove to be a treasure-heap. Under the white ashes that cover it we shall find the fire of old loves and hates, bones of old systems, fragments of the history of the human heart. Nor will novels and romances be needed when we have once come to know the actors in these Provençal dramas, so full of the ceaseless toil and endeavour of humanity, of its agitations, its passions, its controversies, its struggles for freedom, its increase of knowledge, its sorrows, its great men and its greater errors, and its constant succession of humble and unnoticed lives.

CHAPTER II.

FROM THE MOUNTAINS TO THE SEA.

'Here the spring is longest, summer borrows months beyond her own:
Twice the teeming flocks are fruitful, twice the laden orchards groan:
Hail, thou fair and fruitful mother, thus I dare to wake the tale,
Of thine ancient laud and honour. . . .'—II. *Georgic.*

'Point de longs fleuves ni de grandes plaines. Ça et là une ville en tas sur une montagne, sorte de môle arrondi, est un ornement du paysage comme on en trouve dans les tableaux de Poussin et de Claude : des vallées limitées, de nobles formes, beaucoup de roc, et beaucoup de soleil, les éléments et les sensations correspondantes : combien de traits de l'individu et de l'histoire imprimés par ce caractère.'—H. TAINE.

As an introduction to a history one ought not to overlook at starting the influence which is both stronger and more enduring than that of any human system. It is the one which shapes, and, as it were, predestinates the fate of a country—I mean its geographical position, and the unalterable features of its physical geography.

Lying on the high road to Italy the district which we call Provence was trodden by every foot. It was the path alike of the foreign invader who aimed a blow at Rome, and of the conquering soldier who had dared to cross his Rubicon. Along the shore of Maritime Provence, or across the passages of her Alps, poured Celts and Goths, Burgundians, Franks, Vandals, Huns, and Berbers. And the tribes who came to Provence seldom left it. Every wanderer or marauder found here what he most sought, or what he most regretted. The Greeks, if they had to import the olives of Pallas, found here fair skies, pale marbles, violets fit for Hylas, and roses of which Alcibiades might have made his wreath : to say nothing of a sea as 'deeply, darkly, beautifully blue' as that which breaks round the Leucadian headland. The Jews, who drifted hither, first after the persecution of Titus, and again in 1492, after their expulsion from Spain, found here the corn and wine and oil of promise, with terraces, not unlike those of Judea, surrounding 'cities that had foundations' in the sunny hills. The Moors were soon at home in the dusty, *Wady*-like ravines: the crags, the sunshine, and the palms of Provence leaving them but little to regret. For the Phœnician traders there were safe harbours; for the Aragonese a dialect not unlike their own (*Catalan*); Florentines, red-handed from the strife of Guelf and Ghibelline in the Lily City, made themselves new counting-houses in Provence; while the Lombard and Genoese traders found in the Rhone valley a highway for their commerce. These influences procured for the district of the Maritime Alps a rich and a varied past, and in the same manner the exceptional climate and the unique position of the country now ensure for it a future of affluence.

Fashions change, and it may happen that for a quarter of a century some one of the cities of Provence will enjoy a greater reputation, or a greater influx of strangers, than another; but it is certain that what the one loses the other gains, that railways will continue to bring invalids and pleasure-seekers and artists to the Riviera, and that from the Rhone to the Arno one winter city will succeed to the other till the Riviera is one long line of health-resorts. At the present moment the department of the Maritime Alps bears the bell. And no wonder. A rampart of limestone mountains, rising tier above tier, shelters it from the north, while the chain of the Esterels screens its western border. Such a screen is needed, for the Rhone valley, acting like a funnel, permits a constant rush of cold air towards the sun-heated coast. Thus the sweeping *mistral* is formed. There used to be an old saying that

> Parliament, mistral, and Durance
> Were the three scourges of Provence—

and no doubt the third day of a howling *mistral* is a trial to most people. The cypress hedges are bent down, almost to the earth which they are unable to protect, every window shakes, and all night long, across every bar and through every keyhole, this wild wind discourses. Its medley of raving, whining and bellowing is very annoying—and as for the dust, *that* is everywhere! it is in your eyes and in your hair, in your dress, in your ink-bottle, and between the leaves of your books. Meantime your pens split, your shutters crack, your hat flies away, and your hair turns grey; but your spirits are unaccountably buoyant, and the sky, from side to side, is of the palest blue. The sea, on the other hand, looks dark; there is a fringe of surf round the shore, the horizon line is a broken one, and the water is of every shade imaginable, from a deep hyacinth-like purple to a greenish turquoise. This much-abused *mistral* has been christened by the knowing peasantry ' *lou bon vent.*' It really is a public benefactor, for this 'prince of the power' of the air clears the country from damp and miasma, and is therefore one of the great sanitary features of the seaboard.

The streams of a coast which slopes so directly to the sea must run from north to south. They have their sources among the everlasting snows, but their outfall is among the sun-dried sands. It is the incessant currents of air, all these angels of the winds, ascending and descending the valleys and river-beds of Provence, that make and keep the country healthy. Thanks to them we have here no Maremma with its fatal beauty of midsummer, and no Pontine marshes, with their fevers and agues.

The southern exposure of this beach causes an almost daily phenomenon in the matter of the wind. Towards the dawn a *tramontana*, which the boatmen call ' *lou vent de la neige,*' rises, and they may then be seen hugging the land, while in the same way if the wind sets due south they will run close in shore, to catch a *ricochet* off hills which deflect the wind enough to give it a slight change of direction. These experienced judges are of opinion that it is the SE. wind, ' *lou vent de mer,*' which brings the finest weather, particularly if, turning to ' *vent de soleu,*' it goes round all day with the sun. They also denominate this veering wind ' *lou vent dou malhourous,*' because their sails are like the pockets of an unlucky man, empty after having been full. The SSE. wind, the *Siroc*, blows in the upper regions of the air. It gives a pale steel-grey hue to the sky; clouds accumulate, but no rain falls on the south side of the mountains, and the temperature becomes peculiarly trying to nervous people. It has happened to us to leave this coast after weeks of such weather, and to cross the ridges of the hills on the way to Grenoble and Lyons. No sooner had we exchanged the southern for the northern slopes than we found that the clouds and vapours had all condensed in the colder atmosphere, and that torrents of rain had magnified every streamlet into a river.

As a rule the winds of this coast only blow with violence while the sun is high. As soon as he sets, the invisible vapours uniting condense, and drop on the parched shores of Provence the dews that keep its vegetation alive. When in 1882, only four showers of rain fell between the 4th of January and the 5th of April, the dripping grass reminded one irresistibly of the sunshine of Eden, when the 'days' were 'seven,' and when as yet the earth was only watered by such bounteous dews.

Provence is separated by the chains of the Maritime Alps both from Piedmont and from that Genoese territory to which the name of Liguria was anciently given. The Var was long the boundary of this the most eastern province of France; but in 1860, the county of Nice (with the exception of the cantons of Tende and La Brigue) was ceded to the Emperor, who also purchased Mentone and Roquebrune from the Prince of Monaco. In this way the French frontier has been pushed on to the torrent of St. Louis, almost to Ventimiglia, whereby the harbour of Villefranche, and many other sources of commercial and mineral wealth have been secured to France.

There is little level land in the department. One range of hills rises beyond and behind the other: first the wooded hillocks where the hyacinths lurk, then the slopes, so gay with heath and myrtle and arbutus and prickly broom, next the bare limestone ledges, and, last of all, the peaks where the snow-wreaths and glaciers hang, and which, as they meet the clouds, assume the hues and imitate all the aspects of cloudland.

Of the Alps the most northern mass belongs to the Gélas, to that majestic system of upheaval from which the Apennines depend. The first chain, running in the direction of Bordighera, gives rise to the great torrent of the Roya. To the second belongs the fantastic Tête-de-Chien, above Monaco, and the scathed and peeled crags of Eza. These rocks not only come close to the beach, but they rise from the sea in almost perpendicular masses, and are of the most glowing hues above the beach gardens of Beaulieu and of la petite Afrique. The third chain or system, running east and west, goes to join the mountains in the department of the Basses Alpes. Its best-known feature is the Saut-du-Loup, backed as that is by the Cheiron range, of which the head is distant about thirty kilomètres from the sea. The greatest altitude here is, however, very humble when compared with the Pic du Prats (2,438 mètres above the sea), or with the elevation of the two highest glaciers which can be seen from Antibes, viz. the Glacier de Mercantour (3,167 mètres), and that of the grand Mont Clapier (3,346 mètres).

The principal artery of this department is the Var. It receives many affluents, and the space that lies between it and the Siagne (which once formed the ancient viguerie of Grasse) is watered by many lesser streams. These are the Cagnette, the Malvans, the Lubiane, the Loup, the Brague, the Bouillède, the Foux, the Chataignier, the Riou, the Siagne, the Mourachone, and the Argentière.

Beyond the Var you cross first the Magnan, and then the Paillon, that torrent which divides old Nice from her modern *faubourgs*; and, lastly, you meet the Roya, with its fourteen affluents which make such wild work in winter of both roads and bridges. These rivers nearly all possess the same features. First you have the sources, high up among the secret places of the mountains, where little streamlets either break out suddenly through the ledges, as the overflow of some hidden reservoir, or go oozing slowly through the snows of the highest levels. They next make their way downward in half-thawed ripples, till they gather volume enough to cleave themselves a passage through the barriers of the rocks. They then emerge, green splashing torrents, glittering among the uplands, to collect themselves into pools in the fragrant, bosky dells. After this they may meet with the weir of a mill, or with a bridge or two, but then come their two last, their sober stages, the gliding through meadows all pied with daffodils, and finally the slow creeping through the sands out to the salt and restless sea.

These torrents can be very terrible. Take the Brague for an example. As it comes creeping through its flowery banks, it looks so passive and sluggish that one can hardly realise the catastrophe of January, 1872. Very heavy rains fell then with little intermission during sixteen days, and the swollen river ended in forming a lake of two kilomètres in length inside the railway embankment, outside of which there unluckily beat a very heavy surf. These waves, and their shingle, prevented the river from having a clear waterway at its mouth, while most fatally close to that mouth stood the railway bridge. It was supported on one pier, round which swirled the angry eddies, and close up to which splashed the encroaching waves. The line was in danger! The station-master at Antibes telegraphed to Nice to stop the 5 P.M. fast train. But the gale had disturbed the instruments, and his message was not transmitted. Suspecting something of the sort, he next sent off a man on horseback to ford the Brague, and to take the warning to the next station at Cagnes. But neither man nor horse could stem such a torrent, it spread so wide, and it ran so strong. The messenger therefore had to make a *détour* by Biot: so long a one that he was all too late. Meantime the darkness fell. From Antibes the officials could watch the lights of the advancing train as it steamed along through the rain and the tempest. Suddenly the front lamps disappeared, like sparks in the dark. The engine had gone down head-foremost, through the bridge with its broken pier; two carriages fell piled on top of it, until a coupling snapped, then some carriages rolled off on the sea-side of the embankment, and, finally, with a terrible shock, the train came to a stand. How many lives were lost that night has remained a mystery, but the next day's spectacle was terribly suggestive. There was still a lake of water inside the embankment; the rails were snapped and twisted; two carriages with their sides stove in, and which had been in the sea, were now beached on the shingle, and the engine, fast bedded in sand, lay deep in the yawning fissure which showed where the bridge had been. Of the pier no vestige remained, and the eddies of the Brague were swirling among the wreck. A good deal of that wreck must have gone out to sea, but a company of infantry, summoned from Antibes (its men firmly lashed together with ropes), groped about, in a torrent which reached to their waists, to find more bodies, or more means of identifying the survivors.

All who had money or friends had already been removed, but in a carter's inn, about eight minutes' drive from the broken bridge, there lay two friendless, penniless, and unclaimed women, and one man so dreadfully injured that the surgeons had been obliged to trepan him on the spot. He was a musician, and I am told that he ultimately recovered, but his screams were most heartrending as I followed one of the Dames Trinitaires up to the long, low room under the rafters where the so-called 'English' patient lay. In the first bed, near the door, there was a pretty Piedmontese girl of about thirteen, whose black curls were full of sand. Her face was flushed, and her breathing was hard; she had got a congestion of the lungs. Then came the stranger, who turned out to be no Englishwoman, but only a poor German outcast. She moaned and screamed when she reacted in her delirium the terrible struggle in the water. I undeceived the Mère Urbain as to her nationality, but we agreed to say nothing about it; for those were still early days after the war, the peasants' might have shown ill-will, and at Antibes, in the big Hospital where she ruled, the Mère Urbain had plenty of wounded soldiers who would look askance at a German patient.

As for this extemporised hospital, I never saw a sadder sight. The house, to begin with, was filthy beyond description, and the staircase, so dark as to be dangerous, was littered with sacks of grain and bundles of wool. The latter belonged no doubt to the bedding of the past, or of the future, and they were, as became their nature, full of fleas. An unkempt, ill-looking couple kept this *albergo di squalor*, and made a harvest by showing to visitors the surgeons' basin, and other ghastly tokens of the wreck. I shall never forget my disgust, or the wrath of the Mère Urbain, when I drew her attention to a human hand *left lying alone* in one of those shallow baskets which are used for keeping lemons! I had to return to this doleful place on the next, and upon many following days, taking it in turns with a Russian Maid-of-honour to visit the poor German girl, who, as long as her delirium and her great prostration lasted, could only hold intercourse with those who spoke or prayed with her in her own tongue, but the Mère Urbain, as may be supposed, soon reduced the deplorable sick-room to order, and she also swept off all the relics of the wreck, for Christian burial at Antibes. I remember further that the little

Piedmontese, after crying piteously for '*Mamma! Mamma!*' for some days, made a good recovery. As for the poor German, she had a long and tedious illness, but one which afforded her time for salutary teaching. The last time that we heard of her, after Olga S— and I had sent her back to her home near Strasburg, she was respectably married, and she has had every reason to bless that sudden bath in the swollen Brague.

The great flood in the channel of the Foux, in October 1882, was another specimen of what these streams can do. In the space of an hour all the low-lying ground of the Boulevard du Cannet was flooded, much property destroyed, and eight lives lost. The funeral *cortège* of these eight victims, who were buried at the expense of the town, was a very curious and most touching sight. They were followed to the cemetery on the Grasse road by over 5,500 persons, and mourned for there, in their big common grave, with the loudest sobs and cries.

These catastrophes, though they may make a strong impression on the mind, do but little, however, towards altering the face of the country. It is the slow, continued action of natural forces that is truly irresistible: it is what Schiller terms the laying of 'sand-grain upon sand-grain' that is truly creative, and now, as in the beginning, it is the work of the morning and of the evening that leave an enduring mark upon the globe that we inhabit.

A river is an engineering force constantly though irregularly at work, but it must be remembered that the sea which meets its stream is another and an opposing force. The waves collect and roll back part of the sediment which the river lays down, and thus, tideless as the Mediterranean may be, it presents the spectacle of several sea margins, the *cordons littoraux* of the French engineers. Such tiny terraces serve to heighten a beach of which, in vulgar parlance, you hear it said that it is *rising*. This is not the fact, but where the mouth of a stream is turned aside, or dammed back by the action of the waves, it often happens that a chain of brackish lagunes is formed. These in time dry up; evaporation and the growth and decay of weeds ensuring the gradual formation of a soil more or less spongy. At the mouths of the Var, of the Siagne, and of the Brague, the ground thus gained from the sea may be counted by many hundreds of mètres. It was in this way that the great plain below Pégomas was laid down, and had the coast of Eastern Provence, from Marseilles to Ventimiglia, been all as sloping as the shore beyond the mouths of the Rhone, the district would by this time have possessed neither ports nor trade. At Fréjus, this really has occurred, for there is no outfall, the quays of the Cæsars are now 1,600 mètres distant from the waves, and it would have fared with the whole of the eastern towns as it has fared with Aiguesmortes and Narbonne, places once rich and flourishing, but of which the salt and stagnant lagunes are not navigable. There the domain of the mariner has long since ceased, but the domain of the husbandman has not yet begun, so that the towns sleep, emphatically dead cities beside a dead sea.

Eastern Provence, on the contrary, has harbours of great depth, and some of the outlines of her bold coast have not altered for many millions of years. The abrupt headlands driven out into the Mediterranean are unchanged; off them the water measures many fathoms, and between them there are bays of the greatest beauty. Agay, at the foot of the red escarpments of the Mornes, is a harbour of refuge among the Esterels, and the bay so-called of Grimaud can hold vessels of considerable burthen. Cannes, like the Golfe Jouan, has its roadstead sheltered by the fine natural breakwater of the Lérins islands. At Villefranche the depth varies from ten to twenty-five mètres, so that three or four ironclads may be seen lying so close in shore that their topgallants seem to mix with the palms, olives, and carouba trees that fringe this the most beautiful little harbour in the world. Modern roads and villas have hardly been able to ruin the beauty of Villefranche, which, with its miniature fort, its Admiralty Pier, and lazaretto, is as perfect a toy specimen of a harbour as St. Paul-du-Var is of a mediæval strong place. It is rich in colouring as well as perfect in outline, the prickly pear and the aloe fringe its red rocks, and down under the shadow of its belfry and its sunburnt walls you can fancy, if not the landing of the Tyrian Hercules, at least the arrival of popes and of emperors. In the spring of 1866, the corpse of the Tzarevitch Nicholas-Alexandrovitch was embarked here. Every angle or coign of vantage was crowded with spectators when, with slow-chanted psalms, the heavy barge made its way from the pier out to the frigate (the *Alexander-Newsky*) destined to receive the sorrowful freight. The bells tolled, guns fired at intervals, and soon, with a great trail of smoke streaming behind them like mourning pennons, the frigates stood out between the headlands, and the bay of Villefranche was left empty.

I used to think that this mixture of tall masts and waving trees must be unique, but I found in an old-fashioned poem by Orinda [1] the following description of a voyage from Tenby to Bristol, in 1652, which so recalls Villefranche that I will copy it here :—

> But what most pleased my mind upon the way
> Was the ships' posture that in harbour lay :
> Which to the rocky grove so close was fixed
> That the trees' branches with the tackling mixed.
> One might have thought it was, as then it stood,
> A growing navy, or a floating wood.

Though the chain of the Esterels forms rather the boundary of the Maritime Alps than any portion of the department, I will not leave the subject of the mountains and the sea without giving a page to the physical geography of the country beyond the Siagne. 'C'est la région du feu,' says a French geologist in speaking of this district, where the crystalline rocks show all their most rugged features and their most beautiful hues.[2] It is a very wild country, where the tourist may easily lose (*embouscar*) himself in the pathless ravines, and where many a pretty young pedestrian, who reckons on a walk of five miles, may have to make one of fifteen before she gets

---

[1] Mrs. Philips.
[2] I have to thank Messrs. Frith, of Reigate, for allowing me to use three of their very successful photographs.

IN THE FOREST OF THE ESTERELS.

to the stations of Trayas or Agay. The population, it must be added, is exceedingly rough, and not always disposed to be civil to strangers. They are the descendants of the free peasants to whom 'la reino Jeanno,' as they still call Petrarch's beautiful Queen of Naples, gave a right to cultivate the little dells in this the greatest forest of Provence. They did not all live by honest labour either, and even in the beginning of the eighteenth century so full were these dense woods of thieves and marauders that a band of ground on each side of the high road was ordered to be kept clear in case of ambushes. Then what a road! with no inns for man and beast but that Logis de l'Esterel which Misé Brun's misadventures have immortalised! The present *gendarmerie* guarantees the safety of the modern tourist, but the visitor cannot fail to be struck by the miserable lives of the few peasants whom he meets. They seem to spend their time in dragging out the half-charred wood which the fires of every summer leave in the forest, and for which they find a sale in the streets of Cannes. Yet the country possesses considerable mineral wealth. There are, to begin with, the splendid porphyry quarries of Boulouris, where the blocks prepared by the Romans may still be seen; there are amethysts, and veins of a serpentine so beautiful that in the Middle Ages none but the barons might use it for the adornment of their houses. There is an iron mine at Agay, and in the valley of the Argentière some sulphate of lead is dug for the factories at Vallauris. Since 1777, a coal-basin has been known to exist in the Esterels, and the mines of Auriosque, Réyran, and Bozon send both coal and petroleum to Cannes and Toulon. Unluckily the coal is dirty, and in burning gives out such unpleasant gases that it has been found impossible to go on using it for the perfume factories of Grasse.

As the crystalline rocks contain felspar in large quantities they weather very readily, and their decomposition furnishes soil for the pine, cork, and holly woods, and for a vegetation which must be seen to be believed. Hence the rounded forms of these hillsides, on which there is a perennial carpet of heath, cistus, and arbutus. At one time of year you have the snowy and mauve flowers of the cistus, at another the silver spikes of the tall, branched asphodel, while at another the rosy clusters of the oleanders drop upon a mossy couch, fit either for the sleep of Endymion, or for Diana's urgent feet.

The Mont Vinaigre is the highest point of the range (616 mètres), but by far the most marked feature is the headland of the Cap Roux. Its colour and its outline are both remarkable, affording endless studies for the artist and the photographer. It is distant from the Cap d'Antibes twenty-two kilomètres, and forms the western side of the great curve in which lie the bay of Cannes and the Golfe Jouan. Close within its shelter are Gardane and Théoule. To both of those places expeditions can be made by boat. There is a quiet anchorage at Théoule, just below the little, crumbling battery which Richelieu ordered to be built for the protection of the bay. The place is one which may readily rise to importance, for its climate is delightful; invalids can find there the pine woods which are disappearing from the environs of Cannes, and the soil is well adapted for market-gardening. The cultivation of *primeurs* would answer all the better here because Théoule lies as close to the modern railway as it once did to what the peasants still call '*lou Camin Aurélian*': to that great coast road which the Romans cut through its thickets of myrtle and its gorges of porphyry.

CHAPTER III.

THE PEOPLE.

'The true antiquities, those only worthy of our attention, are the slight but visible traces of ancient speech, of ancient race, of ancient feelings and of manners, to which human tenacity has clung through ages of vicissitudes, which barbarism, a new faith, and a new civilisation have not effaced from the land.'—J. KAVANAGH.

FROM the terrace of our villa on the Grasse road the red roofs of the old town of Cannes are visible. Behind them rises the Mont Chevalier, crowned by the parish church and belfry, by the half-ruined castle, and by the great, square *vigie* of Abbot Adelbert, with its lightning-riven crest. On this the Eve of All Hallows the air is scented with the breath of the mimosa, and our balcony is sheeted with the pale blue flowers of the Plumbago. After an absence of six months we have returned to find our hill covered with houses and shops. There is a footpath and a gas-lamp, all testifying to the new order of things in Cannes. Yet there stand the everlasting hills: the bells of the old church are ringing to *couvre-feu*, and we can see the gaunt tower of the Pisan builders through the pale flower-wreaths of this exquisite summer of All Saints. The ideal lies close to the real, and so it is with this Maritime Provence, where the flowers of a season and the ephemerides of a day, flaunt over the graves of a long-buried past.

No visitor can for a moment imagine that this country was always such as he now beholds it—dotted with white villas, and within a twenty hours' journey from Paris. There were always the same mountain crests, if not quite the same gathering together of blue waters which we call 'the Gulf of the Lion'; there were the same wind-currents in the beds of the rivers, the same ghostlike outline of Corsica against the rose of the sun's rising, and the same purple range of the Esterels against the gold of the day's decline. For centuries there has existed the same landscape heated to a white heat, and bathed in the same atmosphere—an ether which in the morning is pearly or opaline, but which at mid-day vibrates with the sunbeams. For centuries there have been the same seedtime and harvest, with snows on the Alpine peaks, and songs of birds among the flowering trees of spring.

But to whom did this fair land belong? Who first cast a net in these waters, or furrowed them with a keel? Who first tilled these fields? who planted the olive, the vine, and the palm? and who garnered the first sheaves in this land of roses, cypress, terebinth, for ever full? Then who on this Provençal shore fashioned the Provençal speech? who built and fenced these cities? who framed those usages of Church and State, which have slowly broadened down, from precedent to precedent? who made society here? who unmade it? and who is now remaking it? Who have been the road-makers and the lawgivers of Maritime Provence, and to whom did her people pray?

Contemporary France is at best a curious piece of

mosaic, and of contemporary Provence it must be said that it is like a basin of sand from its own beach. In that sand you will find many broken shells, but you will also find some undying things. Here is a cornelian, there a bit of porphyry from the Cap Roux, or perhaps of fluor-spar from the Cap Garoube, with a fragment of serpentine that has been washed down by the torrents from the high Alps behind La Brigue. So it is with the Provençal past. As with those many-coloured pebbles, so rolled and differentiated that it needs a quick eye to detect their real origin, it really requires a nice observer to say to what period or system the antiquities and the locutions of Provence once belonged? The people themselves have long forgotten how those huge walls came to be where you see them to-day. The peasant is content to call the line of big, unmortised stones 'leis murassos,' and in just the same way he will answer about the surname of Arluc, that it is '*un nom comme les autres.*' Yet the walls are those of a Celto-Ligurian camp, and this surname of Arluc, coming down to us from the *ara lucis* on the plain of Laval, is perhaps the oldest name in the *arrondissement* of Grasse. The surnames of Maure, Maurin, Maurens, Le Maure, Morel, Moreau, and Moreri, to say nothing of Moricaud, Muraour and Mouradour, all tell their own tale, the first bearers of them having been either, like Négre and Négrin, of African descent, or dwellers at La Maure, or denizens of the hills of the district so long inhabited by the Saracens, and still called Les Maures. Couët is from a Celtic word signifying a wood; but may not Escarraz be derived from $\iota\sigma\chi\upsilon\rho\acute{o}s$ (*iscur*), strong? The proud Grimaud, or Grimaldi, have their derivation from the Gothic *Grimm-walt*, or power of the strong. In Nice the surnames of Bellan, Bellande, Bellandon, go back to the fourth century, but is it true that 'Notre Dame *d'Avigonnet*' (near Napoule) is a corruption of the '*Ave, Diana !*' said by the boatmen of the shore to the Diana of the Esterels? There is no doubt that the many localities now called 'St. Martin' were originally dedicated to Mars, but I cannot satisfy myself whether the popular name for Christmas, 'Calende,' be derived from the Kalends of January, or from *Calène*, the Yule log of the Celto-Ligurians. That log still exists, and libations of red wine are still poured over it at the feast of the winter solstice, just as in many parts of Provence they still light Beltane fires on St. John's Day.

The Greek traders inhabited the seaports, so it is not surprising to find the Greek names recalled of Neapolis (Napoule), Antipolis (Antibes), and Athenopolis, the long since ruined Antea. Yet on account of the incessant ravages of the pirates, and of the later arrival of Jewish merchants who came to monopolise the sedentary professions of the towns, hardly any Greek remains exist in those places. Only the culture of the olive speaks of the Phocæan colonists, and Greek civilisation has left in Provence far fewer traces than one could wish. It is perhaps in the mirthful *farandoulo* that the Greek dance can best be traced, the figures of it being those described upon Achilles' shield, with ' boys and girls to the lute disporting, till the whole city seemed filled with dances, pomps, and feasts.' The *Moresque* dance, on the other hand, plainly dates from that settlement of the

Moors in Eastern Provence to which the Provençals owe their trade in cork and bricks, their *norias*, and their porous water-jars, and the palms which were introduced into Europe by Abdulrahman II. I call all these names and things the real antiquities of Provence, a country of which the making was as varied as it was prolonged.

The Roman roads attest its early importance. The *Notitia imperii* mentions among the nineteen Provençal cities Vence, Fréjus, and Castellane. These lay on the three great roads which intersected the maritime portion of the province. There was first the Via Aurelia, coming by Turbia (*turris via*), Cannes, and Théoule to Fréjus. Secondly, the Via Julia, lying along the upper terrace under the hills of the *arrondissement* of Grasse; and a third road which connected Vence with both the great highways, and then went in a north-westerly direction to Castellane. The best antiquaries believe that the Romans had also a fourth artery, a means of leaving Cimiéz by the valley of the Tinée, and of thus keeping open their communication beyond the Alps. The lines of all their roads, being marked by milestones, bridges, inscriptions, tombs, and altars, may still be identified; and though the authenticity of the bridge over the Riou in Cannes has been severely questioned, some good judges are of opinion that it is a fair specimen of Roman masonry as seen, not in Rome itself, but in the colonies.[1]

[1] I am indebted for this opinion to the taste and acumen of the late Earl Somers, and I find the work of the aqueducts of Clausonne and the bridge at that place, about four miles from Antibes, to be of the same quality. No one ever attributed the remains at Clausonne to mediæval builders.

The conquest of a country which cost Cæsar half his legions being once secured by these roads, rich patricians came to Provence, and the whole face of the country was changed. But the tribes were stiffnecked, and it is to this same obstinate temper, as inherent in the race, that may be attributed some of the most deplorable episodes in their history. Such, for example, was the persecution of the Albigeois, when the villages round La Gaude were depopulated, the wars of the Countesses, the wars of religion, the feuds of the Carcistes, and the excesses of the great Revolution in Provence. The people are wrong-headed, at once passionate and wary, avaricious, and yet fond of holiday cavalcades, noisy, talkative, liable to panics, impatient of control, and unapt to change. So conservative are the peasants that their plough is still that of the era of the Georgics, of which it has the eight-foot pole, the curved *buris*, the bent handle, and the wooden *dentale*, or share. Nor is it of any use to speak here of improvements. All Provençals would gladly find themselves richer, but present outlay costs them such a pang that they prefer to slumber on, in 'old world lethargy,' and to go about in rags even when they may be worth not less than 5,000*l*. Their dislike of a 'Franciot' or 'Parisien' is as intense to-day as if the good King René were still king; and a native of the Northern departments, a stranger to the *langue d'oc*, is looked upon with distrust. He is to be made fun of, and cheated if possible, since under a malicious smile and some appearance of frankness the Niçois can hide many bad qualities. The true Provençal when he speaks French does so with an accent as unlike that of Paris as was the admirable accent once taught in Stratford-atte-Bow! I have heard his talk described as 'French rubbed with garlic,' and really the phrase is a good one if it be meant to describe the racy twang and the peculiar, humorous inflections of such a talker as my dear old friend the late Abbé Montolivo.

Among the peasantry figures of speech are in great request. 'Farewell' is not said: you only bow and say '*A l'avantage*,' meaning to the pleasure of meeting again. The devil is called 'Janicot'; the pig is '*lou noble veste de sedo*,' the gentleman in black silk! Here, as in Italian, diminutives abound: *Bastide* is a house, but a cottage is a *bastidoun*; and Alpe turns to *Amphiho* and *Amphihoun*. A little square is a *pati*; a young child is a *piuchenèto*; while a word like 'valley,' *lou vau*, or *lou valado*, can be modified into *valengo, valergo* (pl. *valergues*), *valeto, valoun,* and *valat*. There is a curious habit of beginning, or ending, the sentences with a word that is irrelevant, or is at least as irrelevant as a word must be allowed to be that has a dozen different meanings—or none! '*Té*' (*tiens!*) probably opens the phrase; '*Vé*' (*voyez-vous*) occurs somewhere in the argument, and '*allons!*' possibly brings the whole to a close.

As for the dialects of the coast,[1] they are both rich and varied, as might be expected where Celts, Iberians,

---

[1] For a notice of these patois of the coast I refer the reader to the *Annales de la Société des Lettres, Sciences, et Arts des Alpes Maritimes*, tome vi. page 357. An admirable guide to the dialect of Mentone is the grammar of Mr. J. B. Andrews, an American visitor who has employed his time to extraordinary advantage, so that he is now a first-rate authority on all matters concerning the district between the frontier and the Var.

THE PEOPLE.

Phœnicians, Greeks, Romans, Goths, Franks, Jews, and Arabs laid down, so to speak, nine strata of elements for the formation of the language of Southern France. In the hands of the Troubadours, that immortal band of two hundred poets, Provençal verses fully proved the grace and versatility of the tongue which is now only spoken by peasants. From town to town and hamlet to hamlet the idioms and terminations still vary so curiously that I will give a specimen of the way in which the most common words alter in districts not twenty miles apart:

	Pater	noster	qui	es	in	cœlis
Nice:	Notre	Père	qui	est	au	ciel
Mentone:	Nuostre	père	che	siès	en	sièl
Biot:	Nuasche	païre	qui	èst	aou	chelir
Mons and Escragnole:	Nostrou	pa	qui	sei	aou	tzè
Vallauris:	Nostro	papo	qui	es	arou	cer
Grasse:	Nostrou	païre	qué	sei	aou	ciel
	Nouestre	pèro	qué	sias	aou	ciel

* * * * * *

	Ave Maria gratia plena				
Nice:	Vou saludi	Maria	pléna	de	grassia
Mentone:	Mi vou salutou	Maria	pièna	di	gracia
Biot:	A vé saludo	Maria	tschéna	dé	grassia
Mons and Escragnole:	Mi vi saludo	Marià	chéna	dé	grassa
Vallauris:	Vé saludou	Maria	chéna	dé	graci
Grasse:	Vou saludi	Mario	pleno	de	gracio

* * * * * *

The masculine termination in *o*, as preserved in the patois of Grasse, carries us back to the time of the Troubadours, and is an eminently Provençal trait. Like the Gaelic of the highlands and islands of Scotland, this native tongue is fast dying out of the towns, but it lives on in remote villages, or among the fishers of the shore, who keep pretty much to themselves. To find many curious customs and superstitions, and some Greek words lingering in daily use, you must go among the fisherfolk, who less than any other class have felt the

DRAWING THE NET.

influence of revolutions and of foreign colonists. It matters little to them who may be the ruler of France, their business is with the Queen of Night, as ruling the waves, and lighting them to their precarious bread-winning from the sea. Their habits and sayings are *autant vieu que li roucas* off which they cast their nets. They know that there is now a great demand for fish in the towns, but then a service from Bordeaux brings daily into the *Pescaria* a quantity of what they contemptuously call 'white fish,' which never came to their bait.

They can point with pride to the gorgeous, hooded *capelans*, to the beautiful transparent angel-fish, to the graceful *girelles*, to St. Peter's fish, and to the silvery *argentines* which lie beside the black *clovisses* and the myriad spines of the sea-urchins. It requires some courage to eat the last-named dainty, but a dainty it really will prove if eaten fresh in some creek, and washed down with white wine. The urchins are very digestible, and recommended to delicate people, which can hardly be said of the more celebrated *bouillabaisse*. Every fisherman can cook it, but it is not every Englishman who can digest it. To many that dish proves 'a broth of abominable things,' and if rich in oil, as well as poor in saffron, it will certainly serve to remind you for many days of your rashness, or your greed, in having made a meal on it.

The number of words in the fisherman's vocabulary derived from the Greek is remarkable. He calls bread *artoun*, and his nets *brégin*; a little boat is a *squifou*, and the thunder is *troun*. This is as it should be, for the Phocæan colonists kept to the ports of Provence; and in the same way it is the gardeners who use the greatest number of Arabic words. They speak to you of *anjubis* (*algibiz*) for a sweet grape; of *jasmin* (*yâsmyn*), *limoun* (*leymoun*), *endibo* (*endib*), *salata* (*salatha*), *serfouil* (*serfoull*), and *trescalau*, for the St. John's wort. This is natural enough, for the Arabs were good gardeners, good druggists, and not bad cooks: in proof of which a dish of rice, tomatoes, and pigeon's liver, as introduced by them, is still valued in the Provençal kitchen.

We are agreed that the race under all these circumstances is not now, and cannot for very long have been, a pure one. Yet every now and again the eye is caught by a marked type. There is not here, as in Florence, a Jewish, or, as in Arles, a distinctly Greek cast of face; but a head of close, black curls, with dark eyes and full broad cheeks and a short but high nose, will serve to show us how the soldiers of Cæsar, or of Vitellius, may have looked. This type, if set off by a greenish jacket and a broad, red sash, is very effective, and proclaims itself as a survival of the Latin element. Up in the hills I recognise a predominance of the Celtic type. The children have blue eyes, and the elderly men in gait and walk so resemble the peasantry of the highlands of Scotland that they would hardly be picked out as strangers in Strath-Oikel or Strath-Conan. We have seen some old women washing at the *lavoir* of Antibes to whom we at once gave the names of Marion Ross, Widow Chisholm, and Peggy Munro, so exactly did they resemble some of our old Sutherlandshire crofters, whose upper lips, short figures, and folded kerchiefs they really seemed to have borrowed. To judge by their appearance some of the women live to a great age. Withered and crumpled like vinestocks, there was a trio that might long be seen sunning itself on the terraces of Cannet. We christened those poor, old women the Fates, but labour in the sun is so hard, and profit on lettuces is so small, that perhaps Clotho, Lachesis, and Atropos were not really as old as they looked. In bad weather the men wear the long, striped homespun cloak which Diodorus Siculus described, but on festive occasions they wear waistcoats cut open to the waist, knee-breeches, and a cloak folded over the left shoulder. In Mougins there is a good deal of beauty, but it is rare in the Maritime Alps, except among the peasants of La Brigue, where it is the rule rather than the exception. The Briguegasque women are neither tall nor short, but have erect figures, and a beauty which, but for the early loss of their teeth, would last beyond the period of the classical *beauté du diable*. In truth we have noticed among them, not only curly, picturesque heads, but loveliness such as Correggio would not have despised in a model. The hair, rippled or curly, is caught back, and covered with a broad black velvet ribbon that forms a pretty and even a dignified head-dress. A short blue or green petticoat lined with scarlet, a dark bodice, and a coloured kerchief folded in two narrow bands across the bosom, complete the costume. These semi-Italian peasants are generally rich, comfortable people, who keep dairies in Nice and Cannes in the winter, but who during the summer return to their mountain farms. There is an odd community of wages in a family, and all the families are connected by marriage, but the women do not marry very early. They are quiet and affectionate, often remaining eight or ten years in the same English family : in fact I prefer them as servants, since among the real natives of Nice and Cannes it is very rare to find qualities suited for domestic service.

The marriages of the peasantry and of the middle class are arranged here either under settlements or under the system of community of goods. By a remnant of

Orientalism which lingers in Provence, the women of the family do not expect to eat at table along with the lords of the creation, and if they are present it is thought good manners for them to sit together and as it were 'below the salt.' But they all sup together on feast-days—for example, on Christmas Eve, to eat the *pan dou Calende*, a thick cake stained with saffron, and which from its huge, round disc was probably made and eaten in honour of Diana, long before the Christian era. The village *Romerage*, or wake, is also a time of eating and drinking, of dancing and gossiping, in the open air. It is on that day that the best costumes and earrings make their appearance, and that the *galoubet* and the *tambourin* are heard. The latter is a long, narrow drum, about a foot in width, and two feet and a half in height, which the player holds between his knees. I have heard a man play on this instrument old airs of which one would like to discover the names and the authorship, but of the dances which they provoke the clergy do not approve, the times of *Romerage* awakening old habits and pagan allusions more honoured in the breach than in the observance.

The peasants of the *arrondissements* of Grasse, of Nice, and even of Puget Théniers, are rich. To find very poor villages, you must go up to the little *pays* on the Esteron and the Tinée; but, whether rich or poor, this population does not care to work for strangers. All kinds of alcoholic drinks are now in fashion, and as wine becomes daily more scarce, the population, both male and female, is markedly less abstemious than of yore. The savings bank is, however, the good angel of the district, and the promise, as it were, of a new and better day for a people who once knew no other friend than the *Mont de Piété*. The savings bank of Grasse has twenty thousand *livrets*, and this is the more creditable, because, though factory workers and their wages increase, landed property diminishes in value. The *arrondissement* of Grasse has in ten years lost forty thousand francs by the ruin of its olive-trees, nor is it likely to recover this loss. The little oil that is now produced does not command a better price, so it is evident that the mineral oils are driving out of the market the coarser oils of the country once used both for lamps and for machinery. Many small landowners are in consequence anxious to part with their land. When the village schoolmaster and his sister have sold, they will proceed to buy shares in some *Société foncière*, or *immobilière*, and will probably lose all their money. Their smaller neighbours will also sell, but then they will go up to Grasse, where, in the perfume factories, men, women, and girls all find employment, where labour is better paid, and Jean will proceed to live *à la carte*, instead of starving on the lettuces of his tiny farm. This perfume trade is popular, and, like the potteries, seems to have the future of the Maritime Alps in its hands.[1] But, as was said before, the native

[1] The works of M. Clément Massier, at Golfe Jouan, give employment to several artists, and to a hundred and twenty hands. These are modellers, sculptors, engravers, enamellers, painters, grinders and oven men, besides the hewers of wood and drawers of water, packers and carpenters. The supply of clay is inexhaustible, and M. Massier, by his taste and energy, has given a great impetus to the business of the country.

population does not care to work for strangers. If you want a job done by the carpenter or the blacksmith you must send five times for him, and if there be a broken pane of glass on a wet day you must make up your mind to its remaining unmended, and for no other reason than 'because it is raining'!

Yet work is highly paid. A mechanic earns four francs fifty centimes a day, and the gardener, who prunes the vines and puts a mat over the heliotropes, expects three francs a day; or, if he resides on the villa, will ask five hundred and fifty francs a year, with a house and fuel. Contracts are rarely finished here to time, and all the heavy labour is done by the Piedmontese. These poor fellows seem to be the Chinese of Europe. Their numbers are inexhaustible; in the winter 1882-3 there were four thousand of them on the new Boulevard of Cannes, and as many more on the works at Cimièz. Many of them have lived so long on this side of the frontier that not only are their children to be found on the benches of the schools, but a percentage of them has been drawn for the conscription, which shows that Provence is again absorbing into herself a strain of foreign blood, which must ultimately alter the type and the temper of her people. The Piedmontese are hardy and enduring in no common degree. They work all day long for seventeen or twenty-five pence, live on dry bread, onions, and oranges, eat nuts and apples, and sleep in the ditches.[1] Yet they have their little theatres, and will sing all day long about their loves.

[1] Too much cannot be said in praise of the night-schools organised, 1883-4, for these poor fellows.

Sometimes Gigi pauses after his verse, then Pépé will whistle a stave, till the singer recommences:—

> O quanto voglio bene a chi so io,
>   Il nome non lo voglio palezare :
> Lo tengo sempre scritto nel cuor mio,
>   Infinche vivo lo voglio portare . . . ,

Then a companion starts another ditty :—

> Credo da ver, bell' Isolina,
>   Un cuore senza amor deve morir.
> Cerca mi in van alla porta di Torino,
>   Senza di te sto io per morir . . . .

and so on, indefinitely.

Yet, in spite of these pure and pretty love-songs, all the crimes of violence that occur are invariably laid to the door of the Piedmontese, and terrible cases of their fury and jealousy have come to my own knowledge. I shall never forget a prisoner whom I once saw being driven by the police across the Place Garibaldi; he was in a cart, and netted over like a young bull. I asked a woman, standing near with a green water-jar in each hand, what he had done? She said it was a *sporcheria*, and it appeared that he had just murdered his wife!

Till the Revolution of 1848, the great ambition of every peasant proprietor, and small *bourgeois*, was to make one of his sons a priest. That it would ensure Peiroun against the conscription, for which Noël or Nourat were too certain to be drawn, was what the mother said, while the brethren and kinsfolk felt it to be a creditable incident in the family history to have an *Abbé* among them. Peiroun might hope to officiate some day, *in pompis*, before a high altar, with all the members of his family present, and might not Pieroun's father, when old and past work, find his chair and his soup in some *presbytère* where there would be room for him beside *M. l'Abbé?* Within the last forty years, however, the number of lads who enter the seminary has fallen off; trade, enterprise, and the many careers of modern life drawing off young men from the ranks of the secular and parochial clergy, while those who feel any peculiar vocation for the religious life frequently prefer to enter some of the religious orders. In many dioceses the supply of clergy already falls short of the demand, and now that military service is obligatory even on those who have crossed the threshold of the seminary, it is to be feared that many posts of duty will be left vacant. Some of the livings are cruelly small. Even with the help of the much-begrudged *casuel* (fees for baptisms, marriages, deaths, funerals, and *obits*), the incumbent of a village on the Esteron must have a hard struggle on a pittance which ranges from 30*l.* to 50*l.* a year. If he has any luck the municipality may eke this out by a small present; but his *presbytère* is a poor little hovel, and hard, very hard, is his fare. As he has the poor always with him, and as an affluent landowner is a thing unknown as a neighbour, it is difficult to suppose that he can save any money, and so, when disease and old age overtake such a village *curé*, he must ask for a pension of 8*l.* from the Minister of Public Worship. If he stands well with his vicar-general and his bishop, this may be augmented by the splendid gift of 2*l.* from the diocesan fund. It is easy therefore to understand that there should not be great competition among the candidates of such a profession, and easy to understand that the holders of such poor livings must charge for the Masses, and other offices, which they are asked to perform.

A rich peasant will not grudge 20*l*. on his funeral; the bakemeats, bells, candles, and the like, mounting up sometimes to even a larger sum. In the hill-villages about Vence, the Italian custom of carrying the dead with open face still prevails, and sundown is here, as in Italy, the usual hour for the funerals of the poor. In Grasse, though the coffin is actually covered, the lid is draped so as to look as if the corpse were displayed; the cap and veil of the deceased presenting a striking likeness to the figure. In the same *arrondissement* we have recently come on the trace of a singular superstition. For the space of nine days and nights it is thought right to leave the house, the room, and the bed of the dead man exactly as he left them. During that period his return is considered possible, and it would argue a want of tact if anything were changed, for better or for worse. As the practice cannot be defended from the sanitary point of view, one can only be glad that the days of expectation do not here, as in Russia, extend to forty.

All the habits of the peasantry are unhealthy—from the swaddling bands of the infant, down to this last compliment paid to the departed. Smallpox is never really banished from the towns, but it is only a wonder that the population is not much more unhealthy than it is, for the plagues of olden times, like the late-lingering leprosy that used to find its home at Eza, proved what dirt *can* do for disease. When I first came to the Riviera I was much interested in the fact that real Syrian leprosy (*Lepra Hebræorum*) was still to be found, and I hoped to see a leper. At last I did—in a crowd before the door of a church on a festival—and I was so utterly scared by the sight of the shining white patches, and by the glaring eyes of the most debased-looking being I had ever beheld, that I clapped my muff up to my eyes, and fled downhill, as fast as if the leper had been pursuing me.

As education spreads, some knowledge of the laws of health and disease will spread also, and it is to be hoped that this may in time correct the extreme nastiness of Provençal habits. Infant mortality is terrible. From motives of economy the children of a family are limited in number, and again from motives of economy the mothers, in going out to work, abandon their babies to the grandmother or to the *crèche*. Thanks to this system the proportion of those who never live to cut their seven-year-old teeth is enormous.

The number of Provençals who can neither read nor write is much diminished: schools have multiplied, rival communities have bestirred themselves in the cause of education, and in the regiments a colonel will often refuse leave, furlough, and other indulgences till his recruits have learned to read. A great deal has been said against the education given by the *Sœurs*. That it leaves somewhat to be desired I can imagine, but, on the other hand, the *Sœurs* are the good angels, and the only ones, of a very poor district. I remember once, along with a friend, examining some children belonging to a convent-school near Falicon, and that we found their knowledge of the New Testament to be advanced as well as correct. The same cannot be said for the peasants who come down from La Brigue, if they are over thirty years of age. One day our Briguegasque housemaid returned from witnessing a Passion-play. She was much touched, and still more indignant. 'What,' she exclaimed, ' had that poor Monsieur done that they maltreated him so? They beat him, and spat at him, and I cried when they pierced his side with a spear!' Our Presbyterian maid and old Benoîte, the Savoisienne cook, were alike horrified at Madeloun's ignorance, for as she went to Mass regularly no one supposed her to be so ignorant of the Life, Death, and Mission of our Lord. We tried to enlighten her, but Madeloun was proof against any theological training. She stoutly denied any complicity in the cruel sufferings of the Lord, appealed to all concerned whether she were not a good daughter, sister, wife, and mother, and as such *incapable*! of such horrid cruelty? Of imputed guilt and imputed merits Madeloun would not hear a word, and though we bought a volume of Scripture stories (with pictures) for her, and Benoîte read them to her in the kitchen, Madeloun remained of the same opinion, 'that poor Monsieur was as gentle as a lamb, that those people were brutal, and that she had had nothing to do with it.'

Religion to the Latin populations is too often a show —a poem acted on the stage of the church, a piece which, thanks to candles and music, is still fairly acceptable, even after many years of repetition, because on a great festival there is always something to look at, *santi belli* (as they call the cheap images) to buy, and a procession in which to take a part. Corporations and congregations are popular, for the same reasons, but there is more love of movement than of devotion in this race, and a festival is looked to more for the fun than for the prayers.

The spread of Liberal opinions keeps the men away from church, but as the male communicants in the parish church of Cannes numbered over three hundred last Easter, it cannot be said that either the Radical demagogues or the influx of Protestant visitors has greatly altered the habit of attendance at this *fête obligatoire*. People go in crowds to visit the churches on Maunday Thursday, and I do not know that I ever witnessed a more touching sight than the mourning group of women who on the evening of that day sang the *Stabat Mater* hymn. It was in a dirty, ruinous, parish church, damp as a stable, and ill paved with bricks. The great door stood open, as if a funeral had just passed out, and the altar was stripped, but before the *reposoir*, where the sacrament was buried, stood some tall camellias, and some candles burned. The women, with their shawls over their heads, as they stood huddled together in the gloom reminded one forcibly of the desolation of the Maries, and of the sorrow and the apparent overthrow of the little Christian community on the evening after the Crucifixion.

That same church had been very picturesque on Palm Sunday, for every grown-up person then had a palm or green spray, while the children carried their curious trophies—a stick all tinsel flowers and bonbons, which is said to be the remnant of the old Greek festival for the return of Theseus after slaying the Minotaur. However that may be, 'these palms,' as Origen said, ' are no longer the palms of Osiris, they are the palms of Christ, and the moment when the priests, on arriving, demand entrance into the church is very impressive. The door is thrice struck on the outside by the foot of the cross, and, with the choristers collected inside, a parley then commences. Admittance is demanded for 'the King of Glory.' 'Who is the King of Glory?' asks the choir. 'The Lord of Hosts, He is the King of Glory,' is the response from without, and then the doors are flung open, and the procession of palms streaming up the aisle becomes the signal for the elevation of the palms of the whole congregation. The church looked like a wood.

Still, because a church is sometimes crowded, or because the peasant, reckoning like his grandfather, by the calendar, sows his seed on the Feast of the Conversion of St. Paul, or looks for rain at Michaelmas, or fears the frosts of *les saints vendangeurs* in May, it does not follow that he is either a devout or a submissive person. Very far from it. These Provençals, like all Frenchmen, believe in equality. They are *frondeurs*, and difficult to overawe. They do not respect dignities, and their *patois* has few locutions expressive of deference or of respect. The scenes at the midnight Mass of Christmas are not always edifying. Some young lads close to me kept up, one Christmas Eve, a fire of jokes and laughter, till I touched one of them on the shoulder, and said to him, 'Chut; lou Pichieut someilho!' (Hush, the Infant sleeps.) The boy first stared at me and my fur jacket, and then stoutly replied, 'He is not born yet.' 'Pardon me,' I answered, 'it is past twelve.'

'Ah, *then*!' he cried, and order was restored in my neighbourhood.

I possess a curious metrical rendering of the Gospels into Provençal, and the direct homely phraseology of that version is very curious. By a certain Marius Décard the Gospels for every Sunday and saint's day were *virados* (turned) into verse, and, what is still more wonderful, he succeeded in doing the same for the Canon of the Mass, and for the prayers during the Celebration. I will only quote a part of the Gospel for the second Sunday in Lent—St. Matt. xvii. 1–19.[1]

> Un jour comm' ooujourd'hui, escalant la Mountagno,
> Jesus s'éro près per coumpagno,
>   Leis très Disciples sanct',
>   Pieroun, Jacques et Jean :
> Et, per qu'ignoures ren de tout ce que n'en éro,
> Jacques et Jean érount doux frèro.

---

[1] As on a day like this Jesus ascended the mountain
And took to Himself for companions
The three holy disciples,
Peter, James, and John:
And (that ye may not be ignorant of how things were)
James and John were two brothers.

   .   .   .   .   .

When they felt to themselves returning
Wonted courage and force,
They took again the little path
Which serpent-like did wind
Along the mountain's side.
Then as they went he stopped their followers' steps;
And Jesus this admonition made:
'Beware,' he cried, 'and lay this well to mind:
Never to any man declare
What you have newly seen—
Make this your secret, in your hearts concealed
Until your death-day, never telling
How drawn up from the earth
You saw God's Son
Towards His Father fly.'

Then follows the account of the Transfiguration in seven verses, and the poem ends thus:—

> Quand agneront repres et l'aploumb et leis forço,
> Et lou courage que ranforço,
> Regagnerount ensems lou pichoun carreiroon,
> Que serpentavo en viravoon,
> Lou long de la Mountagno.
> Es en camin fasent qu'arrestant seis coumpagno.
> Jesus l'y fet' questo montien;
> Gardes-vous (fes-l'y ben attentien)
> De dire, en que que siech, ce que vinès de veire!
> Fés n'en voustre secret, chacun dens voustre cuour,
> Jusqu'oou jour que deis mouort,
> S'envoulant de la terro,
> Vegues lou Fiou de Diou s'envoular vers soun Péro.

I think my readers will appreciate this extract, its naïve simplicity, and the skill with which the scene is presented, and it is not difficult to imagine its becoming popular. Long may such a homely and affectionate acquaintance with the Gospels live in the hearts of the Provençals! for it must be owned that in the towns very advanced views are now fashionable. In Nice Garibaldi, as the real hero of the popular imagination, has certainly dethroned any lingering partiality for religious observances. The *Sœurs* were, in 1882, removed from the management of the Hospice de la Ville in Cannes, and one may even meet a civil interment on the Grasse road. The advanced party there not only has its newspapers, but it has its own ferry-boat, for a steam-launch that plies to the Islands seeks to attract one class of customers by proclaiming the fact that *it has never been baptised*!

With all this, with the most passionate ideal of

personal liberty, the peasantry of the Maritime Alps are marked enemies to progress. They like a prohibitive tariff, they consider every advantage given to strangers as a positive injury to themselves, and they decline to alter their old methods of dealing with their own property.

How they till their fields we shall see when we come to look at the agriculture of the Maritime Alps.

CHAPTER IV.

CORN, WINE, AND OIL.

'The sire of gods and men, with hard decrees,
Forbids our plenty to be bought with ease,
And wills that mortal man, inured to toil,
Should exercise, with pains, the grudging soil. . . .
Nor is the profit small the peasant makes,
Who smooths with harrows, or who pounds with rakes
The stubborn clods. Nor Ceres from on high
Regards his labours with a grudging eye:
Nor his, who ploughs across the furrowed ground,
And on the back of Earth inflicts new wounds:
For he, with frequent exercise, commands
The unwilling soil, and tames the stubborn lands.'

I. *Georgic* (Dryden).

'The field labourer of Northern countries may be but a hapless hind, hedging and ditching dolefully, or at best serving a steam-beast with oil and fire; but in the South there is the poetry of agriculture still. Materially it may be an evil and a loss; but spiritually it is a gain—a certain peace and light lie on the people at their toil: the reaper with his hook, the plougher with his oxen, the girl who gleans among the trailing vines, the men who sing to get a blessing on the grapes—they have all a certain grace and dignity of the old classic ways left with them. They till the earth still with the simplicity of old, looking straight to the gods for recompense. It will not last, but it is here for a little while longer still.'—OUIDA.

MIRABEAU said of the soil of Provence that 'were it to be valued at the price of the best land in France its entire rental would not, in 1780, pay for the cost of all the walls that are used for holding it up.' The countless terraces of Provence are certainly the first thing to strike a stranger, and if that stranger knows anything of the price of labour, his first questions are sure to be, 'Who paid for these walls?' and 'Who is now paid to keep them in repair?' These terraces are simply an instance of the truth of the Scottish saying that 'mony a pickle maks a mickle.' Had they all been constructed in the same half century the rental of the province would indeed have been insufficient to pay for them, but the peasants working at them all day, and often part of the night, through many centuries, have covered Provence with a network of stones. In this way they have preserved to her a soil that is ever ready to run off. Many of the little plots, which really cannot be called fields, rise at an angle of 70° and even of 75°, and but for these walls they might cease to exist after a thunderstorm. As it is, they allow the culture of vines, oats, and plums to creep far up the sides of the hills.

It is said that the idea of so supporting the fields was originally brought from the Holy Land, and as Provence certainly owes both her cork trade and her *blé Sarrazin* to her Moorish invaders, so she may be content to have received her terraces from Templars and Hospitallers, when, fresh from Palestine, they were eager to improve the manors they held under the Maritime Alps.

After the terraces the system of irrigation next calls for attention. If tenants received any compensation for their outlay on irrigation much greater advances would be made; but even as it is the peasant proprietor at least never neglects it. From the 'upper and the nether springs' he waters his field. Countless little, stone channels are built, and from these he can flood the narrow, pan-shaped beds in which he is growing violets or salads. He can let the water pass from one bed to another by simply pushing down the edge of the pan at the side he chooses, and in this way, like the Syrian cultivators of Scripture, he waters his land 'with his foot.'

The whole agricultural and rural life of Provence has this charm of Scriptural associations. Round the wells you see the 'tall 'reeds shaken with the wind.' There is, in bad weather, plenty of 'clay in the streets.' Yonder is the 'threshing-floor,' with its piles of golden maize; oxen plough between the drills, and on that sunny bank a kneeling woman gathers into her apron the last 'shaking of olives.' There are 'rivers that run among the hills,' and then emerge into the 'green pastures,' where the shepherd as he walks leading his sheep 'carries a lamb in his bosom.' The 'waters wear away the stones,' but among the rocks there are 'veins of silver'; and in the beds of the streams hungry, barefoot children seek for 'dust of gold.' Across the mountains go 'paths which the vulture's eye hath not seen'; but in the low-lying valleys 'the wild olive' is grafted, and the fruitful vine is pruned 'that it may bring forth more fruit.' There are 'dews that lie all night upon the branches,' 'hoar frosts scattered like ashes,' thunders which are as 'the voice of His excellency,' 'bands of Orion' across the midnight sky, and 'sweet influences of the Pleiades.' But there are also 'clouds which return after the rain.' There are flowers of the fields 'arrayed' as Judean kings have never been, and 'grass of the field' ruthlessly 'cut down and cast into the ovens.' There is 'wine that maketh glad the heart of man'; there are 'shadows of great rocks in a dry and thirsty place where no water is'; there are 'fenced cities' set upon hills, with 'foundations' in the living rock. There are 'floods that descend' and find out the weak places in the 'bowing-out walls'; there are 'broken cisterns that can hold no water'; and in 'gardens of cucumbers' there are the gardeners' 'lodges,' while there are 'orchards of pomegranates, and of every pleasant fruit.' When spring returns there are 'almond-trees' that flourish, 'locusts and caterpillars' without number. The air is perfumed with 'cassia,' but there are 'little foxes that spoil the grapes,' and many a 'pitcher broken at the fountain.' To make up for them we have 'the potter' and his wheel; in short, a whole world of Oriental images, brought here into daily life, and filling it with associations and with charms.

Provence is a country of extremes—of glaciers, and of sun-dried sands, of winters that are like summers, and of summers that make one regret the few showers of the winter. The same quantity of rain falls annually in Marseilles as in Paris, but in Paris the quantity is spread over one hundred and fifty days which in Marseilles floods the streets in fifty days. In London, out of three hundred and sixty-five days, one hundred and seventy are days of such moisture as to deserve the name of 'wet days.' In Edinburgh the number rises to two hundred and six, while in Dublin it exceeds even this liberal allowance. In Cannes the average never amounts to seventy, and Dr. de Valcourt, who has studied the subject carefully, rates the average over the whole Riviera at fifty-one wet days in the year. But the quantity of rain that falls during those fifty-one days is immense. The peasants are not satisfied unless it also penetrates four mètres into the soil, and they look for the early and the latter rains with the anxiety of persons who know that for the rest of the year they must depend on the dews. Those are certainly abundant, and it is well that they are, for the climate of Provence is very much more arid than it used to be. Such an undesirable alteration has been brought about by a stupid destruction of the forests, which makes evaporation too rapid, and causes the rain that does fall to run off too quickly. So long ago as 1669, a royal edict, taking note of this danger, forbade the cutting of the woods *en blanc étoc*, and they had begun to flourish again when they were in the eighteenth century depreciated by those Economists, called *physiocrates*, who, like the elder Mirabeau, wished to grow corn on every rood of earth. The forests were encroached upon, and the ground so reclaimed put under cultivation. Then came the Revolution, when the peasants, without sharing the theory of the philosophers, had a still more destructive practice, for they put their goats into the woods. Those little depredators soon nibbled and destroyed more trees than their owners felled with hatchets, and the combined effect was disastrous. The late Emperor Napoleon III. gave his attention to this subject, and the hills behind Nice have been all replanted at his command, in the hope of rendering the climate less dry, and of preventing the dangerous floods which the autumnal rains were apt to produce in the district.

The department of the Var remains the best wooded part of France, and in the Maritime Alps the rental of the cork-trees is now large. These beautiful evergreens flourish wherever they find a granitic soil, and along the Argentière, as in the valley above Biot, they form groups that remind one of the wooded dells in the Campagna. It is estimated that over a thousand persons find employment in the trade to which their bark gives rise.

A fine carouba tree, such as we see on the coast about Eza, represents a rental of forty francs per annum, but the principal riches of the Maritime Alps has, until the last half of this century, consisted in the olive-trees. All soils, except a marshy one, lend themselves to this cultivation. There is a popular saying that on the same piece of ground as the best wine you may look for the best oil. There may be some truth in this; but perhaps it only means that the olive is a very gross feeder, and that where it has been plentifully manured its neighbour the vine derives some accidental benefit. The olive is said to have been originally brought to this coast by the Greek traders, and the climate has certainly suited a tree which about Beaulieu attains to the most noble size. The wood, which is valuable, takes a high polish, and has created for Nice and Cannes a whole trade in mosaic furniture. The flowers, which are green and very insignificant, appear about Easter. The fruit hangs long on the trees, ripening slowly as it turns from green to a rich purplish black, and exposed therefore, not only to many changes of temperature, but to the attacks of all sorts of insects. Of all its enemies the *Caïron* is the most mischievous. It is a wicked, little, white worm, that lodging in the pulp soon eats the olive hollow, and which in the last ten years has eaten up 40,000 francs worth of the olives of the *arrondissement* of Grasse. The Provençal olives are never as large as the Spanish ones, but the oil given used to be very fine. The *Nostrale* is the kind on which the peasants of the Riviera mostly rely, but the *Columbano* is also used at Nice for preserving. The harvest, which begins in October, goes on to the end of March. The fruit when it has been beaten off the trees is gathered by women and children, and, after lying for some days in a cool place, is then sent, in sacks of 100 or of 200 kilos, to the mill. In a good year a tree ought to yield 9 kilos of olives and return about 9 kilos 500 grammes of oil. The best sort is delightful for the table, but many of the oils, especially those of Nice, are too rich in what is called *muqueuse*, and as such burn dimly, while they clog the wick unpleasantly. Nothing can be more picturesque than an oil mill, with its shadowy recesses, its deep jars that always seem to be waiting for Ali Baba, and its strange collection of sacks and weights and presses. But next to a perfume factory it is the most ill-smelling place conceivable, whether you stand inside, where the golden oil runs drop by drop from under the horsehair presses, or outside, by the tanks where the refuse festers in the sun. This unpleasant-looking, dark green stuff is, as it hardens, broken up into cakes which are dug out and sold as manure, returning therefore, very possibly, in this shape to the roots of the same trees which originally furnished its materials. The crushed stones, or *grainols*, are a cheap fuel much used by the bakers for their ovens, but they are the terror of the laundresses, as the least mixture of this oily refuse is ruin to the wood ash which is so constantly used here instead of soap.

Nothing can be more beautiful than the view from the town of Grasse, over miles of these olive-trees, of which the pale grey-green foliage forms a quiet-toned background for the sunburnt limestones, the red roofs, the clumps of Aleppo pines, and the beautiful Catalpa trees. The hues of the olive have puzzled artists, whether the trees be looked at in the cool tints of early morning or in the bronzed beauty of the afterglow. Each painter has his own way of handling them. One will deal especially with the angularity of their branches and the roughness of their trunks; another with the airy, smoke-like delicacy of their masses in middle distance; a third will handle them cleverly in clumps, while a fourth, using their masses as part of the lines of his composition, does no more than justice to the part which they play in the landscapes of the south. Yet the difficulty has never really been overcome, and only an approximate success has been gained by anyone over trees so intangible in their beauty. Seen by moonlight they seem to belong to fairyland, while even in the noonday their stems have shadows so sharp as to recall all the pathos of the moonlight in Gethsemane. At once light and massive, at once changeful and evergreen, the olive is like nothing but itself, as it flowers and fruits in its perpetual peace.

After the olive comes the vine. The plant is as old as the world, and as new as the gladness which it daily puts into the hearts of men. It is the most beautiful thing that grows when it is left to ramble from tree to tree; its very tendrils are scented, its autumn leaves are stained amber and orange and crimson, and when its faggots come to die on the hearth they do so at last in 'aromatic pain.' Yet it leads a hard life:—

> We shall see its way is not of pleasure or of ease.
> .... The fruit begins
> Almost before the flower has had its day:
> Even as it grows it is not free to heaven,
> But tied to a stake, and if its arms stretch out
> It is but crosswise, also forced and bound—
> And so it drains, out of the hard hillside
> Fixed in its own place, the food of life—
> And quickens with it, breaking forth in bud
> Joyous, and green, and exquisite in form,
> Wreathed lightly into tendrils, leaf and bloom.
> Yea, the grace of the green vine makes all the land
> Lovely in springtime. . . .
> But so they leave it not—the husbandman
> Comes early, with the pruning-hooks and shears,
> And strips it bare of all its innocent pride
> And wandering garlands, cutting deep and sure,
> Unsparing for its tenderness or joy.
> Then in its loss and pain it wasteth not;
> But lends itself, in unabated life,
> More perfect under the despoiling hand:
> The bleeding limbs are hardened into fruit.
>
> . . . . . .
>
> Then comes the vintage, for the days are ripe,
> And surely now, in its perfected bloom,
> It may rejoice a little in its crown,
> Though it bend low beneath the weight of it
> Wrought out of the long strivings of its heart—
>
> But, ah! the hands are ready to tear down
> The treasures of the grapes: the feet are there
> To tread them in the winepress gathered in,

Until the blood-red rivers of the wine
Run over, and the land is full of joy.

But the vine standeth, stripped and bare,
Having given all: and now its own dark time is come,
And no man payeth back to it
The comfort or the glory of its gift,
But rather now, most merciless, all pain
And loss are piled together, as its days
Decline, and the spring sap has ceased to flow.
Now is it cut back to the very stem,
Despoiled, disfigured, left a leafless stock,
Alone, thro' all the dark days that shall come—
And all the winter-time the wine gives joy
To those who else were dismal in the cold.
But the vine standeth out among the frost,
And, has only this praise left, after all,
That it endures, in long lone steadfastness,
The winter thro'—and next year blooms again,
Not bitter for the torment undergone,
Not barren for the fulness yielded up,
As fair and fruitful towards the sacrifice,
As if no touch had ever come to it
But the soft airs of heaven and dews of earth:
And so fulfils itself in love once more.

. . . .

I speak to those who suffer: they will know,
Better than I, the whole deep truth of it!

. . . .

Measure thy life by loss instead of gain,
Not by the wine drunk, but the wine poured forth,
For Love's strength standeth in Love's sacrifice,
And whoso suffers most, has most to give.[1]

The vine flowers in April, and is therefore only too certain to fall a victim to the *lune rousse*, to the moon after the Paschal one, so apt to come with sharp frosts and blighting winds to ruin the prospect of the year.

---

[1] *The Disciples*, a poem by H. E. H. King.

Even if the vines and the walnuts do not suffer during her reign, which corresponds to the 'blackthorn winter' of our English experience, there are other dangers signalled all along the calendar of the French spring. There are the redoubtable '*Saints vendangeurs*,' St. Croizet, who is commemorated on the 3rd of May, St. Colmet on the 9th of the month, and St. Urbinet on the 25th, and who, as his *fête* falls the latest, is the last and worst enemy of the vine. If there be frost on that day, the case is indeed a bad one for vines that already on the 11th, 12th, 13th, and 14th were reminded of St. Mamert, St. Pancrace, St. Gervais, and St. Pâcome, all grouped under the unpleasant head of '*les saints de glace.*' A vineyard that has been blackened is indeed a sad sight, but there are seasons in which all goes well till the so-called *faux bourgeons* wave ready to be pruned. At this moment the plant is most luxuriant, but as its strength is needed for its fruit-bunches, these superfluous branches with their wandering tendrils are all condemned. I have watched the process in the vineyards of Dauphiny and Savoy. When the last bundle of fragrant leafage has been carried away, probably on the head of the master's daughter, it is her business to plant a small, white wooden cross among her vines, and then, closing the gate, to leave them to God and the sun. The gate will not be opened again till October, when all the merry vintagers troop in. If they are merry then or not depends on the thunder-storms of the summer, for a vineyard that has been *grêlée* is even a sadder sight than one which has been frosted.

F

Some afternoon a storm comes beating up against the wind, and breaks overhead, with flashes and crashes, and such a rattle of hail as makes the heart of the landlord die within him. When the storm has rolled away he goes out to judge of its work. Alas! alas! the path from his vineyard is still running like a river, and a bowing-out wall having fallen into the roadway, he need go no farther to get a sight of the vines. They are all tangled and ravelled, and drenched and hashed, and look as if a park of artillery had been driven over them. A week hence they will look even worse, for the scorching and reddening of the leaves will then show how the sudden chill and the evaporation, after the touch of the ice, have checked the sap and circulation of the plant. In fact the wine-growers of France have many troubles, and between cold and bad seasons, hailstorms and *phylloxera*, their property has of late undergone a deterioration which has reduced many affluent families to the condition of Irish landlords.

The department of the Maritime Alps has some very fine vineyards, though here too *oïdium* and *phylloxera* have touched their health. The vineyards are treated with sulphate of carbon, and with a manure of potass which has been found useful. The labour of so dressing an infected vineyard is paid by the State, the proprietor paying only for the chemicals employed. Two American vines, called here 'Riparia' and 'Jacquet,' are generally proof against the teeth of the *phylloxera*, and the black Catawba grape, the one which has a smell of raspberries, and which covers the Crimean slopes, is now largely cultivated for the same reason in the canton of Nice. But its juice can only be used to mix with other wines, a process always largely resorted to here where the country produces so little wine that for seven out of the twelve months of the year it has to rely on the produce of other countries. The best red wine is that of Bellet near Nice, and the best white ones are those of Gillette and La Gaude. It is also good at Pégomas, where a spur of the hills comes down into the broad alluvial valley which the Mourachone waters. I have often drunk this white wine, which the mistress of the beautiful farm of Terres-Blanches calls Oros, because the *clairette* grape from which it is made grows on the rocks above Pégomas. The process of making a white wine is always a tedious one, requiring greater care than the preparation of a red wine, and there is the fear that a second fermentation setting in inopportunely may turn the whole cask sour. It requires to be racked and cleared very often, and the waste entailed during the repetition of this process makes the wine dearer. White wine will seldom fetch less than from eighteen to twenty pence a litre, while a very good red wine can be drunk, and is drunk in my house, at seven pence the litre.

So much for wine and oil. Now for the corn. Through all the winter days we have seen it pushing bravely in the little fields, drilled in between the vines and the beans, and sheltered by a network of peach- and almond-trees, from which, when spring appears, there will drop a rosy snow.

What would our Northern farmers not give to have anything like these tall, fresh green stalks, in all their healthy straightness of growth, which have feared no winter's rages, and which will be ripe for the sickle before the 20th of June? But on the other hand the Northern farmer would be scandalised at these weeds, at the sword-lilies and the hemlock, and the big arum leaves, and the clumps of borage which adorn the fields. Then sowing and reaping as practised in Provence would strike him as very archaic. And so they are. Machinery for agricultural purposes is unknown, and broad-footed oxen tread out the grain on a paved threshing-floor, to which not even the authority of Scripture could now reconcile a Scotch bailiff.

Yet he would be quite mistaken if he despised the Provençal farmer, even in departments where *la petite culture* prevails. Every means for increasing the fertility of the soil is known and practised, and the small farmer who can produce wheat, maize, pulse, grapes, figs, almonds, peaches, hemp, tobacco, and flax, along with plums, mulberries, haricots, madder, roses, artichokes, and green peas, must be allowed to be a person of no common experience and ingenuity.

In the *arrondissement* of Nice the wheat represents a money value of about 50,000 francs, but the quantity grown is not sufficient to provide for the population during eight months of the year. In this way the *numéraire* of the district (grossly augmented as that annually is by the influx of strangers) does not remain in the country, but leaves it to purchase the bread required for daily consumption. It appears therefore that, in spite of the perpetual sunshine which settles on it, the district of the Maritime Alps is a poor one, nor is there any promise of a golden age for agriculture. Quite the reverse. Wheat, which it costs forty francs to produce here, can be bought on the quay of Marseilles at thirty-five francs, and that after the freight from America, and the duty, and the *octroi de la ville* have all three been paid. This fact is the death-knell of such Provençal farmers whose fields lie in a zone higher than that which can grow oranges, lemons, or flowers for the perfume trade. The taxes are already a fifth of their rental, and the land is no doubt mortgaged for another fifth, so that, considering the rising price of labour, the prospects of the agricultural class may be said to be as gloomy here as they are in Great Britain. I have hitherto spoken, however, only of the case of the landowner; it remains for me to speak of the farmer, and of the husbandman—to whom the ground does not belong, and who have to reckon with a landlord.

CHAPTER V.

ON THE FARMS.

'The distribution of a number of small properties among the peasantry forms a kind of rampart and safeguard for the holders of large estates: a peasant property may, without exaggeration, be called the lightning-conductor that averts from society dangers which might otherwise lead to violent catastrophes.'—E. DE LAVELEYE.

PEASANT proprietors were by no means unknown in France before the Revolution, and in Provence they not only did exist but they also suffered less from the pressure of the feudal system than in the northern districts of the kingdom. During the Crusades, and during the wars of the Countesses, the great lords could not pretend to cultivate their estates. Nor as time went on did it become more possible for them to do so. The family of Grasse, for example, held forty fiefs; the Villeneuves spread all along the coast from the Var to Hyères, and the barons of Baux, who held lands from Arles to Ventimiglia, were the masters of seventy-nine cities, known as *les places Baussenques*. Such proprietors thought of nothing so little as of turning their swords into ploughshares, but they hit on the plan of giving grants of land to their *hommes*, or dependants. The grants to these *caslans* were of two kinds: either in *franc-alleu*, or subject to the *cens*—a duty paid yearly, but to be levied also whenever the ground changed hands, by barter, by sale, or by death. These *hommes* for centuries have cropped the soil and built the terraces of Provence, and have drawn from the ground a livelihood which their superiors, lay or clerical, taxed more or less heavily. The feudal rights of the lords were too many and too complicated to be all enumerated here. They comprised the *corvée*, or forced labour on the lands of the superiors; liability to military service, not always for defensive purposes only, and an obligation to grind their corn at their lord's mill, and to bake their bread at the *banal* oven. Peasants sometimes paid in money, sometimes in fruit, or in hens, and while the Abbot of the Lérins took every alternate basket of figs, the Villeneuves of Vence had a disagreeable way of asking for one pig out of every two. There were also tolls and ferry dues—a penny a foot for every horse or mule; and there was a hard law forbidding the *censitaires* to sell their wine so long as the lord's wine remained unsold. Yet the *censitaires* held on for centuries, and, except when a war or a pestilence decimated their numbers, they made a living of it as best they might. They even bought land occasionally, for they could raise money from the Jews and Lombards on the unexceptionable security of their real property. The Italian colonists settled by the Prior of the Lérins at Vallauris, and those whom the Bishop of Vence originally planted at Biot, held grants of land on the most favourable terms, so that small holdings cannot be said to have been created in Provence by the Revolution.

What it really did was, first, to increase their numbers, and, secondly, to free them from the cruel exactions and restrictions of feudal tenure.

Out of the proprietors in France M. Léonce de Lavergne used to reckon that 5,000,000 were rural owners, and about 4,000,000 were actual cultivators of the soil. Of these 3,000,000 possess, on an average, a *hectare*, or nearly two and a half acres of land. It is easy to see how the freedom of such a farmer makes all the difference to him between comfort and starvation. It has been calculated here, in Maritime Provence, that every grain of corn must bring forth threefold before it represents the bare equivalent of the seed and time bestowed on it. Supposing the return to be only threefold, the *revenu net* would then be none at all. Supposing it to be fourfold, there would still be but little margin left for the husbandman. The royal taxes (reckoned by so many *feux* in each canton) had first to be paid, and then there was the *dîme* of the Church, and finally the feudal dues, from the *cens* on the land down to the baking of the loaf. But the peasant proprietor of to-day has only the first of these burdens to bear. The taxes *are* heavy—about a fifth of the annual value of his farm, but for the rest he may manage as he thinks best. If the harvests are bad then he and his must live more meagrely, and the marriages of his children must be postponed, but if a good year comes, if corn and wine and oil are plentiful, then he is master of his own gains. He has seed-corn to sell, he has no arrears, and if he has not got a lawsuit on hand, he can put by some money, and forget the leanness of past seasons.

Almost every peasant has, or has had, or is going to have, a lawsuit. Sit, as I have done, sketching for half a day on the doorstep of a notary's office, and you will be surprised to see the number of feet that cross his threshold. Needless to say that these litigious habits lead to debt, and that many of the small holdings of France are already mortgaged up to one-fifth of their value. If to this amount of debt overhead any peasant happens to add heavily in his own case, it is easy to see that bankruptcy is not far below the horizon of practical politics for him. At the best of times a very strict economy is required 'to make the ends meet,' and it is a question whether, as education spreads and the wants taught by education increase, the class of peasant proprietors will remain such as it now is. It could not, if it were not that the wants of others are increasing at a still more rapid pace, and that the demand for what a little farm can supply makes the farmer more sure of a sale for his calf, his eggs, his grapes, and his carrots. This is his great opportunity, and it is one which might make his fortune if the movement of modern life did not also reach to his own threshold, and had not sometimes crossed it. The passionate chase after money, and those material pleasures which money can buy, is already spreading downwards from the *bourgeoisie*, and both debt and heart-burnings appear in many humble homes.

Jean and Marguerite Firmin could tell you something about all that. They have lived long and happily on their farm where their little inn was so popular that their wine needed no bush under the creaking sign of the *Cheval Blanc*. It is true that the doorstep has a pool of very dirty water in front of it, that there are sacks of grain on the landing, and that a lot of feathers in a shallow basket shows the fate of the little white cockerel newly killed for your dinner. But the kitchen is a warm place, a savoury mess of *polenta* smokes on the board, and a bit of meat is stewing on the fire. Old Jean has grown stiff with rheumatism, but he has a good face, and his old woman looks at him with kind and anxious eyes. A young woman, with a handkerchief tied round her head, waits sulkily on the carters who are at table. That is their daughter-in-law—one of the new school. She has a bonnet and white stockings in a box upstairs; she dislikes the farm, and the chickens, and the barn where the golden straw is stacked, and most of all she dislikes exerting herself in the house, while her husband is in the field, and his parents are too infirm to work as they used to do. Madame Fanchette is a fine lady in her way. The last time I saw her was at the little station at St. ——; the handkerchief had disappeared, she was, as the Italians say, *vestita da paina*, had on the bonnet and the white stockings, and dangled a little bag in her hand. She was very gay: talking with the *curé* and with the station-master, and with many neighbours, who when they had seen her start for town, on a visit, as she averred, to the dentist, loudly pitied old Jean and his good old Margoton. The new fashions have brought quarrels to the *Cheval Blanc*, and it will go hard to be thought that debt and jealousy, and something worse, may come some day soon should the young farmer's smart wife make many trips to town.

The real drawbacks to the system of small holdings are not felt to be drawbacks in the eyes of the landowning peasantry. It may be too true that the isolated and jealous individuality in which they live threatens the death of public virtue in France, because the peasant does not look beyond his personal interests, and because Arcadian simplicity is generally very selfish. But in France we must rejoice that the landowning and cultivating peasantry exist in sufficient numbers to form some counterbalance to the *doctrinaires* of the big towns, whose theory is that *la propriété, c'est le vol*, and to the artisans, whose practice is communistic. These peasant landowners are still the drag on the wheel, the true conservatives and defenders of the rights of property, and *la petite culture* will find its markets increasing as towns grow up, and as communication becomes more easy.

In the whole department of the Maritime Alps there is not one farm let at a fixed rent. Landlord and tenant are alike convinced that where crops of olives and oranges are concerned a fixed rent would be fatal to both their interests. The leases are all short ones—for three, six, or nine years—and entry is generally at Michaelmas. By far the largest part of the territory of the Maritime Alps is worked on the *métayer* system, and on verbal contracts. Because you see a man carrying a sack of olives, or a bag of violets, or driving a cartful of calves to market, it does not follow that he owns them. He has but a part interest in the freight, being the *métayer* of some landlord, who neither can nor will work his own farm. Who are the persons who take farms on the *métayer* plan? Men accustomed to husbandry, or owners of adjacent plots, or perhaps the former owners of small properties which they have ceased to possess. I will put a case :—

A peasant of the name of Isnard, in the *arrondissement* of Grasse, had a small estate. Four bad olive crops began his troubles, but they were followed by the death of his mule. Isnard himself fell sick, and finally died, leaving behind him a lawsuit, a widow, a lame daughter, two mortgages, and three sons. Of these, the youngest was a coachman in Marseilles; the second was with his regiment at Nice; and Paul, the eldest, had always lived and worked on the farm. The property came to be divided. A *conseil de famille* was held, and it was agreed to put the land up for sale. No sooner was it in the market than it was bought in by what Paul called *la bande noire*, by some notaries, holders of house property in Grasse, Draguignan, or Toulon, who became its joint or its single proprietors. The sale was effected in about three weeks' time, and the widow and daughter migrated at once. They took a room in the nearest little town, where they had some relations, and there they vegetate. There they creep about the chapels, pick olives, collect manure on the roads, and watch the funerals, as they roast their coffee in the little dark street. Paul, the eldest son, is not on good terms with them, for he has often said very hard things to his sister, whose humpback has kept her single, and whose presence in the house had prevented him from bringing home a wife. He determined privately to make an offer for the old house and farm as its *métayer*, and, as soon as his offer was accepted, he

THE FARM.

had the banns for his marriage with Micheline Bazin put up without delay. While they all lived on the farm marriage had been out of the question for Paul: there were already too many mouths to be fed; but now he and Micheline will try to make a living off it. They marry, and their prayer is that their landlord may never set his foot in the place. To do the notary justice, he will not do so, unless it fares with him as old Tusser sings, that

> Jankin and Jennykin cozen him so,
> As to make him repent it, ere year about go.

Then indeed he may come to inquire into things, and quarrels will grow apace, for there is not a point on which a dispute may not be hung. It is the landlord who has to buy both the mule and his harness, to pay the window tax, and to provide a new bucket and chain for the well. If the mule casts a shoe it is the landlord who has to pay the blacksmith's bill, and even if the animal dies it is not difficult to prove that it was in the exclusive service of *lou patron* that it lost its life. On the produce of the olives the *métayer* only gains one-third; but then he has not to pay for the pruning; while on the cereals he secures one-half. The *impôts* (window tax and the like) are all paid by the proprietor, and of the *octroi* dues, that used to press so heavily on Paul and his father, the *patron* halves the expense, whether live cattle or dead meat be taken into market.

In short, the system is one of the most minute and complicated arrangements, all of which are palpably favourable to the *métayer*. It is notably favourable to him if the joint concern between proprietor and tenant should be a *cheptel*, or cattle-lease, as in that case the tenant is, at the expiration of the lease, entitled to one-half the additional value, if he can prove that by and through his means the joint property has been increased. In the face of these conditions it is difficult to believe that the doctrine so applauded in Aberdeenshire (under a very different *régime*) is being broached in Provence Yet so it is, and you are sometimes told that the land *ought* in the end to belong to the man who has tilled it in the sweat of his brow. Considering that all the advances, and all the taxes, are paid by the landlord, the injustice of this proposition is monstrous, and no one ought to be more convinced of its injustice than the Paul who now lives comfortably as a *métayer* on the very spot where his father was ruined as a proprietor. Many good judges are of opinion that *métayage* is an obstacle to agricultural progress, and the whole system has been ridiculed by others, who forget that here too we have a means for the preservation of social order which is worth preserving. When the Paul of whom we have been speaking is a partner with his landlord their community of interests is better than either a fixed antagonism, under the ordinary system of rents, or than the slow ruin of the fields in the hands of a small and poverty-stricken owner.

All proprietors are by no means ruined. On the contrary, some of the cultivators round Grasse are very wealthy, and, being landlords themselves, they have none of that ill-will towards the upper classes which makes the danger to society in countries where the ownership of the soil happens to be concentrated in a small number of families. What they do complain of is the valuation under which the taxes are levied, and the fisc to be paid on every change of ownership. This is exacted whether the *mutation* arise from purchase or from inheritance, and it is estimated to reach throughout France the sum of 8,000,000*l.* per annum. The legal system of transfer is in itself simple and expeditious, and an estate will change hands here in less time than it would take an English attorney to rub his spectacles, adjust them on his nose, and read over the titles. The price of land in the Maritime Alps varies in different localities. In the neighbourhood of the towns it has now assumed a tariff of prices which our grandfathers would have called fabulous. This is owing to the passion for speculation in house property, which went on unchecked till the Whitsuntide of 1883. No man will continue to grow olives in a field for which he can get from three to sixty francs a mètre, and there is no Naboth so stiff-necked as to refuse to part with his vineyard if the Englishman, who means to build a villa on it, will offer to purchase it, at a price varying from sixty to a hundred francs a mètre.

I am surprised that more capital has not been invested by speculators in rose-gardens and dairy farms. A sewage farm would certainly soon pay its expenses in rearing the *primeurs*, for which both this climate and the *petite culture* of the spade and hoe are so well adapted. Every stranger has been struck with the terrible two-pronged *bégu*, the instrument with which a labourer can dig a trench nearly two feet deep.

He stands in front of his work, pulling the earth towards him as it is loosened. Vineyards and rose-fields are dug in this way, and the soil thus prepared is ready to receive the slips at once. Though the physical labour of this method is great, it is thought to pay better than the gentler and often repeated work of the plough. The rule here is to manure every fourth year, but the luxuriant wild plants and the leavings of the clover-crops act as a natural food for the soil. In some districts near Nice the loam is both extraordinarily deep, free of stones, and rich in iron, but roses and violets, like oranges, are very gross feeders, and they require constant mulching with the most stimulating manures. The fields so cropped are generally placed in the neighbourhood of towns.

The Comte de Paris has recently purchased an estate near Mougins, not as a speculation, but for experiments in horticulture. Their Royal Highnesses, who are both fond of gardening, will there have a fine collection of plants, Alphonse Karr's best advice about them, and charming opportunities of seeing what the Provençal soil and climate can do under good management. Nearly every branch of agricultural and horticultural enterprise is capable of vast development here, and any labour so bestowed would be of the sort to ensure public as well as private opulence, to 'maintain a natural tendency of things towards improvement,' and to ensure a magnificent future. It is a pity that for the time being the building operations of the *Société Foncière Lyonnaise* have turned all Provençal heads. New streets and boulevards continue to rise in every direction, and before long the villas from the Siagne to the Roya will form a continuous mass. Fortunes will be made, but they have also been unmade—' *Grande facilité de paiement*' is a charming advertisement, but it really means a system of gambling in lots of land instead of in shares, and as such it has ruined, and it now threatens to ruin a good many of the proprietors and would-be proprietors of the Maritime Alps.

CHAPTER VI.

GRASSE.

'L'activité industrielle de ce moyen âge si orageux est un fait bien remarquable.'—J. AMPÈRE.

THE town lies against the hill, flanked by its escarpments, and supported by that fine natural terrace which first pointed out Grasse for a stronghold to the Celto-Ligurian tribes. A less important town than either royal and parliamentary Aix, or than strategical Draguignan, I greatly prefer it to either of them, and had I been a Provençal great lady I should always have wished to spend my winters in Grasse.

The view from the Cours is charming. Now and again a group of cypresses detaches itself from the mass of olive woods, the distant mountains have the sunshine on their heads, the range of the Tanneron is pine-clad, roses fall in clusters over the terraces, and far below are the stretching coast-lines of Maritime Provence, and the shimmer and glistening of the sea. Besides this sunny Cours there are dark and narrow streets: there are churches and chapels, with the graves of a long-buried episcopate: there is a charter-room with the dusty records and seals of Provençal sovereigns, and little, dusky gardens where the *chanoine's* old woman cuts the lettuces for his supper. There are also tall chimneys, and workshops where the tinsmiths hammer all day long. All these things you may see for yourself on a May morning, but there are two things you would never even suspect unless they were pointed out to you : oldfashioned drawing-rooms with old paintings, little bits of Trianon lingering in these provincial streets, and a labyrinth of cellars where the rose-leaves are stored. Picked in the dewy fields at the very first sign of the dawn, the roses are brought into town before the heat of the May day makes itself felt, and stored in these cellars. You wade up to the knee in their pale, moist, pink petals, and I once lay down and buried myself under them.

Grasse possesses a monopoly in France, perhaps in the world, for the production of perfumes, soaps, oils, and *bonbons*. The olive woods cover 3,000 *hectares*, and sixty-seven hydraulic mills give an annual product of 7,500 kilo of oil for the table. Its perfumed gloves used to be famous, like the leather of Cordova, and, though this particular industry no longer exists, the seventy distilleries of Grasse have a large and always increasing business. The city of Cologne alone orders 60,000 francs worth of the essence of ' Néroly,' made from the flowers of the bitter or Bigarrade orange, each kilo of the flowers furnishing one gramme of the precious substance, and in this way it is easy to understand how 200,000 kilo of blossom are annually worked up in Grasse. Cassia, jasmine, tuberose, violets, verbena, and jonquils are bought up by the distillers, who will pay from six to twenty francs a kilo for cassia-heads. The mounds of jonquils are a very pretty sight when they are first laid down at the factory door, but rather less pleasing is the discoloured heap which consists of the same golden flowers, after they have suffered a 'change' in a caldron of boiling lard. Bevies of girls are occupied by this business: sorting the blossoms, picking the lard, packing the bottles, making the straw-plait for the cases, pasting on the labels, and selling the pretty coloured *sachets* which always attract tourists. The heavy work is done by men. There are foundries for the coppers and stills, with much stoking of furnaces, blowing of glass vessels and retorts, making of packing-cases, and all the carting and carrying of a trade which bids fair to assume really gigantic proportions. Germany, Russia, and, above all, America, send immense orders, and the *attar* of roses now made in Grasse (at twenty francs a drop) will soon compete successfully with the export from the Levant. Essential oil of almonds, and the more deadly extract known as *prussic acid*, are made here, with orange-flower water enough to float a frigate. Orange-blossoms constitute the riches of Cannes, Cannet, Grasse, Vallauris, Mougins, Biot, La Cros, Vence, and St. Paul-du-Var. The scent from this mass of flowers is very trying to nervous people, and as it produces an exasperated and exasperating form of hay-fever, some patients are tempted to run away from this coast, and, hurrying back to England, to arrive just in time for the twenty-ninth snowstorm of the spring. The period of flower-picking extends over thirty days. Crowds of women and girls go to work on the orange-farms, and it is an odd sight to see them perched, like so many monkeys, in the branches of the round-headed trees. There they chatter and sing till the noonday heat silences their voices, and the season is fortunate if it passes over without one or more cases of the peculiar syncope to which orange-blossom-pickers are subject. I have seen a man lie insensible for so long that a doctor had to be summoned, the pollen of these flowers acting occasionally as a poison to the nervous system. Creosote and strychnine can be used as antidotes, but I confess I find an orange-farm a disagreeable neighbour, and am better pleased when *roses de mai* are in season. The *muscadine*, the semi-double, pink rose used for distilling, is aromatic even to the tips of the long green sprays that are bound over in half hoops, like raspberry canes. The pungent perfume of this plant is said to drive away moths, while that of the flower is so delicious, that it is difficult to appreciate the old sanitary rule for Jerusalem, that residents were not to grow roses in the city, or keep a 'Ginvath Varidin' (or rose-garden) close to the walls. The plant and the trade are both of Oriental origin; begun by the Persians, it was known to the Arabs, and to the Jews, who also taught the medicinal qualities of rose leaves.

The French kings patronised the perfumers of Grasse. We hear first of a certain Doria dei Roberti (1580), *médecin du roy*, but also *parfumeur de la royne;* and again of a certain Tombarel, who called himself 'of Florence,' because these men were, in the matter of their art, proud to profess themselves disciples of those perfumers of Florence to whom the Medici were wont to resort for their perfumed or poisoned gloves. Laugier, the perfumer to Louis XVI., lived in the house which is now the Hôtel de la Poste, but the expansion of the flower trade of Grasse since the Revolution is entirely owing to the initiative of M. Pérolle. This generous citizen, the same who presented the Rubens pictures[1] to the chapel of the Hospital, sent two boxes of his wares to Paris, and from this timid venture commenced the trade with the capital and with Europe. Grasse now coins money from flowers, and she will continue to do so through her flowers, after American wheat has undersold the corn, and *phylloxera* ravaged the wine, and disease diminished the oil of the district lying between the Siagne and the Var.

The burghers of Grasse are very wealthy, and fortunes are being made rapidly, to say nothing of those which have accumulated here since the days of the consular city. This is in fact one of the most flourishing towns in France, nor does it require a prophet's eye to foretell that Grasse must continue to prosper. As the sea-winds do not reach up to its esplanade, it will become a health-station, and there are many delightful expeditions to be made from it. If you choose to go in a southerly direction, you can drive to Mouans, with its modernised castle: or to Sartoux, with its Roman ruins: or to Pégomas, with its anemones: or to Pennafort on the Loup. You can also go eastwards—to Tourrêtes, with its mills: to the gorges of the Loup, to Gourdon on its crag, or to Le Bar, the cradle of the Counts of Grasse. All these expeditions among up-

[1] Three fine specimens of Rubens' early style, painted in 1602, for a convent church in Rome when the artist was twenty-five years of age, and when his colouring was still that of his master, Otto Venius. They were painted in three months.

turned ledges of limestone, wooded dells and yawning gorges are enchanting. No winds blow, and the soft air breathes through the pines while the sunshine glorifies the ruins and the little, tortuous streets. What is more, these excursions are fitted for persons of moderate strength and moderate means, but enterprising tourists might by passing westwards do greater deeds than these. They might explore Cabris, and the grottoes of St. Césaire, or the sources of the Siagne, and the native camps of St. Vallier. There are also the ruins of Calian and of Montaroux, the oak forest of Beauregard, and the bridge and mill of Mons in the gorge of the Siagnole. There is the Rochetaillée to be seen, and the Clus de St. Auban, the Roman villa at St. Ferréol, and the little summer-stations of Thorenc and Briançon to frequent. Any traveller who explores this country will be well repaid, whether his hobby be ruins, or sketches of ruins, or deep, shadowy glens with river-pools, or fragrant meadows, or hedges of medlars and jessamine, whether he seek for vestiges of the Templars, or for such strange Orchis as the *O. hircina*, the *O. militaria*, and the *O. albida*.

But to-day, instead of going so far afield, let us remain in Grasse. Let us drink of the well of Crassus, and stand under the gaunt *vigie*, mount the stone stair of the palace of the fair Queen 'Jeanno,' and pray in the chapel adorned by Bishop Mesgrigny, and think how Vauban planned the steps up to the western front of the church. Let us visit the dwellings of a dead-and-gone society, and go down to the gloomy Villa Malvilan to see the Fragonards, and turn over the dusty records of the *Consuls par la grâce de Dieu*, and then, when the daylight fails, let us pace the Cours, and listen to big 'Martin' as he makes the evening air and all the woods quiver with his heavy stroke, of which the blow and the echo keep sounding above the town like the vibrations of prayer through the human heart.

The possession of these Fragonards will some day be disputed with Grasse, for the Louvre is very anxious to possess such fine examples of a master who, if born in Grasse, seemed to realise in his talent all the grace and all the sparkle of the society of the eighteenth century. They certainly look a little out of keeping with the dark corner in which they now reside, but the Villa Malvilan is well worth a visit, and so is the Hôtel Mirabeau. Another great town-house, near Négre's shop, is now a school, but the house of the conventionist Isnard may still be seen in the Place des Aires. It is always easily recognised by its balcony, an interesting piece of hammer-wrought iron, which Isnard was profane enough to have stolen out of a church.

The town-house of the Counts of Grasse no longer exists, and the family has disappeared from the district in which they once held over forty fiefs. To say nothing of a supposed descent from Rhodoard, Prince of Antibes, this family of Grasse is interesting from its alliances and from its distribution over the country. The names of twenty-eight of the Counts figure in Vertot's list of the Knights of Malta, where we read of the Lords of Grasse-Bar, Grasse-Cabris, Grasse-Valette, Grasse-Mouans, Grasse-Montaroux, Grasse-St.-Tropez, and Grasse-Briançon. The first-mentioned of these may be looked upon as the elder or representative branch of this lordly house. Raimbaud de Grasse obtained possession of the fief of Bar in 1255, and it is from his grandson that the many *cadets de la maison* derive their lines. The castle of Bar is still an imposing mass, though the rooms in which Francis I. once spent three days are now used for a *café*. It was on the occasion of the king's return from visiting the lands of his Savoisienne mother that Francis honoured with a visit this Provençal noble who was actually his cousin, through a marriage with a daughter of the house of Foix. This connection with royalty if it procured the excitement and expense of a royal visit for the lord of Bar did nothing more for the stability of the house. Nor did the Counts of Grasse ever possess rights over the town. Charters dating from the days of the Berengers, and of the magnificent 'Jeanno,' had ever served to protect it from the exactions of feudal neighbours who were not allowed to play any great part in its local history.

The branch of Grasse-Cabris, after giving an abbot to the Lérins in 1477, died out, in 1691, in the person of the Abbot of l'Enfourchère, and Cabris was then acquired by the Clapiers, who had been in Provence for more than three centuries, and who were already related to the Grasse family by marriage. It is rather a question who was not? Glandèves and Castellane, Grimaldi and Lascaris, Barras and Villeneuve, d'Agoult and Lombard—we find all these great Provençal names in the list of the alliances of a family which, just before its extinction, could boast of one of the bravest of

French seamen. The family is now represented by a solitary individual. This grandson of the Admiral's is an officer of marines, and at the time of the Washington banquet he was much surprised to receive an invitation, and to find that his presence, like that of a descendant of Lafayette,[1] was desired by America. He learnt then that the gallantry of the Admiral Joseph de Grasse-Briançon has never been forgotten by the republic of the West, to which he lent such great and timely support.

When Grasse was inhabited by the local nobility it was further removed from the trade and movement of the world, but on the other hand life there must have been more full of incidents than it is now. At this moment the chief events are perhaps a rise in the price of cassia, or a fall in the price of soap, the nomination of a new *sous-préfet* (which happens at least once a year), or the death of an asthmatic Canon, or the news telegraphed to the civil authorities that a celebrated Fenian has just been traced to an hotel in Cannes. But when Marie-Catherine-Louise de Mirabeau, Marquise de Cabris, reigned in that big, dark house near the steps up to the Cours, which is still known as the Hôtel Mirabeau, life never lacked for incidents, or for scandals. Louise was the youngest and the fairest of the sisters of the orator. She had the same gift of eloquence, the same power of attracting friends and of making enemies, the same shamelessness, and the same restless energy. Her eldest sister was a nun in a convent at Montargis, and the other, Madame de Saillans, had less singular gifts than Louise, or indeed

---

[1] The late amiable Marquis, Jules de Lasteyrie.

than her parents, who had made all Europe ring with the story of their unseemly disputes.

Louise, when quite a girl, was married to an unsuitable mate, to Jean-Paul de Clapiers, Marquis de Cabris, son of a sharp-tempered old marquise who lived in the town-house of the family, and who had no reason to be proud of her descendant. Part knave and part fool, the vices and the unhallowed imaginations of this Marquis Jean-Paul sometimes culminated in attacks of genuine insanity. His marriage with a girl who joined all the violence of the Mirabeau to all the licence of the Vassans was very unfortunate, and not likely to be mended either by the amours of Louise with a certain unqualifiable scamp, Denis-Jean-Augustin de Janserandy de Verdache, co-seigneur de Briançon, or yet by the appearance in Grasse of her brother the orator. Honoré de Mirabeau, aged twenty-four, and already married, was at that moment under a cloud, and supposed to be living under a *lettre de cachet* in the dull, little town of Manosque, near the paternal acres and the castle of Mirabeau. He suddenly broke out of bounds, and presented himself at his sister's house. When, two days later, the walls of Grasse were found placarded with an indecent squib at the expense of all the ladies of the neighbourhood, it was not unnatural that its publication should be connected in men's minds with the advent of one more of those children of whom their father, the Marquis de Mirabeau, once declared that 'there never had been anything seen like them.' All Grasse discussed the lampoon; the lawyers on the Cours foretold the *causes célèbres* that could not fail to arise from it, and even the nuns behind the *grilles*, who ought to have known better, speculated as to its authorship. M. de Villeneuve-Mouans said that, in his opinion, no one could have been guilty of it but '*Mirabeau et sa triste sœur.*' The brother and sister, who were in truth as much surprised at it as their neighbours, determined to be revenged on the man who made so free with their names. What they determined to do had to be done quickly, for Honoré was not only in flagrant *rupture de ban*, but bound on another errand of some moment in the neighbourhood. He had really come to the south to see if he could not arrange a marriage between a Mademoiselle de Villeneuve-Tourrêtes and a man of the name of Gassaud, whom he suspected, rightly or wrongly, of an admiration for his own wife, *née* Mademoiselle de Marignan. He did go to Vence to consult there with the amiable Sophie de Vence, but he also found time to make himself terribly notorious in Maritime Provence. He and his sister arranged a breakfast in the country, under a palm-tree which is still supposed to mark the spot near Mouans. Covers were laid for four, for Louise was accompanied by her lover, De Briançon, and, to amuse her brother, Louise had invited a certain Mademoiselle de la Tour-Roumoule, whom he was supposed to admire. After breakfast they walked on in the direction of Mouans, and, at about 12.30, they came up with M. de Villeneuve. He was an elderly man, who, bareheaded, but with an umbrella over his head, was at that moment superintending the labour of some work-people. Mirabeau rushed at him, and beat him in the most savage way. Such an outrage could not be allowed to go unpunished. M. de Villeneuve put the affair into the hands of the tribunal, and Mirabeau's lawless absence from Manosque added not a little to the scandals of this lawsuit. All the papers referring to it are still in the possession of the notary whose ancestors did the business of the Cabris family. The details in this instance are, I am told, unspeakably coarse, nor does it mend the matter to learn that the filthy pasquinade which had raised all the stir really emanated from the pen of the half mad and wholly immoral Marquis Jean-Paul de Clapiers-Cabris. The breach between Louise and her family was now complete. Her father, who loved a quarrel for its own sake, whatever might be its merits, took up this matter, and sided, as he could hardly avoid doing, against the mistress of De Briançon. Another *lettre de cachet* was taken out by him, but this time for Louise: who was sent up to Sisteron and desired to repent of her sins at leisure in a convent of Ursulines. Her mad marquis and their only child (afterwards Madame de Navailles) lived on in Grasse with the dowager, and Honoré, after remarking that all the parties in this business had been fools, went towards Aix. When he came to solicit the votes of his equals in that city, he found that the Mouans outrage was by no means forgotten there, and he solicited in vain; so that it was only as the representative of the *tiers état* in the Sénéchaussée of Aix that he was returned as a deputy, and first threw his line in the great deep of revolutionary politics.

Louise, in the meantime, was disturbing Sisteron as she had effectually disturbed Grasse. The Ursulines soon had cause to regret their charge of a lady who, because she had several lawsuits to conduct, invited all the lawyers of the district to her house and table. This, she pleaded, was on account of business, but she presently invited the garrison; admitting this time that she did so for pleasure. She told such anecdotes as not only made the good sisters stare, but presently divided Sisteron into two camps about her reputation. By most people she was spoken of there as a viper! She had however friends enough, and wit enough to carry her point, and after some months full of the most surprising incidents, she managed to get relieved from her sentence, to leave the Ursulines of Sisteron to a well-merited repose, and to return to her parents.

Louise was truly an extraordinary woman. If she had her mother's coarse appetites and unbridled tongue, she was, like her father, gifted with strong intellectual tastes, and her correspondence with celebrated men [1] serves to exhibit one side of her versatile character—a side without which this sketch of society in Grasse at the close of the eighteenth century would be very incomplete.

The years 1788–89 found her again in Grasse, in the midst of what she called 'the effervescences' of a mob which had attacked her castle and threatened her property. Louise, though often on pleasure bent, had so much of a frugal mind, that she complained loudly of the danger to the charter-room at Cabris, and took her measures accordingly. She swept off all her papers to Grasse, placed them at her lawyer's, and had them

---

[1] Her letters, like the rest of the Mirabeau Papers, were placed in the hands of Monsieur and Madame Louis de Loménie. The deaths of those two gifted and charming persons have delayed the publication of the memoirs, and saddened many hearts.

all inventoried and registered, in the hope, as she said, that it might be possible for her one day to be reinstated in all her rights and dependencies. That day never came, but many darker ones were in store. Her husband took flight; the populace grew accustomed to success and crimes; society closed like a gulf above the old *régime*; wit, gallantry, and good company disappeared from the Cours of Grasse; and so did the Chapter, for Mirabeau being dead, the throne and the altar had nothing more to hope for, and the Bishop of Grasse lived in exile, and on alms. The prisons of Draguignan gradually filled with *détenus*, public and private plate was melted up for national purposes, twenty-one judgments were given in Grasse against the *émigrés*, the mills and manors of Cabris were sacked, and Louise herself had to fly from a town of which the revolutionary passions were aptly represented by Isnard.

The hope and prayer of the *émigrés* was to return to France—through ten years of poverty, and of abandonment by the powers who recognised the new *régime*, they nourished a hope which in too many instances was never to be realised. Some families were actually exterminated—all that the guillotine, the flight, and the fields of La Vendée had left, succumbing to fatigue and penury, to the putrid fevers of their lodgings, and to the sickness of hope deferred. Both Louise and her husband were of those who lived to return, and to an altered life, altered in all but this, that their own worst and most extravagant qualities were being reproduced in their only married daughter. But time succeeded at last in doing for Louise what neither convents nor *lettres de cachet*, nor convent bells, nor mother-in-law had been able to do—it tamed her. It was not for nothing that she had crossed the torrent of blood which separated the world she had left from the one on the threshold of which she was to sink down, unpitied and unknown. She returned, neither to Grasse nor to Cabris, the scenes of her extravagance and her guilt, but to ruined Mirabeau, the fountain-head of her strange race. The pea-

CABRIS AND 'LOU CABRES.'

sants had wrecked the castle, but with its collected stones she built herself a cottage, and there, with the greatest patience and devotion, she nursed the second childhood of her miserable husband; and there, wearing out 'the close of her voluptuous day,' she died. Grasse and her Trianon-like house, with the gilt goats' heads (*cabres*) on the alcove, she never beheld again, and of the castle at Cabris there remain now only a few vaults where the peasants store their hay, and some green mounds above the crags where the goats browse and leap.[1]

There is another figure that rises before us as we pace the Cours of Grasse, in marked contrast with either this laughter-loving Provençal dame, or with the painter Fragonard, so inspired by their graces that he could catch the smiles of such light-hearted lemans, and fix them on his canvas for ever. It is the austere form of Maximin Isnard.

Born at Grasse in 1758, he belonged to its industries, married a girl from Draguignan, and went to start a soap work at St. Raphael. Business there did not go on well, and Isnard may perhaps be reckoned among the victims of that wounded self-love of which Chateaubriand averred that it made so many fine heroes of revolution. At all events his wife (Mademoiselle Clairon) grumbled, and seems to have had no instinct of the career which, opening before her husband, was to give a terrible immortality to the name of the conventionist Isnard. His first public discourses got him into so much trouble that he had to fly into Italy, and his whole career was one of opposition. His hand was against every other man, whether as member of the Legislative Assembly, or among the Girondins, or as proscribed till after the fall of Robespierre. In him, as in the Mirabeau family, we find the Provençal gift of eloquence, the qualities of a tribune, and a diction lending itself to every style of argument. His first great speech against

[1] This little sketch, done by the late Honourable Henry Graves, was the last work of the kindly artist, and sent to me a week before his death, in 1882.

the priests who refused the oath pointed him out to the execration of the whole royalist and clerical party. They accused him of atheism. He flung back the accusation, for, like Danton who said, 'We have not destroyed superstition to found atheism,' this fierce tribune preserved some sense of religion. Isnard's reply was, 'I have looked on the face of the earth. I am not a fool: I believe in God, but *law* also is a divinity for me.' The words are remarkable when we remember how many strange years were to elapse before Maximin Isnard, ranging himself on the side of order, wrote a paper on the immortality of the soul, and dedicated it to the much-enduring Pope Pius VII. His early defence of the Revolution was a masterpiece of eloquence. He heard its opponents blame it because it had brought, not peace but a sword. 'What!' he cried, 'would you believe that *this* Revolution, the most astonishing thing on which the sun has ever shone—*this* Revolution, which has robbed despotism of its sceptre, aristocracy of its rod, and theocracy of its golden treasure-heaps—which has uprooted the oak of feudality, and split the cypress of parliament, which has taken the arms from intolerance and the frock from the monk and the pedestal from the peer, which has rent the money-bag of the tax-gatherer, and shivered the talismans of superstition—that *this* Revolution, I say, which is ready to go forth and rouse the nations, to make all crowns bow before the law, and, as such, to shed happiness over the globe—you would believe perhaps that *this* revolution is to accomplish itself in peace?—you believe, perhaps, that no one will try to make such a birth miscarry?—No: the French Revolution needs must go on to its fulfilment.' One can conceive Isnard thundering such words with such a trumpet-voice, to the terror of all the fine ladies and fine gentlemen whose chairs used to be carried about the streets of Grasse when he first left it to go and make soap at St. Raphael. One can fancy the whole chocolate-drinking, card-playing, wig- and patch- and powder-wearing society vanishing before his fiery words, like dead leaves before a November storm.

There is an allusion to the olive-woods of Grasse in one of Isnard's greatest invectives. When sent on a commission of inquiry to Marseilles after the fall of Robespierre, he inveighed against the violence of the Mountain and the crimes of Fréron, in a passage which Cicero or Junius might have envied. 'At every step I take through the south, I find the marks of blood—shed by *you*. Every soul of man denounces *you*—the very stones cry out against *your* cruelty, and wherever I meet with crime there I meet Fréron! I see towers fallen, and I ask, "Did Heaven's thunders level them?"—No! it was Fréron! What hand overthrew those gates?—It was Fréron! Only last night I dreamed that I met the pale spectre of crime wandering among the scaffolds of the slain—and it was Fréron! But for *you* the olive-trees that beautify my native land need not have ceased to be the emblems of peace.'

Isnard never forgot his native place, and after the 18th Brumaire he begged from the First Consul the office of *receveur des finances* in Grasse. 'Give that wolf a bone to gnaw' were the unflattering terms in which Buonaparte granted the request, but he also conferred on the conventionist the title of Baron, which Isnard weakly accepted. This 'ribbon to wear on his coat' alienated from him many of his former friends, and once again Isnard found himself in antagonism with those who had started in the race with him. Ronhard, who represented Grasse in the legislative assembly, was especially provoked at the former 'wolf's' attitude of contrition, and one day when Isnard informed him with some emphasis that he was going '*dans son temple adorer l'Eternel*,' the doctor replied snappishly, '*puisse-t-il oublier que tu fus criminel.*' It is difficult for history to forget it, and one is tempted to prefer to so much titled decorum the scaffold of Danton, who, in dying, confessed, 'I instituted this infamous tribunal, and I ask pardon for it, from God and from men.' Baron Isnard's fine castle and his high park walls are also a curious comment on his threat that if the capital of France proved untrue to the principles of the Revolution strangers might one day have to ask ' on which bank of the Seine Paris had stood.'

We have seen both Louise de Mirabeau-Cabris and Maximin Isnard conducted by strange paths to a late repentance, but the nineteenth century has not given any citizens to Grasse who belong to the same race of the giants. Isnard died there in 1825, and his grandson, the present Baron Isnard, who is the last of his direct descendants, is childless. Madame de Navailles (*née* Cabris) has left no heirs, and the race of Mirabeau (if we exclude the illegitimate son of the orator who bears the name of Montigny) is now represented only by two grandsons of his brother the vicomte, known as 'le Tonneau.'

CHAPTER VII.

VENCE.

' Grasse profondera,
Nice jonchères sera,
Antibes bombardera,
Vence, Vence sera !
Et donnera du vin
A qui n'en aura pas.'—*Vide* NOSTRADAMUS.

' Cette ville a traversé les âges sans rien perdre de son antique physionomie. Elle conserve encore son ancienne enceinte, ses tours, ses portes arquées, ses vieilles inscriptions, ses rues étroites. Sa cathédrale est bâtie sur le temple de Mars et de Cybèle.'—TISSERAND.

'Provence, antique patrie de ces libertés de la commune, filles de Grèce et de Rome, assises de temps immémorial sur une large base.'—CT. ALEXANDRE DE ST.-PRIEST.

OF all the towns of the Maritime Alps, Vence is the one which possesses the richest Church history. Four sees originally divided the coast—Nice, Antibes, Vence, and Fréjus—and for the second of these Grasse was only substituted because the assaults of pirates laid Antibes open to constant dangers of sacrilege and ruin. Of the four, Nice and Fréjus have alone survived, but the records of the two suppressed bishoprics are rich in local interest, and in pictures of local manners. This country under the hills is that of Audimus, of St. Veran, and of St. Lambert; it sent canons and *capiscols* to many Chapters, and it still venerates the memory of several learned and saintly men.

Provence was early Christianised. Legends tell

how, in A.D. 37, a colony of saints drifted to the beach of Maquelonne. And what saints!—Mary and Martha and their handmaid Marcella: while following them came Victor, 'the man who was born blind,' and Maximian, and Lazarus, 'wakened from his four days' sleep, enduring life again,' so as he might present the truths of immortality to the heathen, weighted with such a testimony to the Life Everlasting as never earthly preacher has had at his command. The legend of St. Mary Magdalen in the Sainte Baume is the best known and best loved page in the hagiology of Provence, and Correggio has shown her to us, half hidden by her hair, wearing out in a cavern the close of her remorseful day, with no shelter but its rocks, and no couch but its stones. This story, with that of the foundation of Les Baux by the Three Kings, forms, so to speak, the miraculous genealogy of the Church in Provence, though we hardly touch the *terra firma* of reality when we come to the mission of St. Barnabé, in the district between the Rhône and the Var. He is said to have suffered in the reign of Nero. This herald saint is now only the patron of the poor, little parish of Coursegoules, but his fine, old, Christian name of Barnabé, still lingering in genuine Provençal circles, has contrived to outlive the Raymonds and Hélions of the feudal age, and even to hold its own along with Numa and Marius, as brought into fashion by the Revolution.

The precise date of the evangelisation of Vence has never been fixed. The town lying at some distance above the Aurelian road had long been a favourite stronghold and an entrenched camp of the native tribes.

Roman patricians and priests came to people it, and incense was burning here to Mars and to Cybele, when a Christian teacher, who had turned his footsteps northward, discovered that its citizens were 'too much given to idolatry.' Whether St. Trophimus was that Christian teacher is uncertain, but he enjoys the reputation of having first placed a pastor in Vence (A.D. 161–180). The martrydom of St. Bassus, first bishop of Nice, took place A.D. 250, and that of St. Pons, still commemorated in the valley of the Paillon, occurred about A.D. 260. But Christianity had by this time taken a firm root in the country, and during the episcopate of Audimus of Vence there was already a sacred edifice in the town, under every column of which the builders had buried the image of some false and fallen god. What was so well begun went on equally well, the ecclesiastical annals of Vence remaining both rich and consecutive; and this mainly because its sheltered position preserved it from many of the blows aimed at Nice and Antibes by the barbarians who overran the country.

St. Veran was the greatest of all the early prelates of the see. He was the son of one of the pupils of Honoratus, and his own life was like that of Chaucer's ideal parson :—

> By many followed, and admired by all :
> Such was the Saint, who strove with every grace,
> Reflecting, Moses-like, his Master's face :

In him courage and learning met, and they glorified life under the harsh reign of Genseric. At this early stage of the world's experience to found a religious house for study, prayer, and culture, was to perform the highest act of Christian forethought and usefulness. It is not surprising therefore to find St. Veran building a convent near the present bridge at the mouth of the Loup. The mills of La Dorade which now occupy its site are chiefly built over its foundations, and it is not possible to ascertain what were the original proportions of the religious house whose bells, sounding to matins and to evensong, first woke the echoes of this wooded shore. The career of its monks had to be at once that of men of the altar, and of men of the plough, but the secular clergy were soon to give to Vence another great example of Christian virtue, wisdom, and grace. St. Lambert's name is still venerated in Vence. He lived there in such poverty, and with such evangelical simplicity, that his goodness became a proverb, and, till the Revolution, miracles were said to be worked by his bones. His era was that of the introduction of the Templars into Provence, soon after their foundation in 1118. It was the age in which the Church not only levied the *dîme grosse* and the *dîme menue*, the *droits de parée*, the *droits de prémice*, and the *droits d'autel*, but when it possessed also the monopoly of ideas. It could give its *visa* to one page and fix its brand on another, but it was fortunately represented here by a bishop like St. Lambert, ready to tend the leper, to cultivate the glebe, and to keep in his diocese, with tender human care, the great book of human life for peasants whose lot united the extremity of hard usage to the extremity of hard work.

Vence flourished: for its burghers had begun to grow rich, and to boast of their charters. But life here and at Tourrêtes was something of a struggle for *cazlans* and poor folk. Besides the *treizième du roi*, which was indirectly levied (the assessments being reckoned on so many *feux* to each district of the *viguerie*), there was also the fourteenth of the fruit demanded by their lords the Villeneuves, suzerains who also asked for a twenty-fifth of the flax, and for one pig out of every two—an exaction very hard for the owner of a pig-sty to bear, even when there were no hailstorms to spoil the grapes, and when the galleys of the Barbary pirates were far. The Great Plague, in the time of good King René, was a terrible epoch here, so terrible that Raphael Mosso, the then Bishop of Vence, had to import Pisan colonists to till the valley of the Var. In that way only could a new industrial life be infused into the desolated region.

Provence had as we know many civil wars and many changes of dynasty, but in the towns there lived on a succession of burgher families, always ready to assert themselves, and to render their *consuls par la grâce de Dieu* more independent. 'These magistrates were,' says Sismondi, 'the chiefs of a people who demanded only bread, arms, and walls. Every city felt it had strength only in proportion to the number of its citizens, and each vied with its neighbour in efforts to augment the means of defence. The smaller towns imitated the greater. . . . Cities and towns, the first elements in some sort of what forms a nation, arose and defended themselves.' Archæologically considered, their history is a curious study, and for Frenchmen it has acquired a more than merely antiquarian interest, since, in March 1871, their sympathies were divided between a representative government under one head, and the claims of the modern Commune. M. de Portalis used to say that he considered the government of Provence, with its Governor, its twenty-two *vigueries,* and its many communes, as the beau ideal of all methods for developing self-government without quashing patriotism, for assuring liberty without giving a door to licence. But the great and essential difference between the consular cities of the middle ages and the modern Commune is, that the latter is a principle of disintegration, while the former was, especially here in Provence, the base of a great social edifice. Cluseret, when he conceived of France as of a vast federation of united communes, lost sight of the fact that the old consular city represented the capability, the wealth, and the experience of the *haute bourgeoisie.* Nothing could be more unlike it than the fool-fury of his democratic mob, which had for its leaders, not the best, but the least educated citizens, not the owners of property, but all the dreamers and all the jail-birds. The old organisation had for its skeleton the municipal law of the old Roman world: it provided that the three orders of men who have a majority of interests in common should be represented, and its watchword was preservation. Such was the construction on which Provençal society was intended to repose, and the 'Statuts de Fréjus,' as drawn up by Romée de Villeneuve, let us into the smallest details of its mechanism. It was only when an unequal representation, with arbitrary taxation and clerical tyranny, had disordered its balance and cumbered its working, that the aristocracy, like the Church, became unpopular, and that revolution was brought to the door.

Montesquieu said of feudalism that 'it produces order, with a tendency to anarchy,' and it is lucky that feudalism in France so early found a counterpoise in the growth of the municipality. Useful history may be said to begin with that of the communes. In the eleventh century we find them in Provence assuming coats-of-arms, and in the twelfth demanding greater liberties from barons who had enrolled themselves as Crusaders. The *consuls* found that an excellent occasion for enlarging their borders, and groups of small republics soon covered the south of France. At the best, of course, they were not really free; they were too often like the creature that had ' *ower mony maisters* '—as, for example, in Marseilles, where one division held under the bishop, another under the abbot of St. Victor, and a third from the Vicomte, who in his turn held from the Count of Provence, who owed obedience in part to the French king, but ultimately to the Emperor.

If the magistrates of a town could free themselves so far as to achieve self-government, they called their chief magistrates *consuls par la grâce de Dieu*. The office was not for life, but if a consul died in office his funeral was paid for by the town. A consul of Grasse once declared war with the Pisans, a consul of Antibes promised galleys to the king of Aragon, and all this without consulting their neighbours; but in general their business was self-defence, whether in watching local interests too much at the mercy of the *viguier* and of the *juge du roy*, or in providing for their poor. 'A lively pride,' says M. Séranon, 'in their condition was developed in the townsfolk. The citizens placed their whole affection in their commune, and were proud of the position which they held, and of the name given to their little *états*.' The policy of the sovereign was, as a rule, favourable to these municipalities, and many of them got leave, as *bonnes villes*, to quarter the *fleur de lys*, and to send their mayors to assist at the coronation at Rheims. Aix and Antibes had this honour. Cannes, Mougins, and Vallauris, on the other hand, wore the palm-branch of their patron Honoratus: all these places holding from the chapter of the Lérins. Biot placed a Maltese cross to mark her tie to the Hospital, while Marseilles, Toulon, Antibes, and Fréjus had a right to quarter the Crusaders' cross. Vence, if she made no such boast, was proud of her charters and her archives, of the liberties of her '*consuls, manants, et habitants*,' as she had also good cause to be of the development of her social life.

The spirit of the Renaissance as felt in Vence showed itself in the bias of the townsfolk towards figurative art. The chapels and altars of Grasse and Vence are interesting—indeed, I remember a picture in a little cell-like chapel just outside Biot that touched me extremely by its Perugino-like tenderness, by the grace of that indigenous art which sprang up here as it did in the Tuscan towns. That art, identical with the growth of the commune, bears comparison with the art-life of the smaller Italian republics. By it the churches were beautified; we hear of public lectures on Virgil, of Minorites who drew crowds to their sermons, of portions made for young girls, and of perpetual *obits* for the kindly souls of consuls and canons who while they lived certainly deserved well of their neighbours. Life went on '*rondement, naïvement, à la vieille Française, avec liberté et bonne foy,*' for patriotism is attracted, not merely to the natal soil, but to the institutions and the customs which exist. The inventories of Vence remain, and they have preserved to us the names of Bellot the sculptor, of Clerici the painter, of Giuliani the organ-builder, of Bonetta the architect, and finally of the Canamisi. They were a family of local artists, decorators of the chapels and altars; many of their pictures remain to this day, and it is pleasant to find that they were well paid for the trophies and shields which were ordered from them, and which they executed before Francis I. and his train were received at Villeneuve-Loubet.

The episcopates of Simian and of Grimaldi, the two bishops who preceded the reformed movement in Vence, were by no means rife in local scandals, but the times were evil, and the great offices all in *commende*. Christianity had gone through a series of sad and humiliating developments, and along with the sale of indulgences there was a noticeable lack of personal holiness in the Chapters. Reforms were called for, yet the Reformation in the Maritime Alps had rather a political than a theological importance, which, after the conspiracy of Amboise (1560), it assumed, to say the truth, all over France. In this way society was effectually stirred by it, and the question of moral and ecclesiastical reform was pressed on the notice of some men who might otherwise have missed its importance. The culture of the Renaissance, in which Provence participated fully, had already been tried, but it had been essentially wanting in the higher tones of morality. It had too little of that spiritual earnestness by which alone men's lives are lifted beyond sensuous things, nor had political energy gained much from its luxurious charms. Only the intellectual light it had brought prepared men for freedom of inquiry, and then the study of Scripture acted as a moral stimulant to Huguenot scholars, theologians, statesmen, and captains.

The wars called 'of religion,' which trained many a good soldier, agitated France from 1562 to 1598.

Vence first received specific orders about her Huguenot congregations in 1560. Louis de Beuil de Grimaldi was then in possession of the see, and the castle of Villeneuve-Loubet belonged to a Lascaris, Comte de Tende. As the despot there was uncle to the bishop, and as the chapter of Vence consisted of a Du Port and a De Hondis, cadets of the noblest families of St. Paul-du-Var, it was evident that the issue of any conflict with the Calvinists would turn here on local interests. The bishop took up the question warmly, and when summoned to attend the Council of Trent he excused himself, on the ground of the troubles which 'the new religion' daily evoked in Provence. Three hundred men were raised to deal with them, but the temper of the Vençois rose also, and in 1562 'armed bands of vagabonds and seditious men' met in many places. René de Cypières collected forty horsemen in Nice to defend his co-religionists, St. Jeannet declared for the reformed faith, and the Governor of Vence, who sided with Bishop Grimaldi, could only forbid 'any citizen to lodge or conceal a Huguenot, in any house, garden, or vineyard.'

Domiciliary visits took place, and thirty names were posted 'as absentees for the sake of the new tenets.'

The peace of 1562, actually secured to the Huguenots the right of holding assemblies outside the city walls, and it is to this regulation that Vence owes her Rue des Huguenots, which may be seen to this day. But 1567 was another very troublous year, and troops were posted on every direction, from Sisteron, on the Durance, to the fords of the Var—even in the little eyrie of Gourdon on the Loup — with orders to watch the movements of the reformed party.

GOURDON ON THE LOUP.

The Calvinists in Sospello were very hardly dealt with; but it was lucky for the Calvinists that Lascaris, who represented the royal, Catholic, and therefore the persecuting element in Maritime Provence, was not a blind zealot. He was in many ways superior to the Court party, so much so that he refused to execute the royal orders for any massacre of the Calvinists consequent on the success of the great attack made on them in Paris on the eve of St. Bartholomew. Christopher de Villeneuve shared his determination to be no party to such measures, and accordingly all remained quiet within their jurisdiction. Lascaris died as the fourth war of religion broke out in 1572. His family, like so many others of the demoralised and despotic grandees of that epoch, had a tendency to degeneration, and his inheritance passed into the hands of an only daughter. Henriette de Lascaris, the wife of the most celebrated Leaguer, the duke de Mayenne, became mistress of Villeneuve-Loubet at a moment when her native district was the scene of grave political difficulties. And that time is always rife in private grudges and local quarrels. Just such a bitter feud was the one which now distracted Provence. Carcistes fought with Razats: and men who cared personally little for either creed or catechism threw themselves into the local quarrel. Blood was shed, till the Carcistes, having had the best of it, wrung from the Parliament of Aix terrible sentences against their opponents, as 'raisers of illicit assemblies.' Accusations of magic, of idolatry, and of treason were freely interchanged, as freely as they had been during the great trial of the Templars, and Catherine de Medicis had to go to Aix in person before a peace could be patched up between country neighbours and relations much too nearly connected to lay aside their jealousies so long as any cloak of public interest could be flung over them.

Then the plague appeared in Vence. Butchers and bakers' shops were shut, and the bishop had to migrate to St. Paul-du-Var, where it had not yet made itself felt. In fact the condition of Vence was so deplorable that it was difficult to conceive how even the Leaguers could add much to its misery. But now appeared upon the scene the greatest of all the Huguenot captains, the young, the invincible Lesdiguières—the friend of Condé and of Henri IV., the terror of the Duc de Mayenne—flushed with recent victory, and marching eastwards upon Vence.

What were the Vençois to do? The Leaguers, commanded by the Baron de Vins, levied troops it was true for the Catholic cause, but to join Lesdiguières there hurried all the Calvinists of a disaffected district. How divided the great families were will be seen when we notice that with the Huguenot captain there went the Counts of Villeneuve-Vence, Villeneuve-Tourrêtes, and Villeneuve-St.-Césaire, the d'Oraison, Forbin-Janson, Monclerc, Revest, Montaud, Canaux, Grasse-du-Bar, Villeneuve-les-Arcs, Villeneuve-Gréolières, Villeneuve-Vaucluse, Grasse-Montaroux, and Grasse-Calian. This might seem to represent, even to exhaust, the local families: but not at all: for ranged under the banner of the Baron de Vins were the houses of Villeneuve-Trans, Villeneuve-la-Berlière, Villeneuve-Thorenc, Villeneuve-St.-Jeannet, De Pontevès, Bésaudun, La Palud, La Molle, the Forbin-Solliès from near Hyères, the La Verdière from a glen behind Castellane, the formidable Carces, the lords of St. André and of La Roquette, with the D'Agoult, and their kinsman the Comte de Sault. The whole country from Aix to Brignolles was in the hands of the Leaguers, and Vence bristled with troops, when the news reached Maritime Provence of the murder of Henri III.

Thence arose a momentary hope of peace, the more flattering that De Vins had fallen before Grasse, and that the Bishop of Vence was dead; but the Leaguers, rather than acknowledge the white plume of Navarre, promptly offered Provence to Charles-Emmanuel, Duke of Savoy. Two thousand Italian troops soon heralded on the frontier the coming of this candidate, and so unpatriotic were the Leaguers that the Piedmontese stranger was everywhere well received. It must be said that as far as the consuls of Vence were concerned they at least were very helpless either to choose or to refuse him, and that the only observation they had to make to their new and foreign ruler was 'that there was now nothing left to feed the poor.' While they were thus asking for bread, and while Charles-Emmanuel pressed on to Aix, as to the capital of his new principality, Lesdiguières swept down from the valley of the Durance, and, passing rapidly through the Esterels, divided the Duke of Savoy from his adherents on the Var. In vain did the Leaguers petition their nominee to retrace his steps from Aix: Lesdiguières cut him off, and in June (1582) he appeared before the walls of Vence.

The great Huguenot captain had the reputation of being invincible, and the Vençois had every reason to fear the worst at his hands. No very clear account has ever been given of why this terrible soldier either received, or appeared to have received, a check before a place where he certainly lost a great number of men. He raised the siege, retired beyond the Esterels, and desired the Comte de Grasse to hold Antibes for Henri IV. In this repulse and deliverance the Catholic party discerned a miracle, worked for them, as they believed, by the prayers of the Capiscol of their Cathedral, and by the relics of those famous saints of Vence, St. Veran and St. Lambert. The real explanation of Lesdiguières' change of front was probably to be found in that general movement in favour of Henri IV, which convinced the Duke of Savoy that in Provence he was only playing a losing game. The country had become essentially French, and it meant to continue so; thus when Charles-Emmanuel retired to Turin, Vence made her submission to the Béarnois. Grasse got a new charter from him, and Maritime Provence settled down to her duty under the heir of that Antoine de Bourbon who had once spent three weeks of summer with Francis I. at Villeneuve-Loubet. Many of the Huguenot leaders followed the example of the king when he joined the Church of Rome. Lesdiguières did not do so till 1622, but Scipion de Villeneuve and the lord of Tourrêtes conformed at once: Carcistes and Razats shook hands, and marriages took place between families which had quite recently been ranged against each other in battle.

A Catholic revival now took place. A great deal of new life was certainly infused into the Church by the efforts of St. Francis of Sales, but royal favour is a powerful stimulant, and a strong monarchy gradually gave its tone even to districts which like Vence had once[1] been leavened with Protestant principles.

[1] At this moment the Protestants of the districts of Vence, La Gaude, Cagnes, Gattières, and Carroz, number about fifty persons. The *pasteurs* of Cannes, Nice, and Mentone collect subscriptions for the work of their missions throughout the canton of Vence.

In the reign of Louis XIII. the cities and villages of France were put under the protection of the Virgin;[1] most of the little statuettes of the Mother and Child on the walls and gateways of Provençal towns date from his reign, and districts which had before possessed only some local or distinctive appellation began, from the building of some new chapel, to be called of 'St. Pierre,' of 'Ste. Hélène,' or the like.

Where Catholicism was so dominant, it was fortunate for the Vençois that the bishop's throne was constantly filled by men of great merit. Pierre de Vair, a prudent and conciliatory prelate, brought back to the Church most of the influential burghers who had left her pale, while Antoine Godeau would almost require a volume to do justice to his great acquirements. Born in 1605, his life was full of incidents and full of study; 'the people,' said Dom Bonaventure d'Argonne, 'loved him as a pastor and a father, Rome esteemed him, the Court distinguished him, theologians listened to him, and *everybody read his books.*' The last sentence has ceased to be true, for of many of them the themes no longer interest us, and the taste of the present generation, formed as it is on the prose of Chateaubriand, of George Sand, and of Maxime du Camp, or on the poetry of De Musset and the songs of Béranger, no longer appreciates the taste of the Hôtel Rambouillet. It was there, and at Madame de Montausier's feet, that Godeau fashioned himself. Petted by a circle which called him 'Julie's dwarf,' his good sense and his great parts attracted the notice of Pierre de Vair, the aged Bishop of Vence,

---

[1] August 15, 1638.

who, in dying, expressed his wish to have Antoine Godeau for his successor. One of the twelve original founders of the Académie Française (1634), and one of the forty of whom that learned body was composed (1635), Godeau had waited to be thirty years of age before taking Holy Orders. His tastes up to that time might have been called frivolous rather than serious, and his admiration for the beautiful, red-haired Mademoiselle Paulet, which continued to his death, made his friends suppose that his thoughts would hardly turn towards theological studies, or to a pulpit out of Paris. But his letters at the time of his consecration betray a deep sense of the solemn duty he was about to take on himself, and Richelieu showed his usual insight into character when he named this idol of the Hôtel Rambouillet to the see of Grasse (1636). Godeau said of his charge that he should find more thorns there than orange-blossoms, and so it proved, though his entry into Grasse, in 1637, was a sort of triumph. He found a war going on with the Spaniards, cannon thundering on the Lérin islands, and the funds of the commune exhausted. Worse than this, Antibes, as a nest of Calvinists, defied all ecclesiastical authority, and in 1644, in spite of the complaints and resistance of both their Chapters, the dioceses of Grasse and Vence were united under his charge. When united, they consisted of fifty-two parishes, and their cathedrals were separated by only three leagues of romantic, hilly territory. Godeau dared not show himself in Vence: he was stoned, and the very Marquis de Villeneuve, co-seigneur of Vence with himself, treated him with marked incivility. The bishop, though always temperate and patient, was the first to perceive that his position was untenable, and to advise the king to withdraw the decree by which the union of the sees had been effected. He was allowed to take his choice, and, in spite of the rough reception he had met there, he selected Vence to be his own portion, leaving what he called ' *la gueuse parfumée*,' Grasse, to another suitor, and another master.

Here under the hills he continued to live and work. Nor was he forgotten. We find him summoned to preach at Aix before the king, the queen-mother, Condé, and Cardinal Mazarin. His last years were agitated by the local quarrels of the Vençois with the Villeneuves, as well as by the Jansenist controversy. Like his munificent neighbour, Monseigneur Mesgrigny of Grasse, Godeau adopted a strictly orthodox view of this dispute. He condemned the propositions of Jansenius, traced a splendid sketch of the connection between the Church and the State, built a seminary, and published a commentary on the New Testament, which has been favourably noticed even by Protestant writers. Godeau had now only four years to live, and his eyesight was affected, but it is pleasant to find him surrounded by the good wishes and sympathies of many of the best men and women in France. Madame de Grignan came to visit him before his death, to talk to him about her mother, and to remind him how he had known her predecessor, that first wife of the Governor of Provence who was a daughter of the house of Rambouillet. At length came the Passion Week of 1672, and Godeau, full of years and labour, was singing the *Tenebræ* before the altar of his cathedral of Vence. The last candles were nearly extinguished when the bishop fell, stricken with apoplexy, and so passed, to where, 'beyond these voices, there is peace.'

Surian was a man of a totally different type. He was a shepherd-boy, who had tended his flocks among the heaths of Provence, who had never seen Paris, or heard of the wits of the Hôtel Rambouillet. He ran away with thirty-five sous in his pocket, applied to the Oratorians for help and teaching, and so impressed them with his talents that they educated him with a care to be amply rewarded by his subsequent success. Surian, who has been called the Massillon of the south, was made bishop of Vence in 1727. He lived with great frugality and economy, but saw many evil days when Croat regiments devastated the country, and while the old internecine strife went on in the town between the Vençois and the Villeneuves. Bitter as that quarrel had always been, the eighteenth century was aware of an increasing tension in the popular feeling against the nobles—an aristocracy which lived exclusively in Paris, which made debts there, and which had nothing to commend it or its exactions to the poorer neighbours who had to pay all the taxes. 'Honour and arms,' might still be the watchword of the nobility, but luxury and want now went side by side in many a château, where empty coffers and unpaid bills, splendid arms and torn, dirty linen, long pedigrees and heavy mortgages, were to be found in unhealthy proximity. Society seemed worn out; there was a want of careers and occupations for young minds, the *tiers état* was crippled by unfair restrictions, the different orders of men seemed to stand in each other's way, or to have only opposing interests; there was a hollow-eyed and scantily-fed peasantry; there were scholars averse to recognise in the Church any claim to regulate the actions or beliefs of cultivated and responsible beings; there were courtiers satisfied with the delights of tyranny and lasciviousness; there was a spirit of discontent begetting in men what Plato called ' uncertain and unfaithful ways '— under this clouded and threatening sky the gentle Surian died.

The see was then given to Charles Pisani (of La Gaude), and over his devoted head the thunder broke. He was a good, simple-hearted man, who did his utmost during the three years of famine which preceded the outbreak of the Revolution. But revolutions are not to be stemmed by some loaves of bread, or even by a few kind words. Pisani, though humble, was courageous. He reminded the malcontents of the debt which humanity owed in southern France to a Church *that had existed before the State.* But he could not obtain a hearing, and, after the death of Mirabeau, Pisani had to give up any hope of the return of order in his diocese. Already Monseigneur Boisgélin, the Archbishop of Aix, and the Bishop of Toulon had left their posts, and now, in his turn, Charles Pisani formed part of that great emigration of about four thousand priests, who fled from France, to avoid the hated Oath, death on the scaffold, or the bloodshed of the streets of Paris.

The see of Vence has never been restored. The Villeneuves, who emigrated when the bishop did, though they afterwards returned to the district, have since sold the last yard of their territory, and the old jealousy between the castle, the Chapter, and the *bourgeoisie* is now at rest for ever.

Vence is a very quiet, dreamy place. No one would believe that the regiments of Charles V. once bivouacked in its square, that the bold Lesdiguières had to raise the siege laid to her gates, or that Massena drilled in her streets soldiers who were to go out and conquer the world. Vence now grows violets for the perfume factories, and the dust has gathered deep above the tombs of her bishops, as over the bones of her saints.

CHAPTER VIII.

THE TRUTH ABOUT THE MAN IN THE IRON MASK.

'Il faudra que personne ne sache ce que cet homme sera devenu.'—
LOUIS XIV.

'Toutes les conjectures faites jusqu'alors sur ce prisonnier sont fausses.'
—LOUIS XV. AU DUC DE CHOISEUL.

'Quand on a envoyé ce prisonnier à Sainte-Marguerite, il n'a disparu de l'Europe aucun personnage important.'—VOLTAIRE.

IN the bay of Cannes, and distant only 1,400 mètres from the point of the Croisette, lies the island of Ste.-Marguerite, famous for the State prisons built upon its northern face. The view from the flagstaff of the fortress, over the towns of Cannes and Cannet, is as sunny and varied as the place itself is melancholy. The one is a magnificent panorama of light, life, and industry, bathed in glowing sunshine; the other is made up of sombre rooms, whitewashed walls, and shabby grass-grown courts. Only the steep, paved road which leads up from the Admiralty Pier to Vauban's gateway is picturesque; but soldiers and prisoners alike look bored, and those are the only pleasant days in the week when they are allowed to go over to Cannes to buy the necessary stores.

In the spring of 1687 (as nearly as can be two hundred years ago), this island, with its so-called castle, awoke to a state of unusual excitement. Yet no foreign

THE CROISETTE.

galley was beached to-day on the Tradelière reef, as in the storm that drove Charles V. ashore ; neither was there a Spanish fleet hovering round, as in 1636 ; nor yet did any Barbary corsairs sweep the seas, intent on sacking the monastery, and on carrying off the Church plate of the seven chapels on the Lérins. Workmen, however, moved hither and thither, boats laden with stones and beams lay at the little quay, and tubs of mortar stood in the court beneath the flagstaff. Mass had ceased to be said in the old chapel because a new one was being arranged, and it was even reported that the roof of the governor's house was about to be raised a story. What food for conjecture was here! And the reasons assigned for so much activity were even more delightful! Not only was a new governor coming to reside on Ste.-Marguerite, but he was ascertained to be already in correspondence with M. de Grignan, the Governor of Provence, about the guns of a fortress, where it would be his business for the future to guard a prisoner of rare importance. For more than two months did the workmen labour, and the Abbot of the Lérins soon learnt *for a fact* that the new prison on the neighbouring island was complete, that it had a grated window and a vaulted corridor, with a chapel that might be reached without crossing the open court. It wanted nothing but a prisoner! Speculations were accordingly rife about the keeper and his charge.

Bénigne d'Auvergne, Comte de Saint-Mars, *bailli* and governor of Sens, and somewhile governor of the State prisons of Pignerol and Exilles, was known to be a favourite at Court, and to have enjoyed rapid promotion since, as an *enfant de troupe*, he entered the army in 1638. He was now a trusted tool of the Minister of War, and to him as such Louvois had already committed various responsible charges. Fouquet had lived in his keeping at Pignerol, and from Mathioli he had only parted when, in 1681, he exchanged that fortress for the more remote castle of Exilles. Named governor of Ste.-Marguerite, Saint-Mars had once already inspected his island residence, but as he was ill during his short sojourn there, he had been but little seen, and expectation now stood on tiptoe as the spring days lengthened and as his advent came daily nearer. The gossips of Cannes knew that he was married, and they were prepared to congratulate his wife on exchanging the storms and glaciers of rockbound Exilles for this 'rosette of the sea.' Here was a genial climate and a choice of neighbours, for to say nothing of the Prior and his monks on St. Honorat, Antibes and Toulon had garrisons of troops, and every now and again a galley of Malta would pass, with no wind to fill her sails. All this was true; yet Madame de Saint-Mars, fortunate though she might be deemed, knew from experience that the place of a jailer's wife, as understood by Louvois and as practised by Saint-Mars, was not a cheerful one, and possibly she had no illusions about the island castle which she was about to inhabit.

Late in April, and when the road by Embrun was open and possible for her litter, the governor started from Exilles. He brought with him his wife, his family, his baggage, his company and its lieutenants, his servant Ru, and a '*masked prisoner*,' whom eight Piedmontese

THE FORT AND PRISONS OF SAINTE MARGUERITE.

carried every league of the way in a covered chair. The jailer and his train must have been glad when Grasse was reached. Winter and rough weather had been left behind them in the long zigzags by which they crossed into Provence, and now they marched easily down the sunny slopes by Mougins and Cannet to the coast. Cannes they entered by the old Cannet road, just where the present railway station stands. Then, indeed, the *badauds* noted with joy that Saint-Mars (a little, ugly man, near-sighted, bent almost double, and walking with a furtive step) was the very picture of a jailer, and that he really had brought with him a mysterious prisoner, over whose chair a frame was fitted covered with oilcloth. Watertight this cover was, but surely also most oppressively hot in the rays of an April sun. No one saw that prisoner's face, and no one heard the sound of his voice. A boat was waiting; the governor stepped on board, and the boat, pushing off without delay, carried over to the island prison the man to be known to Louvois and his satellite as '*le prisonnier de Provence*,' but to be called by the world during two hundred years, ' the Man in the Iron Mask.'

Whoever the victim might be, he was exhausted by the journey. Years ago he had been a restless and impatient captive, given to tears and rebellion, but blows and stripes had not been spared, and now, not daring to complain either of the oilcloth-cover of his chair, or of the mask of black velvet which he wore, he did none the less, on arriving at the island, fall sick and keep his bed. His cell was spacious enough. Saint-Mars boasted to Louvois that in all Europe there was nothing to compare to its thick walls, triple iron gratings, and corridor where the prisoner might take exercise without being seen. There were a few prisoners already in the fortress: insignificant Huguenot pastors, who sang hymns to the sea waves, and were beaten for doing so, but there was nothing in their case to divert public attention from the ' masked prisoner.' No human being, his jailer reported, had set eyes on him during the journey southwards. 'All along our route (owing to the way in which I concealed him) people did seek to know who my prisoner might be. They all declare here that he is either M. de Beaumont, or a son of Cromwell.'

For nearly two hundred years has the world, like the gossips of Grasse and of Embrun, tried to guess who the masked prisoner might be? Voltaire was the first to draw public attention to the romantic tale of a princely person, whom as ' the Man in the Iron Mask ' he has rendered famous. All through the eighteenth century the legend grew. First one hypothesis was started, and then another, till at length nothing was felt to be too wonderful, or chimerical, to be put forward as the explanation (?) of the misfortunes and mystery of ' the Man in the Iron Mask.' This was sure to be the case in the eighteenth century. History then consisted of the repetition of certain conventional facts, and no light was suffered to be thrown upon the arbitrary measures or upon the telltale record-offices of absolute kings and their irresponsible ministers. If any man got into disgrace and so found his way to a prison, or into one of its *oubliettes*, so much the worse for him. No questions were asked about his fate, and any reversal of his sentence was hopeless. Private influence of course might be brought to bear, but as often as not it happened that men in disgrace had no friends, and prisoners out of sight were so emphatically out of mind that ministers of state have owned to completely forgetting the name, as well as the sentence, of some miserable captive grown grey in the gloom of the Bastille. The State prisons were full, and popular officers like Saint-Mars found in their charges a means of economising upon all the allowances, and of thus growing rich through the responsibilities of their position.

Very few facts are known about the man who lived for thirty years under the safe keeping of Bénigne de Saint-Mars. I will make a memorandum of them here, collecting them from the letters that passed between the jailer and the Minister of War. When Voltaire wrote his brilliant conjectures so many years ago, the existence of these letters was not suspected. When M. Topin, only a few years ago, determined to make us believe that Mathioli had worn the 'mask,' he also had taken little pains to look for the secret where alone it could be found—viz. in the letters of the period. These letters exist, in the Archives of War, and in the Archives of Foreign Affairs.[1] We have further the diary of De Jonca, the Lieutenant of the Bastille, and, finally, we have the extracts from the register of the parish of St. Paul, long kept in the Archives of the Hôtel de Ville of Paris, and fortunately preserved in print, since the originals perished during the Commune of 1871.

[1] The references to them in Jung's volume are exhaustive and correct.

The facts are as follows :—

The 'Mask' was a *man*—that is to say, he was neither a child, nor a boy, nor a greybeard, when Louvois first caught him, and consigned him to Saint-Mars' care.

The letters of Louvois first indicate a warrant taken out against him, with orders to waylay him if possible. He was actually taken at the fords of Péronne, March 1673, and hurried to the Bastille, where Louvois says *that he saw him*. He was then sent off to Pignerol, and was smuggled after dark into its dungeon on April 7th, 1673, and then for the first time Saint-Mars beheld the man of whom Louvois had written to him, but whose name had never been mentioned in any of the despatches. The papers belonging to this political prisoner were also seized near Péronne; a man of the name of Nallot being fortunate enough to secure them for Louvois. Most unluckily, those papers are now a-missing. Nallot, who seized them, died a few days after his exploit, and his death, whether by the hand of some enraged conspirator, or by the order of the crafty Louvois, is one of the many enigmas of this strange affair. Louvois continued to write about the 'Mask,' as 'the man you know about,' or as 'the prisoner of Péronne,' but neither by Louvois, nor by his father Letellier, nor by his son Barbézieux, *was the name or the Christian name of this victim ever written*. What Louvois does say about his character is this: 'Though obscure, he was none the less a person of consequence; that he was a prodigious scoundrel, who, on a very important matter, had cozened many persons of distinction;' that he was 'to be hardly treated and jealously secluded from every eye;' and 'you are to give him only the things necessary for life, with no comforts whatever.'

Under this pleasing *régime* the 'Mask' began his imprisonment. Saint-Mars complied with all the minister's orders, and sent him a plan of the tower in which his enigmatical charge was lodged. We find in the public archives the names of all his other prisoners, with the record of their arrivals, departures, deaths, or changes of lodging, nor can there be any dispute about the governor's own removal from Pignerol, April 1674, when appointed to the charge of the fortress of Exilles. With him there went away only two prisoners, whom he called his '*deux merles*'—a Jacobin friar (arrested for treason), and the 'Man in the Mask.' Exilles is situated in a snowy gorge on the north side of the range of the Mont Cenis, and there jailer and victim continued for thirteen years to reside, till their removal to Ste.-Marguerite, *viâ* Embrun, Grasse, and Cannes, in 1687. The 'Mask' dwelt in his famous 'new prison on the Island' till the autumn of 1698, when Saint-Mars, having lost his wife in Provence, gladly accepted the highest promotion that a minister had to give, and went up to Paris, to become Governor of the Bastille. The 'Mask' travelled with him, and ate at the same table, but a loaded pistol lay beside Saint-Mars' plate. De Jonca, the Lieutenant of the Bastille, was in waiting to receive them. The 'Mask,' placed for a few nights in a temporary lodging, was finally incarcerated in the Tour Bertaudière, and in a south room. But he had now been a prisoner for more than a quarter of a century, he was no longer young, the change of climate tried him, and he fell sick. Nélaton, a surgeon, says that he saw his tongue and felt his pulse, but that he never saw the face of '*le prisonnier de Provence.*' He died rather suddenly, without the last sacraments, just as winter set in, November 19, 1703. The register of his death is signed by Riel, the surgeon of the Bastille, and his funeral is entered in the parish of St. Paul as that of '*M. de Marchiely.*' The funeral cost forty livres. His clothes and his mask were burnt, and there, but for the legends that have grown up about his birth and his fate, the tale of the 'Man in the Mask' ought to have ended, when one more unfortunate went to his death in the prisons of Louis XIV.

It is not true that his mask was of iron. It was made of black velvet, but it had a steel spring in it. It is also a fiction that he wrote his name on a silver plate and threw that out of his window, to be picked up by a boatman of Cannes. Saint-Mars' letters show that one of the Huguenot pastors once wrote on a piece of pewter and was beaten for doing so, but though the linen of the 'Mask' was always steeped to prevent correspondence through the laundress, Saint-Mars never detected the 'Mask' in any attempt to use his shirt as writing-paper. He was over the middle height, tall, and well-made, and towards the close of his life he told the governor's servant that he was sixty years of age. He spoke French, but with a foreign accent, sang, and was fond of music. There is no trace in all the letters about him of his ever having been treated as royalty.

When at Pignerol his clothes were expected to last for three years, and when he left Exilles his bedding was reported as only fit to be burnt: indeed there can be no doubt that Saint-Mars amassed a large fortune by stinting those State prisoners for whom the Government made him a very liberal allowance. The 'Mask' belonged to the Church of Rome, confessed, heard Mass, and communicated at stated times. When first imprisoned he was passionate and clamorous, but he found submission the better policy, and he ended by attaching to himself both the servant Ru and the lieutenant De Jonca.

Now that we are in possession of these few facts we shall see how far wide of them range the eleven hypotheses about the 'Man in the Iron Mask.' He was said to be—

1. The Comte de Vérmandois, son of Louis XIV. and of Louise de la Vallière. His sister, the beautiful Mademoiselle de Blois, afterwards Princesse de Conti, was passionately attached to this young soldier, and her grief knew no bounds when he died of the smallpox at Courtrai, on November 18, 1683; '*muni de tous les sacrements de l'Eglise.*' The 'Mask' lived twenty years longer.

2. The Duc de Beaufort. This rough and harebrained person, though he did give some trouble during the Fronde, was never anything but, so to speak, the clown of the Bourbon family, to which by his illegitimate birth he belonged. The fact of his death at Candia, on board the 'Monarque,' and the succession of M. d'Yvonne to the post of admiral, are all matters

of history. As he was born in 1616, he would have been eighty-seven in the year of the 'Mask's' death. There is no proof or hint that the '*prisonnier de Provence*' was almost a nonagenarian.

3. The Duke of Monmouth. It is conceivable that Frenchmen should entertain this opinion, but it is not necessary to convince Englishmen that the son of Charles II. and of Lucy Waters died on the scaffold in 1685, while the 'Mask' was safe in Exilles.

4. The Armenian patriarch Avédic. This touches on one of the genuine romances of history, of which the career of M. de Ferréol should fill one volume, the disappearance of Avédic a second, and the papers of poor Mademoiselle d'Aissa a third. I can recommend these themes to all who care for facts far stranger than fiction. Avédic really was for a time a French prisoner, his imprisonment happening in this way. M. de Ferréol, a gentleman of Dauphiny, first got himself sent as ambassador to Constantinople and then occupied himself with the religious and political intrigues of the place. Jesuit missionaries were at that time very zealous, but just as M. de Ferréol sympathised with their objects, so Avédic, the Armenian patriarch, looked on the Catholic party with hatred. The French ambassador in return hated Avédic, 'the mufti who governs the Empire,' and he was able to bring about the disgrace of a minister who was certain to have plenty of rivals. Avédic was deposed and exiled, but the bold stroke of having him kidnapped by a French vessel originated in the scheming head of De Ferréol. Landed at Marseilles, Avédic contrived, by means of

a Greek named Spartali, to make his fate known, and as he was seen alive in Turkey in 1706, he could not possibly have been the '*Marchiely*' buried from the Bastille in November 1703.

5. Nicholas Fouquet. The Superintendent who had been the right hand of Mazarin's government, and the friend of Madame de Sévigné, the lord of Calais, of Havre and of Mont St. Michel, the patron of Corneille and Molière, and the pretender to the favours of Mademoiselle de la Vallière, was certainly a prisoner who needed to be shut off from every helping hand. His guilt was of the deepest dye. Having the fleet at his disposal, he had formed a project for a civil war of which the plan exists to this day in his own handwriting. He was arrested at Nantes, and sent to Pignerol to the care of its incomparable jailer. But Saint-Mars always *names* Fouquet in his letters to Louvois. He writes of Fouquet's tears, illness, repentance, and inquiries about his wife and family. He even names Fouquet's valet, and, after describing his apoplectic seizure, he mentions the Superintendent's death at Pignerol in the arms of his son in 1680. This death did not occur till after Saint-Mars had ceased to be personally responsible for him, for he left for Exilles (taking his '*deux merles*' with him) in 1674.

6. An elder brother of Louis XIV., but not a son of Louis XIII. The 'Grand Monarque' being born in September 1638, a brother who was his senior must have been sixty-six years of age when the 'Mask' only owned to sixty. There is little to be said either for or against this imaginary being's claim to the mask, since we

possess not one single fact from which to argue. It has, perhaps for this very reason, been the most popular version of the mystery attaching to a prisoner of whom Louis XV. said that 'he never harmed any one but himself.' Wild as was the original invention of the life of this poor bastard prince, it had to become the foundation of a legend still more romantic. While on Ste. Marguerite the 'Man in the Mask' is averred to have been the father of a little boy who was sent over to Corsica, and there given into faithful hands. The only message transmitted to its guardians was, 'Il fanciullo vi viene da *buòna parte*,' and my readers need not be asked to discern in such an infant the founder of the Napoleonic family and dynasty!

7. A twin-brother of Louis XIV. The whole story of his birth, and of the warning sent by the shepherds to Richelieu, may be found in Grimm's Correspondence. It reads delightfully there, but unluckily it is not supported even by probability. The delivery of the queen was witnessed by seventeen noble persons, but Richelieu, so far from being anxious or ready for action, was not even present. He had left Paris in July, for a tour in the northern provinces, was at St. Quentin when the birth took place, and only returned to the capital in October, after an absence of many weeks.

8. A son of Mazarin and of Anne of Austria. The relations between the queen and the Cardinal were often questioned, and by no one so much as by that Duchess of Orleans who was a Princess Palatine. The Cardinal died in 1661, and any son of his might naturally enough, after his death, have become the

object of persecution, but we have no trace of that child's fate during the twelve years that must be accounted for before Saint-Mars received him (then a full-grown man!) at Pignerol at the Easter of 1673.

9. A son of Cromwell. Here again the dates make the idea preposterous.

10. A son of Anne of Austria and of the Duke of Buckingham. The English ambassador admired that queen, and was once forward enough to express his feeling, but forty-eight years elapsed between the adieux of Anne and of Buckingham and the incarceration in Pignerol of their imaginary child. Where and how were those years spent?

11. As historical researches have increased the ten suggestions I have enumerated have gone slowly but surely out of fashion, till only one claimant remained for the honours of the Iron Mask. Many historical dictionaries, and the work of M. Topin, gravely assure us that it was worn by Ercole-Antonio Mathioli, an agent of the Duke of Mantua, who sold the secret of a French intrigue about the cession of Casale. Named originally to Louis by the Abbé de l'Estrades, he was called up to Paris to see the king, who paid him 100,000 livres. But he sold his secret to the persons most interested in the miscarriage of the French design upon Casale, intrigued beyond his depth, and was ultimately denounced by his accomplices. Mathioli fell a victim to his own devices. He was himself overreached and arrested, and was received by Saint-Mars at Pignerol on May 2, 1679, six years after the 'Mask' was sent there by Louvois. In all Europe no facts were better known than Mathioli's

small treachery and its instant punishment. No sort of mystery was made about either it or him. He wore no mask, and he kept a servant, and Saint-Mars invariably in his letters mentions both by their proper names, though he does not speak of this cozening Italian as much as he does of Fouquet and Lauzun, those splendid instances of the instability of fortune. When Mathioli was troublesome he was beaten, and once, when he was ill, Louvois sent orders to bury him like a common soldier. He did not die then, and Saint-Mars (when he took his '*deux merles*' to Exilles) left him behind in Pignerol. There Mathioli lingered till the 'Man in the Mask' had left both Pignerol and Exilles, and had lived for seven years behind the gratings at Ste. Marguerite. Then (1694) orders came from headquarters to dismantle Pignerol, and to transfer Mathioli and his servant to the island prison in the Bay of Cannes. He came, but, being in very bad health, he only survived the journey twelve days. There was as little secrecy about his death as there had been about his fault. On April 30, Saint-Mars wrote to tell the authorities in Paris that Mathioli was dead, and to ask what he was to do with his valet. The demise of the Mantuan agent in Provence was recorded by its historian Papon, who had learned it from the almoner Faverol, and by no possibility could this poor, scampish Italian who could not speak French, and who had only lived through twelve spring days on Ste.-Marguerite, have been '*l'ancien prisonnier; l'homme de Péronne; le prisonnier de Provence*,' as Louvois and his successor described their nameless victim in the mask. That man we know went into Pignerol seven years before Mathioli, and he died in Paris nine years after the Mantuan. A fanciful resemblance between the words 'Mathioli' and 'De Marchiely' is positively the only hook on which to hang the assertion that that cozening agent was the *mystery*—the man who wore the mask.

But truth would be strange, much stranger than fiction, if, instead of any of these royal, semi-royal, and wholly imaginary beings, there had really sinned, suffered, and died a Monsieur de Marchiel—a man in middle life, bold, adventurous, and accomplished; a man who, 'though obscure,' to quote Louvois' words, 'was not the less of importance;' a foreign emissary; the travelling agent in a conspiracy to poison Louis XIV., with his principals in London and Amsterdam, and also in very distinguished circles in Paris. Such a man there really was. A plot to murder the king was discovered by Louvois, who believed, and who made the king believe, that his former mistress, Madame de Montespan, was privy to it. To conceal her guilt Louis made as light as possible of the danger he ran, while on Louvois devolved the task of unravelling the threads of this most portentous intrigue. He gave orders that a suspicious agent, a traveller known as Louis d'Ollendorf, as the Chevalier de Kiffenbach, as M. Harmoises, or des Armoises, and as M. de la Tour, but more commonly as M. de Mareschal, de Marcheuil, and de Marchiel, should be waited for at Péronne. That adventurer was accordingly secured at the ford, between the night of the 28th and the morning of the 29th of March, 1673, and was instantly forwarded to the Bastille, where Louvois states to Saint-Mars that he had an interview with him. What passed between them Louvois does not state, and he is silent also as to the contents of De Marchiel's papers, which had just been seized by his agent Nallot. The sudden and immediate disappearance of Nallot is, as I have said before, one of the enigmas of this mysterious affair. His death, however brought about, has been a great misfortune from the historical point of view. In fact it has been an irreparable one, as Nallot alone could have divulged the secret of De Marchiel's papers, and the nature of the errand on which he was travelling, in the interest of employers of far greater rank than his own.[1] It is certain that Louvois knew it, and that possessing such a secret the War Minister was able for the future to defy both enemies and rivals; to threaten all the greatest people in France—yea, Turenne and Condé themselves; to make his father participate in his honours, and to leave his reputation, and his papers, in the hands of the son who became his successor. The great plot, whatever it may have been, was utterly frustrated that dark night at Péronne.

Plotters and prisoners at that moment filled the State prisons of France, nor was it till 1778–80 that the tribunal known as the *Chambre ardente* took cognisance of crimes which had such strange elements of necromancy, cruelty, perfidy, indecency, and treason. But justice was not even-handed; and, being without

---

[1] It is just possible that the prisoner may have in confession divulged both the nature of his guilt and the names of his employers, and that his statements were sent to Rome. If this were so the archives of the Vatican hold this secret, in addition to many more.

the knowledge which Nallot for those few days possessed, we are now quite at a loss to understand why this De Marchiel should have had so great and so lasting a share of Louvois' interest. Why was he not, like Lemaire, discharged, and ordered never again to enter France? or, like Rohan, Van Enden, and Des Preaux, beheaded? or, like Gallet, hanged, to save further trouble? He was sent to Pignerol, and, though his *name* is never once mentioned, he evidently remained the object of such incessant solicitude to the minister and to the jailer that he ran no chance of being, like the Comte de Montemayer, forgotten in his dungeon. His life was spared for some reason which Louvois never divulged, but which possibly was one of personal rather than of national importance.

Who was this De Marchiel? and is there anything known about him to identify him further with the masked prisoner? He was a Lorrainer, and probably a bastard of some creditable house, for the families of Ollendorf, Kiffenbach, La Tour, Armoises, or Harmoises, whose names he alternately assumed, were families not only then existing in Lorraine, but all inter-connected by marriage.[1] He is known to have lived in Paris and

[1] Jung expresses a hope that in Lorraine further researches about these families may yet throw some light on the mystery. The name of Harmoises once oddly enough did figure in a mystification in Lorraine, an impostor so called having tried to personify Jeanne d'Arc. I have been able through the kindness of M. Favier, librarian of Nancy, and of the late curé of Contrexéville, to satisfy myself that the family of *Armoises* is now extinct in the country. As for the name of *Maréchal*, I found it as late as 1738 certainly worn by persons of good birth, for a certain Ladislas Maréchal de Barcheny is mentioned as ' *l'écuyer du feu roy de Pologne* ;' but at this

in Brussels, to have served in a cavalry regiment, and to have run away with a married woman, while he corresponded with those political malcontents of whom Rohan, the lover of Madame de Montespan, was the head. Those plotters had another travelling agent, De Tréaumont, who was a Huguenot, but De Marchiel was assuredly a Catholic. He spoke several languages, was musical, and had both the tall figure and the energy that belong to the *rôle* of the soldier of fortune. Like Madame de Brinvilliers' lover, Gaudin de Ste.-Croix, he sought in treasonable conspiracies the distinction, the excitement, and the luxuries he loved, but his career ended at Péronne; his life from that day became a blank, and his name was a secret till he was ' *nomé sur le régistre M. de Marchiely, que l'on a payé 40 livres d'entèrement.*'

I give this hypothesis as the last and perhaps the best solution that has ever been put forward. I give it for what it is worth, for material proofs can never be acquired without those papers which Nallot seized, and of which Louvois—abundantly as he wrote about '*l'homme de Péronne*'—never divulged the contents. History cannot be built upon conjectures, nor can an historian work from deductions only, and nothing whatever has been *proved* by the minister's letters, or by Jung's *résumé* of them, except that the ' Mask ' was none of the other eleven persons he has been supposed to be.

---

moment it seems to belong rather to the class of artisans. It occurs in the hamlets between Troyes and Nancy, as Maréchal, Marchal, and Marchial: and is in such common use that it cannot serve to prove anything, or to identify anyone.

In 1672-1703 there were plenty of rogues in French prisons, and the charge of a prisoner of State in middle life and of average health was as good as an annuity to the governor of a royal prison. Saint-Mars was ever a favourite with Louvois. The minister was not likely to fall into the error of telling his friend all that he himself knew about treasonable plots and plotters, and it may be that Louvois simply meant to do Saint-Mars a kind turn when he sent him, as a very paying boarder, 'a man who, though obscure, was not the less of consequence.' Whatever was his motive, or whatever the crime of De Marchiel, they have between them contrived to bestow a strange sort of immortality on the prisoner whose name will live for ever as that of 'The Man in the Iron Mask.'

CLOISTERS OF ST. HONORAT.

CHAPTER IX.

ST. HONORAT.

'Ce n'est pas d'ailleurs en quelques lignes qu'on peut écrire l'histoire religieuse, littéraire, dramatique, souvent troublée, quelquefois glorieuse, d'une société qui a vécu près de quatorze siècles.'—LENTHERIC.

LENORMANT, when speaking of some antiquarian investigations, once said feelingly that 'when our native soil is in question no search can be too laborious or too minute.' The foundations of Christianity in southern Gaul, and the labours of its Gallic evangelists, make such common ground for us all of the early Christian sees, that a man must be, I think, singularly devoid of emotions if he is not aware of any warmth of feeling when for the first time he lands on the island called 'St. Honorat.' There a good and brave man planted the Cross, and there monasticism, which in the East had adopted a faquir-like singularity, wore its gentlest and its wisest aspect. The Convent of the Lérins had many learned and many pious scholars, but it had no *pillar-saints*, and the rule of Honoratus, instead of isolating men from one another, united them by such strong ties that the monastery became the home of all the wise, and a philosophical school for Europe during the darkest centuries of her history. The life which was one of prayer and of holy observances, was also one of manual labour. So rent and torn was the Empire that under her barbarian conquerors it might have been doubtful whether any civilisation could have survived had not the patient monk preserved some of its graces in his garden, his chapel, his cloister, and his cell. Our business to-day is with the founder of the great religious House in the Bay of Cannes.

It is early in the fifth century. Leontius is Bishop of Fréjus, and both Vence and Cimièz have their churches, while at Hyères there is a school of cenobites who imitate the solitaries of the Thebaïd. Honoratus, immediately after he was converted to Christianity, was seized with the desire to visit the East. It was from the East that civilisation first came to Maritime Gaul. Long relations with Greece and Carthage had enriched a coast where earth, air, and skies possessed already a something Oriental in their beauty. It was from Syria that Christianity had dawned; Jerusalem, Antioch, and Alexandria were all names of power, and still in the daily offices of the Church men heard the most pathetic of prayers arising in Greek, '*Kyrie eleison, Christe eleison, Kyrie eleison.*' In every respect the age of Honoratus was more nearly connected than we can now realise with Palestine, and with the first brightness of His Rising who had dispelled the thick darkness of the peoples. But the father of Honoratus forbade the journey, and his elder brother Venantius laughed at the proposed pilgrimage. Saddened and discouraged, the young disciple saw no hope of carrying out his plan, and devoted himself with such patience as he could acquire to works of almsgiving and mercy in his own home.

Tradition, which places that home in one of the north-eastern provinces of Gaul, goes on to say that Honoratus was a tall, handsome, fresh-coloured youth, with chestnut hair. Such as he was he did not shrink from one of those frightful lepers who used to roam the country, and lurk in solitary places. He received this poor wretch with tenderness, and, taking him to his own room, began to anoint his most miserable sores. Suddenly the scarred face of the leper became a radiant one. Honoratus, blind with excess of light, sank on his knees before a patient who was none other than the Lord Jesus in person, and then heard a voice bidding him be of good cheer. It was declared to him that his brother Venantius would not only withdraw his opposition to Christianity, but would become one of those elect disciples who by their virtues encourage and enlighten others. So it proved. Honoratus presently found that Venantius was a convert, and then the brothers applied themselves to finding a guide willing to accompany them to the morning-land of their faith. Capraisius, a learned man and grown grey in prayer, lived on one of the islands near the mouth of the Rhone.

He felt sympathy for the two young disciples whose hearts burned to tread the soil of Palestine; he joined himself to them, and they started on the journey which was to be so memorable for Gaul. Venantius died at Messina. He never reached the distant and sacred goal of his travels, but in dying he exhorted Honoratus to courage. 'Fear not,' he cried, 'fear not, oh my brother, for God intends thee to do greater things for Him!' There is surely something pathetic in this death by the wayside, in the message sent back to the father in his distant and pagan home, that he was bereaved of his firstborn, as well as in this humility of the elder brother who meekly realised that he at least was not destined to leave upon earth any victorious footprints. As for the future which he foretold for Honoratus, that has far exceeded their largest hopes, and for the one brother, lost in early manhood, Honoratus was destined to receive, both during his lifetime and after his departing, a long succession of spiritual brethren, of the sons and the workers for God.

But in the first freshness of his sorrow it seemed as if travel had lost all its charms. He would not go to Jerusalem without Venantius, so he hastened back to Gaul, and, as tradition says, to the companionship of his sister. That gentle and beautiful girl, who had also embraced Christianity, had received at her baptism the name of Margaret, in honour of the fair saint of Antioch who vanquished the fiery dragon.

The first hermitage of Honoratus was the *baumo* or grotto of Cap Roux. There for many months he saw the waves rise and fall, and heard the winds (*mistral* and *libeccio*) rave round that noble promontory. Did he never regret his Eastern travels, and never at the dawn be found dreaming of Jerusalem set round with hills, or of Antioch's marble pavements, and of Alexandria's sacred lore? Or was he content to hope that

> Not by Eastern windows only,
>   When daylight comes, comes in the light:
> In front the sun climbs slow: how slowly!
> But westward look—the land is bright![1]

Distant about half a league from the shore, and as if anchored in the Bay of Cannes, lie the two islands which the country folk call the 'rosettes of the sea.' Honoratus heard that they were named Lero and Lerina, and he found that, rising only a few mètres above the level of the water, they were covered with woods, and separated by the narrow channel of Friuli. All around them lie reefs of rocks, some of which would seem to deserve the title of islets, since one is now called of St. Ferréol, and another, the little '*Translero*' of antiquity, is the 'Tradelière' of the Cannes boatmen.

Honoratus was charmed with them. They were solitary, for the old settlement of 'Vergoanum' as mentioned by Pliny, like the 'cities' once noticed by Strabo, now presented no features; and probably for this reason, that Lero, the larger of the two islands, does not possess a single spring of fresh water. Lerina, a natural shelf of rock of about half a kilomètre in extent, was a desert. The air he noticed was balmy, and the thickets were full of odorous and health-giving plants. There were the wild sarsaparilla, the milfoil that banishes melan-

---

[1] Clough's *Poems*, vol. ii. p. 195.

choly, the resinous pines, the sleep-giving henbane, and the fennel and the aloe that strengthen the eyesight. This seemed to be the very place for a hermit's home. But it had two great drawbacks. In the first place Lerina swarmed with poisonous snakes, with brown, barred adders, squirming among the sunburnt stones or hissing from among the lush grasses. In the second place, there was no well, or spring, or streamlet—'water, water, everywhere, but not a drop to drink!' The legend tells how the saint first summarily disposed of the serpents, and then pondered how to obtain a supply of water for an intended monastery. On one spot grew two tall palm-trees. Thither he repaired, and striking the ground three times in honour of the Trinity, which he invoked ('*pregua la trenitat*'), he bade the waters flow. A sparkling and abounding fountain instantly burst forth. The limestone rocks often contain such springs, the outcome of a subterranean deposit of fresh water, and to this day 'St. Honorat's well' continues to supply the island and the monastery called ' of the Lérins.'

Honoratus determined to settle on this enchanting and enchanted spot. His convent was built. No doubt it was at first a rough and homely affair—possibly wattled like the cells of Marmoustier, where St. Martin first ruled over eighty monks clad in serge and goatskins. But of this new monastery it was a primary rule that no foot of woman might pass its threshold; in fact its founder, like his imitator St. Senanus, thought it best to forbid any woman to land on the island. Thus Margaret, banished to the adjacent island of Lero, found herself as much shut off from her brother as in the days of his early travels. She reproached him finally with his neglect of her. Honoratus replied that so far was he from being indifferent to her, that it still cost him many struggles to wean himself from her affection and from all worldly concerns. He had in fact come to the determination to visit her only once a year. Margaret burst into tears. 'Let me at least know at what season I may look for your coming. It will be the only month in the year for me.' The saint replied that he would come 'when the cherry-trees were in flower.' For many days did Margaret weep by the little *caranquo* from which she could see the landing-place of Lerina. The cherry-trees were bare. But Margaret prayed earnestly that they might not only flower early, but keep their flowerets late and long. To her surprise and delight the trees burst into flower. She sent over a branch to the convent, and Honoratus came. The days grew to a week, and the weeks grew to a month, and still those fair blossoms of a fruitful tree might be seen, hanging white in the island gardens. Honoratus came again, and this time he comforted his sister. He told her that her strong crying had prevailed at Heaven's high gate, and that he had himself learned how precious is an affection like hers in the eyes of Him who measures time by Love, and not by years.

Opinions differ as to the exact date of the settlement on the island. Some place it as early as A.D. 375, but the best authorities, like Mabillon, say that it ought to be fixed at A.D. 410. It has often been asked, What was the rule of its founder? From the early notices of the 'Règles de Lérins' it is plain that a rule was both used inside the convent and admired outside of it, but it cannot now be recovered. It was superseded by that of St. Benedict, and all trace of the original has disappeared. We may infer that it was not very intricate. If it did not aspire to being very comprehensive from the theological point of view, we must remember that the aims of Honoratus were all moral and spiritual ones. The two truths grasped most strongly by him were the Fatherhood of God and the brotherhood of men, and his rule was intended to form men in a rude age. He sought to teach them that faith, love, light, order, diligence, and peace are at once the true freedom of the human will and the best consecration of the human spirit. He taught them that life can so go on in study and in prayer that death presents at the last hardly any palpable change; that religion, so far from narrowing men's hearts, brings us a larger sense of the presence of God, and of the Communion of Saints. In this way he permanently enlarged the horizon of his Christian associates, and the popularisation of his teaching did, in the fifth century, serve to unite all the congregations that adopted his rule. Very striking in that dark age was the action of Christianity in binding society together. The Church had not yet asserted her right to punish error in the persons of those who held it, the times were felt to be evil, and Christianity acted on mankind less by dogmatic utterances than by forming a Church, and by proclaiming an aim of brotherly concert under the banner of her Invisible and Immortal Head.

Honoratus was not allowed to end his days on the island which he loved so well. The Church had need of her leading men, so he was chosen bishop of the premier see of Arles, and there, at a very advanced age, he died. . His heart, ever full of an intense appreciation of the burden of evil, reverted fondly to his quiet convent, and he used to visit the Lérins once every year; but now he was to start on a much longer journey, and for a more silent House. It was at the Epiphany, before the cherry-trees flowered, in the year 427, that he left a Church which he had quickened to a deeper and a richer life. He did so among the regrets of Churchmen. The champion at once of a Divine morality and of a Divine charity, he had warred only against violence and intolerance. He never imitated them, and he has thus left behind him the reputation, not only of a holy life, but of a simple, persuasive speech, and of a singularly sweet and patient temper. About his miraculous gifts, as well as about the details of his real work, there is much that is dark and fragmentary. We can at best only peer at them through the shadows of a remote past; but the figure of the saint stands out distinctly, and 'surely,' cried one of his disciples, 'if ever Charity should consent to sit for her portrait, she will borrow the features of Honoratus.'[1]

[1] A very curious *Vida de Sant Honorat* was written by a monk of the Lérins, Raymond Feraud, who fought under Charles of Anjou. The poem, in 10,000 lines, is a singular picture of mediæval ideas, legends, and manners, and the miracle by which St. Honorat saves the innocent Gualbore de Bellande, under the ordeal by fire, is very dramatic. A ruined tower of the castle at Nice, where this tragedy took place, is called the 'Tour de Bellande' to this day.

The disciple who thus fondly described him was Eucherius, and he, like Hilary, watched by the deathbed of the prelate. The vacant see was presently offered to Hilary, whose forebodings regarding his own advancement were justified by the many troubles and responsibilities of his episcopate. The Church of the West seemed not content with those doctrinal subtleties and definitions which it already owed to the Alexandrian schoolmen, but it agitated itself afresh with questions of grace and freewill. Those were points which St. Augustine once endeavoured to set at rest, but which, so far from being laid, appeared in the fifth century, and were again, like uneasy ghosts, to reappear in the seventeenth century, with the Predestinarians and the Jansenists. As the monastery of the Lérins was one of the first philosophical schools in Europe it did not escape this conflict, or the reproach of semi-Pelagian tendencies. How far the teaching of its members—Salvianus (called of Cologne), or of Faustus of Riez (called the Breton)—was or was not heretical, cannot now be clearly settled. The writers are long since dead. They cannot be cross-examined as to which side of the controversy they really leaned, while from certain passages, and their contexts, a good deal might be both proved and disproved.

Of all the theologians whom the house produced, the greatest beyond doubt was the one who is still called 'St. Vincent du Lérins.' He was of northern, some say of Belgian, extraction, and as a soldier he had opportunities of seeing the miseries of his country and the incapacity of the Cæsars. He entered the convent on the Lérins. There, transplanted to a small, wooded island, he tasted the calm but austere delights of the monastic life. There, placed between the two immensities of the cloudless sky and the dark blue sea which seem to repeat each other when they meet on an unbroken horizon, he was able to forget for a little 'the shipwreck of the present world.' He began to turn his attention, less to the furious tumults of the heathen, or to the futility of rulers who always imagined some 'vain thing,' than to the purity of Christian dogma. His 'Commonitorium' became instantly famous. It kept its credit through the Middle Ages, was early translated in Scotland, and admirably edited by Baluze in 1660, while in our own nineteenth century it continues to receive a good deal of notice. This is not because of its pretensions, for it is a very modest little treatise, divided into thirty-three short chapters, and purporting to be written by 'Pellegrinus, the least of the servants of God.' Something it assuredly owes to a style which has been compared to that of Tertullian, but the book is supremely interesting to theologians. It maintains that Holy Scripture contains all things necessary for salvation; but, as regards the interpretation of Scripture, it confronts many of the popular heresies and heresiarchs of the day with the remark that, 'a unanimous or almost unanimous consent of the Fathers should be taken as authority.' Few uninspired sayings have been so acceptable or have been so often quoted as St. Vincent's test for orthodoxy: '*Quod semper, quod ubique, quod ab omnibus creditum est.*' He bids men shun the perplexities of 'various error,' while it is certain that no preceding writer has thrown so much light on the interpretation of Scripture. He handles severely the heresies of the Donatists, Nestorians, and Arians, but he aims his blows chiefly against that doctrine of Predestination which, as being an innovation, cannot, he contends, stand his test of antiquity, universality, and consent. His book is very interesting from the way in which it anticipates, as it were, the utterances of the Athanasian Creed. The resemblance between some passages is so striking that, in the absence of any proof as to the authorship of that Symbol, it has sometimes been asserted that it came from the pen of St. Vincent of the Lérins. The reader can judge for himself:

Commonitorium, Cap. XII.	*Credo.*
'Perfectus Deus, perfectus homo : in Deo summa Divinitas, in homine plena humanitas.'	'Perfectus Deus, perfectus homo : ex anima rationali et humana carne subsistens.'

Himself a very judicious and careful student, he inveighs against a loose and irregular use of texts. He always puts the authority of Scripture first, and, while using tradition as a guide and interpreter, he adopts a strictly conservative attitude as regards the 'profane novelties of voices.' He never sets up tradition as a rival to Scripture, and his theory is one of the most important in the history of human thought. By no subsequent theologian has his subject been treated so as to receive much additional clearness, and I need not point out how, in the centuries that have elapsed since he wrote in his cell on the Lérins,[1] men have both gone

---

[1] He died about 450.

far beyond him, and fallen far behind him, in their methods of investigating dogma.

His work with those of Eucherius, and with the conferences of Cassianus, form what we may call the classics of the Island Sanctuary.

Lupus was another of its monks, but his fame was not earned by the pen. When Attila was returning from Orleans, he crossed the Seine above Troyes. Ruined by former invasions, that city had neither walls nor garrison to oppose to the fiery Huns. Lupus, the bishop, went out in his robes to meet a conqueror who agreed to spare the city if he might enter it and have its bishop for a hostage. The inhabitants fled to the woods with which this part of France is still thickly covered.[1] 'Enter, scourge of God,' cried Lupus, 'enter, and march where the wind of the Divine wrath drives thee!' But at that moment, says the legend, a thick mist enveloping the whole country hid Troyes from the sight as it also preserved it from the cruelty of Attila. The life of Lupus, after he left the convent on the Lérins, was one long warfare, now with these barbarian invaders, and now with the Arians of the north-eastern provinces. Till quite lately, the dragon which he is said to have conquered was yearly carried in procession through the streets of Troyes, and his wars with heresy have secured for 'St. Loup' a place among the mythical dragon-slayers of France.

It is hardly possible to exaggerate the importance of French monasticism during those early centuries. It

---

[1] The district between Troyes, Chaumont, Contrexeville, and Mirecourt, provides nearly all the oaken furniture of France.

was the monks who rendered Christian a new world reclaimed from utter barbarism; it was the monks who taught the Gospel, who preserved the vestiges of classical learning, and this humanising mission is the glory which can never be taken away from them. They were the priests, the chroniclers, the gardeners, the doctors, the schoolmasters, and, above all, the missionaries of Europe.

By none of the missionaries educated on the Lérins was the name of its founder more cherished than by St. Patrick. It is perhaps on this account that many of the legends told of the Irish missionary are identical with those originally ascribed to Honoratus. Take, for example, the clearance out of Ireland of venomous reptiles, which is borrowed from the destruction of the serpents on the Lérins. It is the nature of the myth to change its local habitation in this way, while it preserves the spirit of the action, or of the miracle, which it embodies. By far the most touching point in the history of St. Patrick is the tradition of his cruel sufferings in youth at the hands of the heathen Irish. So far from bearing any ill-will to those savage masters, his mind dwelt on their miserable darkness. As the truths of Christianity took an always firmer hold of him, his memory reverted more incessantly to the scenes of his early slavery. Burning with Divine charity he determined to make himself the apostle of a people who had done him nothing but harm. His self-chosen task of converting them must, as he well knew, be all the harder because Ireland had entirely escaped the civilising influences of Roman rule. No roads had opened up a country where wild in its woods and morasses its savage peoples ran; no great wall had ever been built to curb the raids and forays of rival clans; no villa of the proconsul set a pattern for elegance or comfort; no cohorts enforced discipline, and no Christian bishops had come, as in Gaul, to fill the places vacated in the towns by Roman officials.

The parents of St. Patrick, who were Christians, offered no opposition to his wishes, and during a stay on the Lérins he at once perfected his own education and prepared himself to be a missionary among the Irish Celts. The bold, simple, objective teaching of St. Patrick, as it has come down to us in the 'Book of Armagh,' may be taken as a specimen of the way in which the monks of the Lérins proclaimed the message of their faith. In the halls of Tara the daughters of King Lodghaire asked St. Patrick and his friend if they were not fairies (*Dhuine Seidhe*), or men of the hills. The saint replied, 'Would it not be better for you to confess to the true and living God than to inquire of us concerning our race?' The next question of the Irish princesses was, 'Who is God?' and this elicited one of the most beautiful confessions of faith that has come down to us from the primitive teachers of our Church. I will only quote a few sentences from it, and I have selected them, less because of their reference to the Erin where St. Patrick uttered them, than on account of an evident allusion to the sunny Lerina where he once prayed and studied.

> God inspireth all things . . .
> He sustaineth all things—

> He giveth light to the *light of the sun.*
> He hath made *springs in a dry ground,*
> And *dry islands in the sea.*

Might not those illustrations of the Creator's power have been suggested to him by the famous well of Honoratus, and by the sunshine which warms the islands in the Bay of Cannes?

THE CASTLE ON ST. HONORAT.

CHAPTER X.

THE MONASTERY ON THE LÈRINS.

'From men thus abstracted from the commerce of life the Church would, from time to time, receive new treasures of learning, and new lessons how to live above the world. And even if any of them should be called away and leave no visible fruits, think not, ye seekers after a sign, think not that they must therefore have been of the idlers of the earth : for what know ye of their influence upon those around them? how dare ye scan the mystery of their faith in God ? What did Simeon but "wait"? What did Anna but "fast and pray"?'—J. R. HOPE SCOTT.

THE era of legend and of tradition is left behind by the time that we reach the date at which Amand, as Prior of the Lérins, ruled over three thousand seven hundred monks, and substituted the rule of St. Benedict for the first simple statutes of the founder. With modifications, that rule continued to be observed on the island and in the dependent houses till the time when neither reformed congregationists of St. Maur, nor Cassinists of Padua, had charms sufficient to allure disciples to the convent on St. Honorat.

We now approach the era of Charlemagne, between whose conquests and those of Clovis there is all the difference between power and brutality. The mind of that great emperor was even more powerful than the sword which he had wielded in life and which is buried with him in Aix-la-Chapelle. He made war on barbarism, and to dissipate its darkness he founded schools. Another of his great objects was the unity of the clergy, and to promote this he placed it under the safeguard of that temporal power which he first really secured to the popes. On these two piers—learning and uniformity—he designed to build an empire more enduring than his campaigns, or even than his life. His nephew, St. Bernard, once visited the Lérins; and we may be sure that that noble monastery did not escape the attention or the sympathy of the emperor. The worldly possessions of the convent increased; its chapels became famous, and pilgrims from all parts of France and Germany repaired to its seven shrines. He who visited them seven years in succession got a palm-branch from the Prior, with the assurance of the forgiveness of his sins in this world and in the next. Once upon a time there lived in the mountains of Provence a poor man, who, having already resorted thither six times, begged his master to allow him to make his seventh and last visit to St. Honorat. But his master was one who feared not God, and who had no compassion for the servant, whom he roughly bade to go tend his pigs, and to speak no more of wandering to the shrines of the Lérins. The poor swineherd, after weeping and bewailing himself, fell into a deep slumber.

In his sleep he fancied himself again on the beautiful island. There his ears were ravished by the chanting of psalms, and by the soft murmur of the sea breeze among the pines. He forgot both his hard lot and the ill-temper of a master as swinish as his herd, when he received with rapture from the Prior that palm which crowns the seventh pilgrimage to the seven shrines of the Lérins. Suddenly he awoke. It was at the edge of a cork-wood; the lanky swine were crunching acorns all round him; the island sanctuaries were far away, and no bell here rang to prayers—yet, lo! by his side the much-coveted palm-branch lay: for an angel had brought it to comfort him!

The dependencies of the monastery of the Lérins gradually reached all along the coast from Genoa to Barcelona. But as its riches increased, and as silver shrines and jewelled reliquaries accumulated in the island, the convent became an always greater temptation to pirates. As early as the beginning of the eighth century, the Moorish chieftain Moussa ravaged the coast, and did so almost unopposed. In fact, Gaul, when possessed by Franks, Burgundians, and Visigoths, was the scene of such disorders that it was incapable of self-defence, and lay open as a field where Normans, Saracens, and Vandals might sack and pillage at their will.

Contemporary with the weak reign of Louis le Débonnaire (814) was the life of the celebrated Haroun-Al-Raschid, whose pirates not only landed in Provence and in Corsica, but, carrying terror up the banks of the Tiber, burnt the basilica of St. Paul's-without-the-walls of Rome. In 846, these pirates landed beyond the

Esterels, and, after establishing themselves at the Garde Fraxinet, between Fréjus and Hyères, they pushed up into Dauphiny, and even into Bresse. In 940, Fréjus was sacked by the Moors; and in 972, St. Mayeul became their prisoner.

Every movement causes a counter-movement, and there can be no doubt that these constant invasions of the Saracens did much to stimulate the pious passions of the Crusaders. They roused in due time the patriotism of William, Count of Marseilles, of Gébelin de Grimoald, and of Isarn, Bishop of Grenoble. They felt how decisive to them was the question, whether Europe was or was not to be subject to a Semitic sway? They raised troops, and delivered their districts from invaders who had held their footing good in southern France for more than a hundred years.

But the monks on the Lérins had no troops, and they had treasures. It became necessary for them therefore to make a stronghold to which to retire when threatened with fire and sword. Abbot Adelbert II. began the square tower, or *vigié*, of Cannes; and in 1088, the castle of the Lérins was built. 'It is,' says Lenthéric, ' the true type of those strongholds, at once military and religious, which from the eleventh to the fourteenth century rose along the coasts of Provence. In them every detail recalls the passions and the violence of the Middle Ages, of those centuries so full of strong convictions. All the stones employed for this now dismantled building are mutilated remains of the Roman epoch.' The building is now a shell, but is none the less remarkable for its proportions. All the columns

M

are antique, and on one may be read the name of Constantine, while other blocks seem to have been the gravestones of the earliest colonists. This great tower served as a *vigié*, as a beacon, as an arsenal, and as a library. It was certainly not built too soon, nor was it altogether successful after it was built, if we may credit the tale of the terrible massacre of 1107.[1] That fell at the time of Pentecost, when the island must have well deserved the description which St. Ambrose once gave of it: 'Among such fresh springs, such leafy groves, such smiling vistas, and such scented airs, the earth seems opening Paradise.' All nature was serene, and the festivals of the Christian year had run their course. Only St. Porcaire, the Abbot of the Lérins, was uneasy. He had been warned in a vision of a danger threatening the community; it could not be a mere fancy, it must be an intuition sent to him by that Paraclete whose seven-fold gifts of wisdom the Church then invokes, and never invokes in vain. He therefore bade his monks be wary. They were to bury their treasures, and, while prepared for the worst,

---

[1] *Cartularium Abbatiæ Lirinensis*, cccvi. 'Sita est insula quedam apud Provinciam undique circumcepta freto Tirreni equoris que ab incolis vocitatur Lirinus, quingentorum martirum cruore atque capitibus Domino Jhesu Christo olim dicata, cujus victoriæ dux et signifer extitisse legitur sanctus abbas Porcarius, debacante super eos gente Sarracenorum: inter quorum sepulcra condiuntur ossa venerabilis Alfgulphi, ejusdem loci abbatis et Dei martiris egregii. . . . Hoc autem munus libertatis et honestatis quod monasterio concedo in honorem sancte Dei genitricis Marie et beatissimi Honorati confessoris Christi fundato, confirmo et propria manu coroboro hoc testamentum, ut inviolatum persistat nec quilibet temerario ausu infringere presumat.'

IN THE CASTLE OF ST. HONORAT.

must earnestly commend their souls to the God in Whose Hand are the destinies of the greatest and of the most obscure. The vision came true, and only all too soon. The Abbot was saying Mass, when shouts of pirates crying '*Allah! Allah!*' broke in upon the chanting of the choir. The corsairs had landed: the white turbans and the dusky faces of the pirates were already at the door, and five hundred monks, along with St. Porcaire, bit the earth that day. Many more were carried off as slaves. The victorious Moors having left, as they believed, not a soul behind on the island, sailed off for Agay. There four of their Christian prisoners contrived to escape. They first hid in the forest of the Esterel and then made their way back to the Lérins, where they were welcomed by two companions, who during the massacre had managed to hide among the rocks. From this small nucleus the life of the monastery had to be built up anew.

It may not be uninteresting to anyone who will take the trouble to read these pages on the Island, to endeavour to realise what this great mediæval monastery was like.

The first thing that struck the eye was the main square of the building, with its cloisters, on one side of which the church was built. Inside that church the most remarkable thing was the curtained-off choir, where the brothers sat in their stalls, and from which the sound of chanting proceeded as the monks repeated their vesper psalms, or the pathetic Office for the Dead. There were in the square a large schoolhouse, the well, the library, the hospital, the rooms for guests, and the houses of the Abbot, Prior, and novices. With dormitories, refectories, stables, wine-presses, cellars, laundry, goat-stable, fruit-room, kitchen, forge, looms, slaughter-house, oven, barns, byre, and pigsties, the convent covered a large space of ground; but there were no mills on this island, and no vineyards. Their flour-mill was at Mougins, and their planks were sawn at L'Abbadie, near Pégomas, while their vineyards lay round their summer-house of Vallauris. The officials of such a House had many duties, and were necessarily of many grades of importance. Let us pass them in review, and fancy that we see them in their black habits as they lived:

There was first the Abbot: generally a Grimaldi, or a Castellane, or a cadet of some other great, local house, such as that of Villeneuve.

2. The Vicar-General.

3. The Claustral Prior, to whom belonged the keys of the house, church, chapels, castle, and lodges.

4. The Sub-Prior.

5. The Sacristan. His duty was to see that the lamp burned continually before the altar. He had to supply the oil for this purpose, the incense, and the candles used during service, as well as the great *brandon* of red wax, which is lit on Maunday-Thursday and burns till Pentecost.

6. The Dean, whose residence on the island was obligatory.

7. The *Camérier*. In his department was the furniture of the cells and chapels.

8. The *Pitancier*, who drew the rights from Napoule,

valued in the time of Dom Balthazar Moricaud at 2,900 livres.

9. The *Vestiaire*, who had to get the serge from the looms, and to keep in order the hangings, stoles, altar-cloths, and robes.

10. The *Cabiscol*, or precentor. Subject to him were the chanters and choristers. It was his duty to train the voices, and to conduct the musical services of the convent. The preservation, like the preparation, of all scores and instruments fell to his share.

11. The *Infirmier*. To him were confided the four surgical instruments, the probe, the lancet, the razor, and the pliers. By him were prepared the white and the golden ointments, the salves and unguents, for all of which he collected the herbs most in repute. His jars were full of electuaries, while bundles of herbs and rolls of linen lay ready for use in the hospital. He put his faith in certain times and seasons and combinations of the planets as being favourable for the exhibition of his remedies; thought madness dependent on the moon, but held melancholy to be fairly amenable to borage and hellebore, to milfoil and pimpernel, while the rest-harrow cured delirium, and the star-thistle stopped the plague. In consideration of his trouble, and of his charity in giving out such remedies as tarragon and absinthe and feverfew for the fevers of the poor, he had a right to all the alms collected in Cannes on the festivals of All Saints and All Souls, while the lands of Cannet were especially apportioned to the infirmary. It is even thought that there was a 'convalescent home' in that sheltered locality, under the protection of the two strong towers

of Danis and Placette, which the monks built there in the fourteenth and fifteenth centuries.

12. The *Econome*, or book-keeper.

13. The Treasurer.

14. The *Procureur*. He had to register and preserve all the papers bearing on the legal and civil interests of this great community. His office is sometimes spoken of as that of the notary, or '*bailli de la curie de Lérins.*'

15. The Librarian. As the Lérins was a Benedictine house a great deal of copying and studying was done, but till the fourteenth century the number of volumes in conventual and collegiate libraries was really small. There was wealth of calendars, and psalters, and choir-books, but, for example, the Dominicans of Dijon were thought to be rich when in the fourteenth century they possessed a hundred and forty volumes, of which twenty-nine represented patristic learning.

16. The Cellarer.

17. The Registrar of Woods and Forests.

18. The Almoner.

19. The Master of the Novices.

20. The Mayor of the Serf Labourers.

21. The Porter.

22. The Armourer.

23. The Gardener.

24. The *Ouvrier*, whose place was equivalent to that of clerk of the works. The masonry and roofs of the house were under his charge.

Each of these officials had a staff under him—a large staff if the work lay in the kitchen-garden or in the vineyards; and besides the regulars there was a body of lay brothers (who took the three vows but did not observe the rule), who were hewers of wood and drawers of water, who tended the cattle and fed the pigs, and either saw to the nets or worked the boats that plied between Cannes and the island, or even carried saintly messengers to Rome.

Cannes belonged to the monastery of the Lérins—that is to say, the Abbot was its feudal superior—and the town paid to the convent a tax on all its produce. Corn was rated to owe one-tenth, wine one-eleventh, flax and hemp one-fourteenth, and so on; but then, on the other hand, it was an Abbot who added a few feet to the pier, and who built the tower on the Mont Chevalier. In fact the whole dignity and interest of this piece of coast is so centred in the Convent on St. Honorat that we wonder how the House ever came to ruin.

The Great Schism of the West was the first thing that damaged it, for the Popes of Avignon had no friendly feeling for it, and, what was worse, they invented the system of putting the abbeys into *commende*. In this way the abbot could be a layman—some prince or baron, who was useful to them, and who never drew less than a third of the rental of the House. A great change of feeling necessarily took place. Such an abbot-commendatory was a hireling and a stranger, an embodied piece of grasping worldliness; while the Prior, left to reside in the cloister, had no control of either the riches or the interests of his House, but fulfilled its duties with nonchalance, and in narrow circumstances.

By 1500, this abuse, like many others, reached a climax. As an example, we need go no farther than a certain Agostino Trivulzio, presented in 1517, by Pope Leo X., to the see of Grasse. His nomination was not unsuitable. Grasse was, as St. Ambrose said of Provence, 'more Italian than Italy itself,' and the bishop came of a noble Milanese family. But this same Agostino appears in the list of the bishops of Toulon, and in that of the bishops of Bayeux, and while he was chief shepherd of three French sees this pluralist was also commendatory-abbot of Nanteuil and of Fontfroid. He never so much as visited Grasse, and he died in Rome, where his tomb, in the church of S. Maria del Popolo, may be seen to this day. It is curious, however, to hear the way in which the very pope who had appointed him thundered, at the Council of the Lateran, against this system of the *commende*. Too many interests were, however, involved in it, so the abuse went on, and it went on to be that disintegrating element which gradually but surely brought the monastic houses to ruin.

The monks of the Lérins lived on the very worst of terms with their abbots-commendatory. Sometimes they had the best of it, but once, when the Abbot happened to be a high-tempered and crafty Grimaldi, they got very much the worst of it. He treated them simply as serfs attached to the soil of his fief, removed them one and all, and had them replaced by some regulars of the Order of the Cassinists of St. Justina of Padua.

But even this stern measure did not secure peace, and the quarrels continued till the middle of the eighteenth century. The years that were so painfully fertile in jars produced nothing else of great or good, and the calm which fell at last on St. Honorat was less that of ordered discipline than of moral inaction. In 1740, a body of Cluniacs was introduced; but the new blood could not revive a life that stagnated, while all around this dying monasticism there lay a world of thought and business—a world struggling to be born.

Among Protestants there is a common impression that when the Revolution of 1789 came, it found the religious orders in France idle, affluent, over-fed, and full of empty pretensions. As representing an ignorant intolerance, they are supposed to have then fallen victims to the just wrath of a populace whom they had robbed of bread for the body and of freedom for the mind. Nothing can be farther from the truth. The institution was more than two-thirds dead, and the houses, in six cases out of ten, already worn out and condemned. It is true that for too long the sluggish and egotistic lives of the regulars had possessed nothing in common with the fortitude, simplicity, industry, and wisdom of St. Honoratus and of St. Benedict. Neither was the stagnation of the eighteenth century that Peace, passing all understanding, which rebukes the fire of human passions, while it lightens the grievous pains and fills the vacant spaces in solitary human hearts. The founders had truly made of their institution 'a great centre for national and religious life;' but the world now demanded different specifics, and it confessed to having very different ailments from those of the fifth century. The vast multiplication of convents rendered them a mistake, while, thanks to the system of the *commende*, it was not uncommon to meet, as Mr. Gibbon did, 'an *abbé* who, by renouncing the world, had secured to himself an income of 100,000 livres a year.' That this income was perhaps spent in the ante-room of a Madame de Pompadour naturally did not do anything towards elevating either the system or the men.

By the last half of the eighteenth century Frenchmen had become philosophical. The libraries, even of country-houses, were full of the works of the Encyclopedists, and the jokes and anecdotes of Grimm were more in demand than the 'Commonitorium' of St. Vincent of the Lérins. The court and the camp had more charms than the cloister, so professions became scarce, except among women, and few men of note adopted the religious life. The convent of Port Royal had been perhaps the last expression of monastic fervour of which monarchical France was capable, and its results were not such as to tempt the next generation to repeat them. The press had become a power, for a new aristocracy, that of literature, began to assert itself. In a very rude age the monastery had really incarnated the doctrine of brotherhood, and there men had learnt 'how good and blessed a thing it is for brethren to dwell together in unity.' But now a new philanthropy had its votaries. Jean-Jacques Rousseau had just argued before the Academy of Dijon the equality of men, and though it might have been difficult to deduce from the pages of his 'Emile' a definite theory of education, yet the book, like the rest of Rousseau's works, did, by its style and its enthusiasm, herald a new era of thought, of sympathies, new claims, new aspirations, and new efforts—when different methods both of primary and of secondary education came to replace the old ones, and when learning no longer lived on herbs in a cell, hard by the one where the painter laid his palette, or the prior told his beads.

The Government never took on itself to abolish the institution of monasticism, and even under the tyranny of the old *régime* it was not forbidden to men to live together in communities. The State only determined to cut off some dead branches, and it obtained canonical sanction for its operations. Worldly as it was, it felt a sort of clemency for those seats of ancient learning, the cynosures of so many pious fancies, records in stone of an age when contemplation brought heaven down to earth, when pious hands first cleared away thorns and briars from the fields of France. 'Time,' it has been said, 'trieth Troth,' and time in this case brought to judgment both the method and the men. No revolution did it, only time succeeded where pirates and heretics had failed. The cloisters had the same dim religious light, the gardens had the same careless beauty, the orchards the same russet fruits, while over the valleys, where the rich abbeysteads stood between breadths of cornland and vineyards, there brooded the same sylvan peace. Only the spirit that is in man had changed, and practical Frenchmen could no longer fit themselves to a conventual life. Thus it happened that near Rouen there was a priory in which only one monk remained: many congregations were suppressed for lack of members, and the Government ordered three hundred and eighty-six useless religious houses to be shut.

A bull of Pius VI. did, in 1787, unite the abbacy of the Lérins to the see of Grasse, and when, in 1788, the pontifical commissioner came to look into the affairs of a House already canonically suspended, the fact transpired that there were but four monks in residence on St. Honorat. The seven chapels had lost their popularity, and pilgrims no longer flocked to their shrines; only the *plant of pardon*[1] still showed its spikes of yellow flowers on the beach where martyrs had died under the blows of Moorish pirates. The moment had arrived for the secularisation of St. Honorat. In this case, as in every other, the Government undertook to indemnify the survivors. An inventory of the property was made. The list proves how wide of the mark is the popular picture of cellars full of old wine, and of sideboards covered with old plate. The very library was by no means intact, and the four monks, as they had had little to enjoy, had now very little to leave. Dom Théodule, the Prior, was a native of this district. Perhaps he loved his island, with its shrines and its myrtle-flowers, with the washing of the waves, and the sound of the fishermen's bells when they drew their nets by night in the bays where the corallines grow. Perhaps he had for years counted the stones of the great House whose tower was familiar to him since childhood; certain it is that Dom Théodule never went out of sight of his lost priory. He retired, with his pension of 1,500 livres, to Vallauris, and died there, in the house of his sister, Madame Gazan. Dom Marcy, on the same pension, became Vicar of

---

[1] *L'herbo dou Pardoun*, the *Cineraria maritima*.

Antibes: not quite an ignoble berth, as Antibes, once the seat of a bishop, was extra-diocesan and in the direct gift of the Holy See. Dom Lassans died the humble *desservant* of a hamlet near Grasse; while Dom Chardon, after drifting as far as Avignon, died there a professor in a public school. Thus the old order gave place to the new, and thus on the Lérins died Love and Zeal.

The year 1788 was followed by the more stormy one of 1789, and soon the seaboard of the Maritime Alps was startled, not by the ringing of any Angelus bell, but by the voice of Mirabeau, which was as the roar of the *mistral*, by the shouting of the 'Marseillaise,' and by the booming of the English guns. The spring of 1815 brought Napoleon to land within sight of the Lérins, but by that time the monastery had become a heap of ruins. In its palmy days it once had an Abbot so fond of meditation that every night he was wont to pace the path between the seven chapels and the little mole. It was reported that long after his demise the ghost of St. Virgile haunted his accustomed walk. Assuredly in the early days of this century St. Virgile could have noted nothing during his walks but an abomination of desolation, for the rank stalks of the fennel and the smilax tangled above the place where his abbey had stood.

The Bishops of Fréjus-and-Toulon made a note of these desecrated shrines, these empty altars, and this deserted beach. Both Monseigneur Richer and Monseigneur Michel wished to get possession of the island, and as the property had been already twice put up for sale, to be bought, first by an English clergyman, and then by a French actress, there was hope that it might again come into the market. Accordingly the late bishop, Monseigneur Jordany, was fortunate enough to buy it in. The Jordany belong to Cannes, and a Jordany had once been Prior of the Lérins, so it was a double gratification to have obtained possession of the island. A colony of brothers of the Third Order of St. Francis was first placed there. Their business was the cultivation of the soil, and the training of orphan boys on a model farm, but they have latterly been replaced in the monastery by some Cistercian monks. The pious gifts of Catholic visitors have enriched the new foundation, and the tall belfry of the new convent now serves as a landmark to mariners from St. Tropez to the Cap Garoube. Visitors of the fair sex are not permitted to enter the convent, and they are of course proportionately anxious to do so. I was once deluded by a friend who can prove a descent from Edward III. to hope that because I have some of the blood of King Robert the Bruce we might together have been able to gratify our curiosity. I should then have had it in my power to report to my readers about the cloisters of the Lérins. But H.R.H. the Comtesse de Paris undeceived me. She told me that the late amiable Queen of the Netherlands was the only woman who has entered there *as by right*, and that though she had herself crossed the threshold an express permission had previously been obtained from Rome. I must therefore ask gentle readers to be content with a photograph, and gentlemen to visit for themselves a House of which I am told that the monks are pardonably proud. The brothers are also very much pleased to speak of the rights which render their estate free of municipal dues. Cannes formerly depended from the Lérins, and, but for the existence of certain admiralty rights of foreshore, it appears that even now the Mayor of Cannes could not set his foot uninvited on the island of St. Honorat.

It is unfortunate that the books of the old library have not been recovered. The papers were originally sent up to Grasse. During the Revolution they ran many risks and were carted off to Draguignan, where they lay for years at the *sous-préfecture*. They are now at Nice, and the great disorder in which they were found augured ill for such a classification as might lead to a discovery of their merits. The *Société des Lettres, Sciences, et Arts des Alpes-Maritimes* has, however, taken the matter in hand (1883). The big, brown, wooden book, containing a hundred and fifty-two leaves of parchment, has been catalogued and reprinted,[1] and in this way we possess a list of the gifts, grants, sales, and privileges of the monastery during the ninth, tenth, eleventh, and twelfth centuries. A second series, comprising the charters from the thirteenth to the eighteenth century, is in preparation. The Prince of Monaco possesses one curious and original document from the charter-room of the Lérins. It is

[1] *Cartulaire de l'Abbaye de Lérins, publié sous les auspices du Ministère de l'Instruction Publique*, by MM. H. Moris et Ed. Blanc. The printing press of the convent was employed for the production of a volume which can be bought from H. Champion, 15 Quai Malaquais, Paris.

literally as well as figuratively a 'rent-roll,' for on a roll, eleven inches wide, but fourteen feet in length, is preserved a list of all the fiefs, lands, and tenements belonging to the Abbey. Each entry is attested by the local notary, and the document is one of the greatest interest for the topography of all the districts once controlled by the abbots of the Lérins.

The plate and silver shrines, which were deposited at Grasse when the abbey was united to the see, were early sent to Marseilles to be melted up for national purposes, but there are a few relics of St. Honoratus still preserved in the diocese. The *Châsse* is at Grasse. It is a small, arched, wooden chest, with curious archaic figures, representing scenes in the life of the saint, such as his arrival on the island, and his conquest of the serpents. One of these, a monster apparently fourteen feet long, plays the heroic part in the composition. The *Châsse* is empty, but the church possesses a bone, and Cannes also has a relic of him, which is carried through the old town on the festival of the Saint. I met it once, being escorted by M. Barbe the *curé*, with a dozen priests, and a hundred white-veiled children, but this small, annual procession is all that survives from the olden time. It must have been a good deal more animated when the pilgrims from Riez, appearing in Cannes, fought the Cannois for the right to walk first, next to the great crozier of the Abbot, in the triumph of St. Honorat's Day.

Thus fades the renown even of those who have 'built churches and chapels:' thus sinks in clouds the little day of every human system. 'God,' said a wise French preacher, 'only effaces to write a fresh inscription.'

The speech of Monseigneur Jordany, when he recovered the island of the Lérins, showed that he had read aright the 'fresh inscription,' the larger message of the nineteenth century. He dwelt on the virtues of Honoratus and of his disciples, but he told the crowd, 'that both saints and martyrs, both bishops and fishermen, both priests and men of the world, belong alike to God, and have a message from Him to the world.' It would hardly be an exaggeration to add that we are all, Catholics and Protestants, the children of the Middle Ages, and that the bells of this cloister, like those of the fabled city sunk under the sea, stir our hearts. They remind us of a time when the founder had an ideal, an ideal which was that of the Beatitudes, and an impersonal zeal for the coming of the Kingdom of God.

CHAPTER XI.

NICE.

Il y a un pays, où la nuit sans voiles,
Pleine de parfums, de sourdes rumeurs,
Laisse scintiller une mer d'étoiles—
Des étoiles d'or, tremblantes lueurs.

Il est un pays, où l'oiseau qui passe
Gazouille, et bénit l'éternel printemps,
Pays de jeunesse ardente et d'audace,
Où les cœurs épris ont toujours vingt ans.

Ce pays—c'est toi . . .
Noël Blache.

'Les événements effacent les événements—inscriptions gravées sur d'autres inscriptions—ils font des pages de l'histoire des palimpsestes.'—Chateaubriand.

THE county of Nice is like a beautiful woman, and her history is that of the conquerors who were at once her lovers and her lords. She has never had a continuous life of her own, and she has had many vicissitudes; only the sky is still bright with all her smiles, and the sea of the *Baio des Anges* is salt with all her tears. A strong life runs in her veins, snow-clad mountains stand round about her, her red earth brings forth wine, and roses, and scented herbs, her sunshine gives hope to the dying; she was, and she is, and she ever will be, so long as the sunshine lasts, beautiful, perfumed, rich, laughing, and warm. Yet her history has hardly been a happy one. Its storms would fill a volume, and I propose therefore to throw it into the form of some chronological tables, which can be consulted at pleasure, or passed over at will.

The country has ever been wasteful of human life. These hills that slope to the sea have at all times tempted strangers and invaders. The Ligurian races succeeded to the Pelasgic builders on Mont Agel, and a Celtic emigration into the Maritime Alps took place, perhaps two thousand years before Christ. No date can be fixed for it, or for the exploits of the Tyrian Hercules at Villefranche and Monaco, or even for the foundation of Cimièz.

The legend of the foundation of the earliest Greek colony in Provence is as beautiful as the sea which first bore to the mouth of the Rhone the galley of the Phocæan youth. It is a legend, yet if it be true, as Schiller says, that 'a high soul underlieth childish play,' then this story may be held to be descriptive of the way in which Provence, like the king's fair daughter, has over and over again given herself to a stranger, has adopted and absorbed into herself new strains of blood, and has given to her population a tinge, now of Greek, now of Moorish, now of Jewish, and now of Genoese blood. At the present moment the currents of Anglo-Saxon and of Piedmontese life are sensibly altering the populations of the coast.

But here is the legend of the first Greek settlers, as told in Marseilles, a place still so Greek in its colouring. Nann, the king of the Ségobriges, held high festival. His chiefs sat round his table. They were brave and they drank deep, as they filled a bowl to pledge fair Glyptis, the only daughter of their king. White-robed, with hair that fell to her knees, Princess Glyptis slipped into the hall. She was to choose a mate to-day from the *braves* who were her father's most trusted friends. They all drank to her, and as they praised her loveliness, they whispered, 'On whom will her choice fall?' To whom would Glyptis give the cup now brimming in her white hands?

> None but the brave,
> None but the brave,
> Deserve the fair!

But the fair have their caprices. Glyptis had known these *braves* since her childhood. She knew their jokes, their thick beards, their gruff voices, their exploits, and their drinking-songs. A strange face near the door caught her eye. Ah! *that* no doubt was the Phocæan youth of whom King Nann had spoken, and whom he had bidden to his table to-day, so that young Protis might, on his return to the isles of Greece, tell his fellows how men feasted in the halls of a king all whose soldiers were brave, and whose only daughter was beautiful. Glyptis gazed, and hesitated. The land from which this stranger came was far away—nearer to the sunrising than the white cliffs of her home; but there men spoke in a softer speech, and looked not unlike the gods to whom they prayed. The maiden looked again; then she glided through the rows of the Gaulic chiefs which had opened to let her pass, and she placed in the hand of Protis the cup that was her troth-plight. Every fairy tale ends in the same way: 'and so they were married, had sons and daughters, and lived happy ever afterwards.' That is the old, orthodox *finale*, and the legend of Glyptis and Protis is no exception to the rule. They did live happily, and they founded in the dominion of Massalia a city of which Chateaubriand could say that she was 'Athens' youngest rival.' Nice and Antibes (Antipolis) were children of this parent Massalian colony, but being weak they had more to fear from the fierce native tribes. It was the Greeks of Antibes who first summoned the Roman legions to their assistance. This occurred B.C. 237; and the conquest of the district was so obviously tempting to the Romans that their first *promenade militaire* was followed by others, and the Latin element thus introduced into the Maritime Alps was destined to be soon, and for ever, the dominant one.

	B.C.
Passage of Hannibal into Italy	222
P. C. Scipio lands at Villefranche	201
Romans defeated at the fords of the Var	186
Cannes destroyed by Q. Opimius and the 22nd legion	155
P. Flaccus defeats the tribes	127
Aix, in Provence, founded by the Romans	126
The *Via Domitia* made	125
The *Castrum* of St. Vallier built	125
Pompey goes into Gaul	77
Siege of Vence by the Romans	60
Victories of Augustus as recorded at Turbia	13
Tiberias gives freedom to the cities of a coast of which Cimella (Cimièz) was the Roman, or military, capital, and Nice the emporium of Greek trade	A.D. 14
Mission of St. Trophimus	(?)
Mission of St. Barnabas	(?)
Battle of Arluc, near Cannes	72
Amphitheatre of Cimièz built (Hadrian)	130
Pertinax born at Turbia	193
St. Bassus, first Bishop of Nice	200 (?)

	A.D.
Martyrdom of St. Pons at Nice	261
Diocletian persecutions in Gaul	302
St. Hermentarius, first Bishop of Grasse	?
St. Acceptus, first Bishop of Fréjus	?
St. Eusebius, first Bishop of Vence	?
St. Honoratus founds the Convent on the Lérins	circa 406
Appearance of the Visigoths	406

The Roman civilisation was so perfect in laws, in architecture, in military strength, and in social refinements, that any man now foretelling a return to

ROMAN BRIDGE OF CANNES.

barbarism would have seemed as one who dreams. Flourishing towns were threaded like pearls along the Aurelian Way: Fréjus, Cannes, and Antibes had their theatres; Arluc and Mandelieu their altars of Venus; Clausonne and Vallauris their aqueducts; Vence and Grasse their temples to the twelve great gods; Turbia had its trophy; Napoule and Auribeau their granaries; Cannes its bridge; Fréjus and Taurentium their ports; while farther to the eastward there were villas on the

Cap Martin, a wall at Mentone, and a circus at Ventimiglia.

The destruction of Cimièz must have been a great blow, not only to the power of the proconsul, whose villa occupied the brow of the hill, but to the whole social organisation of the coast. No more beautiful spot than this old Roman capital! The steep hillside bristling with vigorous groups of trees, the rosy orchards and the noble olives, all make up a most charming picture. Below, in the valley of Paillon, is the stony river-bed, and the white roads that lead into the rocky gorges of St. André and Tourrêtes. No winds blow at Cimièz, and a gentle sadness hung at once over the silent Roman villa, and over the shadowy paths that led up to the convent and the white tombs of the dead, till some staring modern boulevards came to drive away these visions of an historic and of a religious past. But seated for an hour at the door of the church under these spreading ilex trees, between the ruined amphitheatre and the Christian graves, we can pass in review a long succession, both of the soldiers who studied war, and of the sons of peace. Ediles and proconsuls and centurions here planned either military business, or the gladiatorial shows of a circus built to hold four thousand persons, and then, after the delights of the theatre, they would tramp away in the early dawn to Antibes, to the port where the triremes rode, and whence these Roman colonists drew their supplies. Nice, with her harbour of Limpia, was occupied by the Greek traders, for whom very dark days were now in store.

	A.D.
Nice and Cimièz sacked by Burgundians	414–32
Martyrdom of St. Vallier, Bishop of Antibes	473
Appearance of the Ostrogoths	510
Conquests of the Franks	537
Cimièz destroyed by the Lombards	571
First Saracen invasions	713–35

We have noted the introduction of the Latin element, so I must pause here to speak of the first Semitic wave that struck on the coasts of Southern Europe. After Christianity had been driven from her old strongholds—Palestine, Egypt, and Carthage—a new danger threatened her in the development of a spirit of military fanaticism among the disciples of Islam. This has in some ways proved a blessing in disguise, since long before Southern Europe could recover from the assaults of the barbarian races of Cimbri, Ambrones, Teutons, Vandals, Visigoths, Ostrogoths, Normans, Lombards, and Huns, her Semitic colonists had a richer civilisation. These new comers were called sometimes Saracens, or people from the *Yark*, or East; sometimes Moors, or people from Western Mauritania. They were nominally Mahometans, but they really held a mixture of Egyptian, Persian, Sabæan, Chaldean, and Jewish creeds. Essentially nomadic in their origin, we shall see them become first sailors and then colonists, able like the fairer Moors of Granada to reach the highest places in arts and refinement: 'standing,' says Deutsch, 'together with the Jews, at the cradle of modern science.' The Berbers, who were the rougher element, may be said to be now fairly represented by the modern Kabyles, and by the Arabs of the Tell.

The Feudal Age.

	A.D.
Saracens land on the Island of St. Honorat	730
Second invasion of the Saracens	739
Antibes and Cannes given by Pepin to Thibaud	750
Charlemagne gives fiefs to G. di Ventimiglia	770
Charles IV. gives Provence as a fief to Bozon I.	879
Bozon II., titular King of Arles	948
Consuls appointed in Nice	1008
Tower of Cannes begun	1070
Castle on St. Honorat begun	1080
Order of St. John of Jerusalem founded	1099
Berenger, Count of Barcelona and Forcalquier, acquires the fiefs of Provence	1112
Pope Gelasius comes to Provence	1116
Provence divided between the Counts of Toulouse and the Berengers, Counts of Barcelona and Forcalquier	1132

This is the age of chivalry; Crusaders, Templars, Hospitallers, and Troubadours jostle each other on the stage. Arabic and Jewish learning filter through the Pyrenees, and the Albigeois heresy advances beyond the territories of the Counts of Toulouse and of Provence. The world is young, but growth is in every limb. The feudal princes are powerful, and country life—a thing unknown to the Romans—begins round the castles of the great barons. The communes are, however, still more full of vigour, a strong patriotic life of commerce and self-government animating the towns of Provence. It had to struggle both against the barons and the tyranny of the Chapters.

	A.D.
Earliest charter of Grasse	1181
Albigeois crusade	1206
Statutes of Fréjus drawn up by Romée de Villeneuve for Raymond-Berenger IV.	1235
Béatrix, youngest daughter of Raymond-Berenger, married, at Lyons, to Charles of Anjou	1246

	A.D.
Charles's ships built at Nice	1246
He goes to the Holy Land	1247
St. Louis lands at Hyères	1254
Charles, at the instigation of Pope Urban, starts from Nice for the conquest of Sicily	1263
Charles, after the murder of Manfred, crowned King of Sicily	1266
Massacre of the Sicilian Vespers	1282
Charles II. (the Lame) gives a charter to Grasse	1287
Charles II. builds Villefranche	1293
Charles II. surrenders the Templars to Philippe-le-Bel	1307–8
Robert I. (the Wise) sides with the Guelfs	1318
St. Roselyne de Villeneuve dies	1329
Jeanne, heiress of Provence and of the Two Sicilies, marries her cousin, Andrew of Hungary	1347
Andrew is murdered : the Queen marries Louis of Tarento	1348
Jeanne and Louis land at the Ponchettes of Nice, and go by Grasse to Avignon	1348
Jeanne sells Avignon to the Pope (Clement VI.)	1348
The great plague visits Nice and Biot	1349
The Lascaris and others rebel against Jeanne	1352
Civil war	1354
Jeanne gives a charter to Grasse	1366
Jeanne adopts as her heir Louis of Anjou	1380
Civil war in Provence. Charles of Durazzo proclaimed as Charles III. Jeanne flies to the Tour Drammont, and sails from Agay for Naples	1381
Civil war. Antibes sacked by the Armagnacs	1390
Castle of Napoule begun	1390
Tower of Cannes finished	1395
The Grimaldi get possession of Monaco	1395
Genoese corsairs sack the Lérins	1405
King René embarks at Antibes	1452
Fréjus burnt by the Barbary corsairs	1475
After the death of René, Provence, ceded to Louis XI., is united to France	1488
Palamède de Forbin-Solliès, first governor for the King	1489
Jews expelled from Spain by Ferdinand and Isabella : emigration into Provence	1492
Passage of Charles VIII. through Antibes into Italy	1494
Louis XII. creates the Parliament of Provence	1517

NICE.

	A.D.
Charles of Savoy fortifies Nice, and weds a princess of Portugal	1521
Pope Adrian VI. comes by Villefranche to Nice	1522
Visits the Convent on the Lérins	1522
Wars of Francis and Charles V.; the Emperor comes to Nice	1524
He takes Villeneuve-Loubet, Vence, Grasse, Antibes, and Cannes	1524
Augustin Grimaldi, Bishop of Grasse and Abbot-Commendatory of the Lérins, disloyal to the King	1524
Battle of Pavia	1525
The Knights of Rhodes found a house in Nice	1527
They get Malta from Charles V.	1529
Immense floods	1530-31
Descent of the Barbary pirates at Napoule	1530
Charles V. burns the forest of the Esterel	1536
He comes to Cannes, and leaves in a fishing-boat	1536
Napoule burnt by the Moors	1536
The Pope Paul III. and Francis I. meet in Nice	1538
Charles V. lands at Villefranche	1538
Treaty of Nice, called '*de la Croix de Marbre*'	1538
Louis d'Adhémar de Grignan, governor in Provence	1540
The Turks who besieged Nice repulsed by Doria	1542
They take Nice	1543
Charles III. of Savoy succeeded in Nice by Philibert, who marries a daughter of Francis I.	1553
Huguenot church in Napoule	1554
Battle of Lepanto	1571
Plague brought to Cannes	1580
The League in Provence	1587
Pompée de Grasse murdered at Mouans	1588
Napoule burnt by the Duke of Savoy	1589
Fréjus and Antibes taken from the Leaguers	1589
Who sack Antibes and Cannes	1589
Lesdiguières enters Provence	1590
He obliges the Duke of Savoy to give up Cannes, Grasse, and Antibes	1592-99
But suffers a defeat before Vence	1592
Henri IV. joins the Church of Rome	1597
Charles Emmanuel of Savoy enters Nice	1603

	A.D.
His son, Victor Amadeus, marries Princess Christine of France	1619
Siege of Cannes	1633
War between France and Spain	1635
The Lérins taken by the Spaniards	1635
Guitaud governor of the Islands	1637
Miracle of Laghet	1652
Vauban's works at Nice	1675
Vauban's works at Antibes	1680
Cassini's observations	1682
The Masque de Fer goes to Ste.-Marguerite	1687
War with Savoy: Nice taken by the French	1690
Mathioli dies in the prison of Ste.-Marguerite	1694
The Masque de Fer leaves Provence for the Bastille	1698
Military operations on the Var	1703
Pégomas ravaged by the troops of Savoy	1707
Marshal Berwick razes the Castle of Nice	1710
Vauban fortifies Ste.-Marguerite	1712
Nice is restored to Savoy	1713
Peace of Utrecht	1713
Monseigneur Mesgrigny, Bishop of Grasse	1720
Plague at Marseilles	1720
Charles Emmanuel III.	1731
Fragonard born in Grasse	1732
War with Spain: the Infant Philip enters Nice	1744
The enemy, whose headquarters are at Cannes, presses through the country as far as Draguignan	1745
English ships take the Lérins	1746
War with Maria-Theresa: General Brown quarters himself in Vence, Biot, and Grasse	1746
Inhabitants of Cannes fly to the islands	1746
Evacuation of Grasse	1747
Mirabeau born	1749
Earthquake (of Lisbon) shakes this coast	1756
Masséna born at Levens, near Nice	1758
Barbaroux born at Marseilles	1767
Corsica handed over to France	1768
Napoleon born, August 15	1769
Cannet made into a commune	1773
Suppression of the order of the Jesuits	1773
Death of Louis XV.	1774

	A.D.
Death of Charles Emmanuel III.	1775
Napoleon goes to France	1778
The Bishop of Orleans, last Commendatory-Abbot of the Lérins	1779
Pisani, last Bishop of Vence	1783
The monastery on the Lérins closed, and its four monks dispersed	1787–88
Napoleon goes to Valence and to Marseilles	1787
Assembly of the *états* of Provence	1788
Mirabeau named deputy	1789
Riots at Vence and St. Jeannet	1789

The convocation of the provincial assemblies at Aix and at Lambesc was rapturously hailed in Grasse, where Prunières was bishop, but where Mougin de Roquefort was mayor and *viguier*. He it was who first in Maritime Provence called by the name of 'Revolution' those demands which, in imitation of the patriots of Dauphiny, he formulated for his country. Those demands were not only reasonable, they were elementary, but, as the weeks went on, passions grew fiercer, and holy zeal turned to blind fury. The whole country was in a ferment, and an emigration began which was to make a radical and a lasting change on the face of Provençal society. The ceaseless wars of Louis XIV., the disorders of the regency, the profligacy of Louis XV., the sufferings of the peasants as described by Vauban, the weakness of Louis XVI., the unpopularity of the queen, the lack of popular representation, the selfishness of a more than half-ruined nobility, the corruption of Churchmen, the decay of piety, the philosophical and deistical tendencies of the eighteenth century, the hopeless embarrassment of the national finances, with three years of famine, had all prepared the way for these catastrophes.

	A.D.
Troubles in Grasse	1790
Suppression of the Bishoprics of Grasse and Vence	1790
Death of Mirabeau	1791
Numbers of *émigrés* go to Nice	1791-92
Castle of Bar destroyed by the mob	1792
Riots at Grasse	1792
Castles of Cabris, Montaroux, and Calian sacked	1792
War on the right bank of the Var	1792
The French army enters Nice	1792
Napoleon with the artillery in Nice gets a step, and becomes *chef de bataillon*	1792
Masséna commands a battalion in a regiment of volunteers of the Var	1792
A bridge over the Var built	1792
Louis XVI. beheaded	1793
The Terror proclaimed	1793
Nice wishes to be united to France	1793
Masséna retreats from St. Martin-de-Lantosque	1793
Battles of Sospello and Utelle	1793
Riots in Nice	1793
The allies evacuate Toulon	1794
Hoche named to command in Nice	1794
Madame Letitia Buonaparte lives at Antibes	1794
Fighting at the Col de Tende	1794
Buonaparte lives at No. 1 Rue de Villefranche	1794
He walks to Vence	1794
Four hundred Piedmontese repulsed by Scherer	1795
The Directory	1795
Napoleon nominated to the command of the army of Italy	1795
He is again in Nice	1796
Nice is made into the department of the Maritime Alps	1799
Masséna defends Genoa	1800
Suchet occupies Cagne, and Pascalis Antibes	1800
Alberti held Lantosque	1800
Napoleon made consul for life	1802
Dubouchage prefect of Nice	1803
Napoleon declared Emperor	1804
Is crowned King of Italy	1805
Pius VII. reaches Nice on his way to Fontainebleau	1809
Pauline Buonaparte lives in Nice, at Villa Avigdor	1810

	A.D.
Masséna disgraced by Napoleon	1811
Pius VII. passes through Nice	1811
Rejoicings in Grasse for the birth of the King of Rome	1811
Abdication of Napoleon	1814
Nice is restored to the House of Savoy	1814
Passage of Austrian troops	1815
The Prince of Monaco returns to his principality	1815
Napoleon lands at Golfe Jouan	1815
Joachim Murat resides in Cannes	1815
Masséna, Duc de Rivoli and Prince d'Essling, dies	1817
Lord Brougham's first visit to Cannes	1831
Charles Albert comes to Nice	1836
Pier of Cannes opened	1838
Battle of Novara: Charles Albert goes by Laghet to the Var, and sleeps at Antibes	1848
Island of St. Honorat bought by the Bishop of Fréjus and Toulon	1858
Battle of Solferino	1859
Nice ceded to the Emperor of the French	1860
Emperor offers the title of Duke of Nice to Thouvenel	1860
Mentone and Roquebrune sold by the Prince of Monaco for 4,000,000 francs	1860
M. Gavini de Campile, first prefect of the A.M.	1860
Railway open from Fréjus to Nice	1864
Emperors of France and Russia visit Nice	1864
Death of the Tzarèvitch Nicholas-Alexandrovitch at Nice	1865
Death of Lord Brougham	1868
Demonstrations in Nice after September 4	1870
Great floods: bridge of the Brague breaks under a train	1872
The Marquis de Villeneuve-Bargemon prefect of the A.M.	1872
Tower of Cannes (previously damaged 1786 and 1796) struck by lightning	1875
The Queen of Holland winters in Cannes	1876
Burning of the Opera House in Nice	1881
Queen Victoria visits Mentone	1882
Great snowstorm on the coast	1883
Exhibition at Nice	1884
Death of H.R.H. the Duke of Albany at Cannes	1884
Great financial crisis in Nice and Cannes	1884
The waters of the Vésubie brought into Nice	1884
Cholera breaks out on the coast of Provence	1884

Facts can be entered in these tables of dates, but Nice must be seen to be realised. The beauty of its site, the majesty of its mountain ranges, the variety of its aspects, the loveliness of its *vallons*, like its cosmopolitan crowds, its Carnival, its noise, its smells, its bouquets, its dusty torrent-beds, its palms, its shops, and its long white promenade, all seem to be conjured up by the fancy. It is the most noisy and the most lonely place in the world. Twenty or thirty years ago it possessed a very agreeable society of strangers, grouped round the nucleus of the local nobility and officials. These met of evenings in a simple way, or spent long, sunny days among the woods and hills. But all that is now a thing of the past. The quantity of the winter visitors has greatly increased, the quality has greatly gone off, the old colony has been sadly broken up, and the boast of a fashionable guide-book is true when it says that here, as a rule, '*les relations sociales sont faciles, exemptes d'obligations gênantes et des exigences de l'étiquette.*'

The environs of Nice give as much pleasure as its mongrel crowds inspire disgust. The valley from St. André to Tourrêtes is as rugged and bold as the gorge of the Chiffa. Falicon lies smiling to the sun, while the deserted village of Châteauneuf is on the other hand desolate beyond words. From the Aspromont road the view up the valley of the Var strikes me as unique, for the river comes stealing out from the feet of the hills, and the villages group themselves on every rocky knoll.

Then I know no coast so beautiful, especially if

you turn to Villefranche, with its fort and towers and its fairy roadstead, where the big frigates swing almost on a level with those church bells which for centuries have announced to red rocks and blue-green waters all the dramas of human life, the landings of popes and emperors, the deaths of peasants, and the burial-days of kings. Beaulieu is so beautiful that the opening of a sea road through its woods was positively an event for public rejoicing, but not so the cutting of its woods to build villas for visitors to Monte Carlo! Eza is the most picturesque thing on the coast, whether seen from the high road into Italy, or gazed at from its sunburnt beach. I call it sunburnt, and yet I do not forget its splendid carouba trees, or the little garden where the Abbé Montolivo, a first-rate botanist, grew so many rare plants, among the boats and nets and all the fishing tackle that divided his heart with his flowers and with the Municipal Library of Nice.

Even more delightful than the coast is the scenery of the *vallons*. They are of great extent and variety, according as you push your explorations far into the hills, or remain within a walk of the town. Some very beautiful spots, like the *vallons* of Fabron and of Mantega, can be reached with little exertion. The first of these opens behind the Château de Barlas, on the Antibes road; the other is reached by a path at the back of the Memorial Chapel of the Tzarèvitch, near St. Etienne. In its fern-fringed recesses where even the sunbeams only rarely penetrate, there is a solitude such as a hermit might travel far before he met with again. Spring there is redolent of fancies, of flowers and scents; the peasants still seem unsophisticated; children sing in the canebrakes; under the olives the great, white hoods of the arums look like the tents of the fairies, and delicate coronillas hang veils of green and gold over every steep. As you rest among the myrtles you cannot believe that you are within half an hour's walk of the station at Nice, but rather fancy yourself to be very far indeed from the 'madding crowd,' and from its 'ignoble strife.'

CHAPTER XII.

THROUGH THE COUNTY OF NICE.

'Il revenait par les ruelles en pente qui longent les anciens murs d'enceinte du château, ruelles désertes encombrées de broussailles et de ces grandes herbes de St. Roch (bien à leur place dans ce coin moyen-âge), et ombrées de l'énorme ruine déchiquetée en haut du chemin. Le village qu'il revoyait, baraques anciennes quelques-unes abandonnées, sentait la mort et la désolation d'un village italien.'—A. DAUDET.

THE fastnesses of the Maritime Alps can only be reached through the valleys: by following to their sources the Tinée and the Vésubie, which pour their waters into the Var. I have long had the greatest wish to explore the country which lies between these two streams, and to push my travels to the eastern limits of the department. But 'circumstances over which I had no control' have on two occasions rendered it impossible for me to carry out an intended visit to the Alpine districts of Eastern Provence. I must therefore ask my readers to be as much pleased as I am to read an account of them from the pen of a more fortunate traveller. A few years ago Mr. James Harris, Her Majesty's Consul in Nice, accompanied the then Prefect of the Maritime Alps, the Marquis de Villeneuve-Bargemon, in an official tour through a country which English tourists have few opportunities of knowing. Mr. Harris says of his journey that it lasted a week, and that it was undertaken in June: not too late a season for the excursion, since he and his companions saw a great deal of snow, and realised much of the misery of the hill populations, who suffer from goître, and look half-starved on their cakes of chestnut-flour. I have Mr. Harris's kind permission to make the following extracts from his journal:

In the first carriage were the Prefect, Baron Roissard (deputy), and myself; in the next came the General of Division and his staff; and in a third went some military and civil officials, including an army surgeon, our goal being Puget-Theniers, and our business an inspection of the conscripts liable for service. . . . Having skirted the left bank of the Var for two hours, we passed on the one hand the villages of St. Isidore and St. Martin, and on the other the valley of the Esteron, the hamlet of La Gaude, and the cliffs of St. Jeannet. We here entered a narrow gorge called 'l'Echaudan,' where we noticed the junction of the Vésubie with the Tinée. The former is a rushing torrent of bluish snow-water, and the latter is as yellow as the Tiber. This is a curious feature; but still more noteworthy is the fact that though these two streams through summer and through winter pour a great volume of water into the Var, but a fractional part of their volume ever appears at its lower end, or at the mouths of a great torrent which seems to have absorbed their contributions into its vast and stony bed. . . . Before reaching Villars the country had become uninteresting; but I sketched during an inspection of recruits, and was glad to notice, when we left Villars and the valley of the Ripert behind us, that the limestone cliffs were becoming more bold and precipitous. Presently the village of Touët-de-Beuil came in sight—a mass of dark, overhanging roofs perched half-way up the hill on our right, four hundred and forty-one mètres above the sea. We ascended to the village, and entered the church which is at its farther end. In the centre of the nave is a grating, and on looking through it we could see a small torrent leaping in a series of cascades to join the Var. The church, which is dedicated to St. Martin, spans this torrent by means of an arch, and is, as far as I know, unique of its kind. . . . Puget-Theniers and its *sous-préfecture* were reached in due course. The town is unsketchable, and but for its souvenirs of the Templars, whose garden occupied the site of the present Grande Place, it would be uninteresting. It lays claim of course to having been founded by the Romans, and to have been governed by a prætor under the orders of the Prefect of Cimella (Cimièz). In the eleventh century the abbots of the Lérins acquired jurisdiction over the churches of Ste. Marie and St. Martin, privileges which they owed to the piety of two of the Balbi family, lords of the fief, and married, the one to a Castellane, and the other to a Glandevèz.... The road from Puget to Guillaumes being unfinished, it was necessary for us now to mount the mules provided for the party, and to commence the ascent of the Col de la Crous. This meant a ride of three hours, and a visit to a small mine of copper which some enterprising Englishmen have begun to work eight hundred and twenty-two mètres above the level of the sea. Guillaumes, which we reached before sunset, is most picturesque, backed by curious needles of limestone, which, rising as they do out of the steep mountain-side, look like a continuation of the fortifications of a town that, like so many more in Provence, can boast of a castle built by Queen Jeanne. It will speedily be able to boast of a new bridge and road, putting it in direct communication with Puget-Theniers and Nice. In fact, the question of roads is everywhere the most prominent one, and wherever we appeared the Prefect was besieged with verbal petitions about them. 'When was *le gouvernement* going to take into its serious consideration the wants of *ces populations déshéritées*?' Then was the moment for producing the deputy, and Baron Roissard always declared that their interests were so safe in *his* keeping that so long as they granted *him* their confidence there was no fear of their missing 'the realisation of their most legitimate aspirations.' The peaceful nature of the said 'aspirations' shows how far we are removed from the old warlike days when Charles VIII., Louis XI., and Francis I. made this frontier town the basis of their operations against Savoy.... The valley of the Guébis, which was followed from Guillaumes to Péone, is both steep and narrow, and Péone is a lonely spot. Founded originally by some Spanish workmen, a legend accounts for its subsequent prosperity by telling how the heir of the odious Lord of Beuil was once carried off and hidden in a cave by vassals who threatened to let the child die of hunger unless the stubborn Grimaldi yielded to their just 'aspirations.' The inhabitants of Péone charitably rescued the poor little hostage, and obtained in consequence rather extensive grants.... At the top of the wild Col de la Crous (2,849 mètres) we had to traverse large fields of snow, in which our mules sank up to their girths, and we were not sorry to call a halt at the village of Roya, whence a steep valley runs down to join that of the Tinée. The scenery now began to improve at every step; the wooded and precipitous glens were beautiful, and it seemed as if at every moment we must have our progress stopped by some sheer descent into the bed of the Tinée. But the mule-path that zigzagged down the face of the mountain led us safely to the level of the river, and as we approached St. Etienne-aux-Monts the inhabitants trooped out to meet the Prefect with many signs of rejoicing. . . . St. Etienne lies in a basin where the Ardon runs to meet the Tinée, and beyond the gorge of Jallorques, which leads to St. Dalmas-le-Selvage, may be seen the snowy heads of the Enchastraye. The prosperity of this place, which used to have a large seminary, depends on its water-meadows and on the dykes that preserve them. In the days of the Romans, Diana had a temple on a spot, called *Delinsula*, and in the fourteenth century a shrine was built here by the Templars called La Madonna grande, and adorned with an excellent fresco—a painting far superior to anything I have seen in this country. Durante mentions it in his 'Chorographie du Comté de Nice.' The parish church is a fine structure, one which resisted the earthquake of 1564. . . . Next morning we rode down to Isola—a town which has been twice carried away by the torrents, and twice reconstructed. When we left Isola in the afternoon, we realised a little of the fury of the Tinée, for on arriving late at St. Sauveur the whole party admitted to being deafened by the unceasing roar of a river which had sounded in our ears for many hours. The whole district bore evidences of its terrible power. . . .

The families of Balbi and of Grimaldi were successively lords of St. Sauveur, a place of which the name goes back to the tenth century, but which has an abundance of Roman remains to testify to its far greater antiquity and importance, when its Latin conquerors had a fort to keep the Ectini in order. Our adventures may be said to have ended here, as we found a carriage-road leading to Rimplas, another Roman position, under the inaccessible crag between the mountains of Sisette and La Magdeleine, in the valley of the Blore. Here we saw the ruins of a castle built by Alfonso of Aragon, and burnt by Marshal Belle-Isle in 1747. This miserable village once belonged to Peter Balbo; but he was deprived of his estates because he sided with the Angevine party against Charles of Durazzo, and his fiefs passed into the hands of the Grimaldi, lords of Beuil, who, since 1380, had already held thirty other fiefs in the uplands of the county of Nice, and lived on very bad terms with their neighbours the Caïs of Roure and of Gilette.

A tolerably fertile plateau is descried from these heights. It is called Valdeblore, and contains the villages of St. Dalmas, La Roche, and La Bollène, celebrated for their cheeses. The road continues to ascend till the *col* is reached which separates the valley of the Tinée from that of the Vésubie, from which a view is gained of those northern peaks which in their turn divide the Vésubie from the Gesso and its watershed (into Italy), opposite the Col della Finestra and the Col di Fremamorta. The Mont Gélas and the Clapier, preserving even in June their mantle of snow, are the great features in the view during the descent upon St. Martin-de-Lantosque. This ride occupied more than a couple of hours. . . . St. Martin, which is rather a popular summer station, possesses one very steep street and several inns, of which the Hôtel des Alpes and the Hôtel de la Poste are the best, while a considerable number of villas have sprung up in their neighbourhood. The scenery is really remarkable, but it becomes even finer at Roquebilière, an hour and a half to the south of St. Martin, where magnificent groves of chestnuts spread in every direction. To the left of this place, and on the plateau of Berthemont, stands another summer station, boasting not only of a good hotel, and of some hot sulphur springs, but also of an excellent carriage-road which connects it with Nice, and with La Bollène, a place in great repute among the Niçois, who, in spite of its mosquitoes, resort to it during the hottest months of the year. If one of the curious sights of St. Martin be its Sanctuary of the Virgin, which acted as a hospice for travellers near that great crag through whose *finestra* the daylight is seen, equally interesting in the environs of La Bollène is the walk up the valley of the Gordolasca to the Lago Lanzo, where, throughout the whole summer, miles of snow remain unmelted at an altitude of eight thousand feet above the sea. Lantosque stands about a mile and a half below La Bollène, picturesquely perched on a rocky promontory, from which it was very nearly shaken, once in 1348, and again in 1566, by the severe shocks of an earthquake. As the descent upon Nice is made, the mountain gorge grows wider, and the Vésubie is crossed at a point where a mule path leads up to Utelle. This is a very ancient place, once held by the Templars, and still possessing a church of the earliest workmanship, with massive towers, and fine twelfth-century carving. The road now follows the left bank of the Vésubie, rising gently till at Duranus it attains a height of six hundred feet above the bed of the stream in the perpendicular precipice which has received the name of the 'Saut des Français.' . . .

This ominous name commemorates a reverse of the republican troops under Masséna. Nice and the county of Nice are full of traces of that 'spoilt child of fortune.' Born in Levens the little, dark-eyed Jewish lad who began life as a potboy, and was intended to finish it as a fencing-master, was reserved for a strange destiny. He developed also qualities very alien to his race; he had genuine military abilities, and a barbarity of which the Duke of Wellington said, in referring to his retreat, 'that it had seldom been equalled, and had luckily never been surpassed, as it was revolting to human nature.' He died rich. When he surrendered his command to Marmont, and retired to Bordeaux, he took with him 800,000 dollars, but his life was shortened by debauchery, and one cannot forget that, brave as he might be, he was never at heart thoroughly loyal to either the Emperor or the Bourbons. There is a spot near the Quatre Chemins, on the Genoa Road, which the Niçois like to point out as having been the place of the Marshal's breakfast, just as the Vençois show the house where he lived, and the spot where he drilled his volunteers. But this 'Saut des Français' has less pleasing associations. In 1792, Masséna led the vanguard of a division charged to hold the valley of Lantosque. He had with him the commissaries Férus and Baudoin, and these three pure republicans spared their fellows neither requisitions nor domiciliary visits. Thus their names became feared and hated throughout the whole district, nowhere more heartily than in Levens, which had had the honour of giving birth to the future marshal. The castle of Rainaldi was sacked, flocks and herds driven off, and the inhabitants were terrified, when the appearance of six thousand Austrians at the Col della Finestra delivered them from these exactions. But these first excesses led to an obstinate resistance to French supremacy, and the fastnesses of the Maritime Alps were for two years the scenes of many strategical movements, executed too often in spite of deep falls of snow and of great want of provisions. At this 'Saut des Français,' some republican troops were hurled into the Vésubie by the inhabitants they had so long harassed and illtreated, and the people of Levens and of St. Blaise could not conceal their satisfaction when Masséna, thanks to the jealousy of his rival Anselme, found his way into a prison in Nice, not very far from the quay that now bears his name.

Of the marshal's native place of Levens, Mr. Harris says, 'It stands in a plateau commanding so fine a view of the basin of the Var that it is easy to realise that this must have been a military position of importance. Nothing now remains of its fortifications except a couple of arches, but its destruction is of a date far anterior to the revolutionary epoch, since Charles Emmanuel, Duke of Savoy, destroyed it in 1622. From Levens to Nice the descent occupies rather more than two hours.'

Mountain excursions from St. Martin-de-Lantosque may be made in every direction, whether in search of flowers and ferns, or of more exciting sport, and though mountain storms occur at all seasons, it is only after the equinox that invalids need fear the approach of cold weather. The Comte and Comtesse de Caserta have a villa just beyond the town,[1] and from this point His Royal Highness starts on long expeditions through the Alps, in pursuit of the chamois, the wolf, and the lynx. Artists might find plenty of work here for the pencil, and I remember Mr. Freshfield once saying to me that they seemed to him to be most strangely neglectful of the beauties of a district which he considered as savage and as noteworthy as those of any region yet explored by the Alpine Club. A few years ago the dresses and costumes of the peasantry added to the picturesque element in any sketches made at St. Martin; but old customs are fast disappearing, and with them the clothes, dances, tunes, and merrymaking of the peasants, who are learning to dress like '*Franciots*,' and to build *pensions*. Yet in spite of their progress towards nineteenth-century fashions, it must be long before these upland pastures, these wild gorges, and these sunburnt, little villages cease to have a freshness and a typical charm of their own.

[1] I am indebted for the view of St. Martin-de-Lantosque, which forms the frontispiece to this volume, to the kindness of H.R.H. the Comtesse de Caserta. It is one of a series of photographs made by her husband of the environs of their Alpine home.

ST. PAUL-DU-VAR.

CHAPTER XIII.

ST. PAUL-DU-VAR.

'Le soleil de St. Paul est le plus beau de la Provence, et le pays où croissent les plus belles oranges de toutes espèces qui sont là en plein vent, hiver et été, ce qui ne se trouve point ailleurs, hors à Hyères, car elles ont gelé à St. Laurent. Ce territoire est couvert de vignes, d'oliviers et de figuiers, et dans la même terre on y voit communément de ces trois sortes de plantes disposées par alignement avec des blés entre deux, de sorte que le même héritage porte du blé, du vin, des olives et des figues. Tout cela est cultivé avec beaucoup de soin, mais le mal est que la sécheresse les désole et rend très souvent leur travail inutile.'—*Rapport de Vauban, déposé au dépôt général des Fortifications*, tom. ix.

'Arbre, place, ravin, herse, église, château et rocher, tout cela se tient, et forme un tableau charmant et singulier qui ne ressemble qu'à lui-même. Le contraste de ces âpres déchirements avec la placidité des formes environnantes, est d'un *réussi* extraordinaire. Les peintres qui comprennent le vrai sont d'heureux poètes. Ils saisissent tout à la fois, ensemble et détails, et résument en cinq minutes ce que l'écrivain dit en beaucoup de pages : ils font le portrait des aspects sentis, portrait pénétrant et intelligent, sans l'effort des pénibles investigations.'—GEORGE SAND.

WHETHER you start from Nice or from Cannes it will take you rather more than two hours, with a pair of horses, to reach St. Paul-du-Var. The place is seventeen kilomètres from Cannes, six from Vence, and about fourteen from Nice, but hardly five from the station of Cagnes, from which a good walker will reach it in little more than an hour's time.

I have been six times to St. Paul, and each time that I have seen it it appears more interesting, beautiful, and unique than on the former visits. It is, in truth, so unlike our workaday world of hotels, villas, railway-stations, and shops, that a gifted and artistic companion was right when she said to me, 'One can hardly believe that this place is *real*, and that we are not seeing it in some happy dream.'

It is very real, however. It has its modern life of births, deaths, and marriages, and its ancient history, dating from the ninth century, while it was to the struggle between Francis I. and Charles V. that this little place on the Var owed the strength of its fortifications. Its extraordinary beauty it owes to a combination of form and colour, and of the bold and unyielding lines of its masonry with the most graceful, varied, and harmonious natural outlines. To reach St. Paul from Cannes you must take either of the roads which pass by Villeneuve-Loubet, and in both cases you must, before reaching La Colle,[1] turn to the right, and leave the valleys of the Loup and the Lubiane for that of the Malvans.

I will imagine to-day, however, that the reader means to approach it with me from Nice. In that case we either take the train to Cagnes station, meaning to follow the course of the Cagnette into the hills on foot, or, leaving Nice by the bridge of the Magnan, we can drive on to the great bridge over the Var. Underneath us then lies the vast, stony bed, and the little, wandering streams of water that in dry weather represent the Var,

---

[1] La Colle is the birthplace of Eugène Sue.

the most formidable of all the Alpine torrents, which for centuries constituted the boundary of France on the side of Nice and Italy. On each bank stand the great parallel dykes of Vigan, a colossal work, so colossal that Vauban thought 'no one could ever get back a thousandth part of what it would cost to confine between banks the strongest and the most ill-conditioned river in France.' A road must now be followed by us which will land us presently among the figs and the orange gardens of St. Laurent. Throughout all the Maritime Alps it is a generally conceded point that if you wish to eat the best figs and to hear the purest Provençal spoken, you should make some stay in St. Laurent-du-Var. It is a rich little *pays*, though naturally it did a bigger business before the railway came to carry all the traffic past the place which had been for so long the established frontier-town and toll-house. The town, with its square belfry, groups itself well on the bank, and by looking up the wide and wandering bed of the river a fine view of the Alps is to be obtained. The sweep of the Var round the foot of the hills is perhaps actually less striking here than it is when observed from the opposite side, or from the Aspromont road, but still it is very beautiful, and full of that charm which a subalpine landscape always possesses for me. You have beauty here, without any of the desolation or the oppressive gloom of the genuine Alpine pass, and you have also a sharp contrast between the rich, happy, and highly coloured foreground, so full of human life and endeavour, with those white mountain peaks that, in a grim kingship, seem to tower over all.

Up there no song of reapers is ever heard, only the crashing of the avalanches and the cry of the *geiers* that sweep round the glacier as it grinds a slow passage down the mountain-side. Down here mule-bells tinkle, children sing in the brakes of the tall reeds by the river, and man goes forth to his labour till the evening.

At this moment the hour is still early, but the mists have cleared away from the heights of St. Jeannet, so we will turn our horses' heads that way, to return presently, and to cross the ridge of La Maure. St. Jeannet is itself only a dirty scrambling village which received its name from the Knights of St. John of Jerusalem. As a place it does not repay a visit, though we read of it in the 'wars of the Countesses' and in the religious wars of the League, when it was a stronghold of the Huguenot party. There is nothing remarkable about it now, except the popular saying that all the women in it are witches. There have been some such reputed 'witch-villages' in England, and I think that in India there are still some to be pointed out. The saying probably arose in a fixed jealousy between near but by no means friendly tribes; and in the Middle Ages the accusation of witchcraft sufficed to excuse any amount of uncharitableness of word and deed. At La Gaude the inhabitants at one time professed the Albigeois heresy, and were exterminated for their pains, so it is possible that some old *odium theologicum* is at the bottom of this unflattering saying about the ladies of St. Jeannet. It is only when you have reached the town itself that you realise how possible it would be, by the way of the high *plateaux*, to scale a rock which from the low country looks as inaccessible as anything that can be conceived. The cliff of St. Jeannet is a bold, overhanging headland, as it were, of limestone; a natural bluff, formed by the abrupt termination and weathering of one of the lateral spurs of the hill. The sharpness of its outline and the warmth of its colouring render it a landmark for miles. It deserves, in fact, all the praise which I have heard Mr. Lear the artist bestow on it, when he told me that not in Corsica, and not even in Calabria, had he met with a landscape of nobler forms than this natural terrace under the hills from St. Jeannet, by Tourrêtes, Vence and Grasse to St. Césaire—in a word, from the basin of the Var to the head of the Siagne.

From the earliest period of European history the fords of the Var had been felt to be of great strategical importance: well worth fighting for, and still better worth defending; thus it happens that all these hamlets of St. Jeannet, le Broc, St. Paul, Gattières, and La Gaude had a troubled history. Over and over again have they been harassed by troops. At one time the Moors took a fancy to the district, and settled themselves on a spot known to this day as La Maure. It is said that La Gaude derives its name from a Celtic term signifying a wood, and the district was certainly once much more densely wooded than it is now, for the vineyards have a great reputation, and every year one may notice that some patch of coppice has been cleared and built up into terraces, so as to increase the quantity of white wine which La Gaude supplies. We will buy some in St. Paul for our breakfast, and if it is more than five years old we shall find it worth drinking. The wine in question is of a pale amber colour, and it keeps as well as it carries, but, like everything else in Provence, it would be improved by a little more care being bestowed on it. I remember once fainting in the little, dark street of St. Paul, and a woman giving me some white wine, in which the wing of a wasp and the hind-leg of a fly floated about, along with other extraneous matter that had found its way into the bottle! No white wine can be sold at so low a price as a red one, not because of any especial value of the straw-coloured *clairet* grapes, but because its preparation implies so much more time, labour, and waste. It has to be racked so often that a considerable quantity is lost, and there is always the danger of a second fermentation setting in, and turning the whole cask sour. As far as I have been able to learn, this wine of La Gaude cannot be drunk under seventy-five centimes by the grower, and it costs in the retail trade from 1 fr. 50 c. to 2 francs the litre: whereas a very sound red wine can be got from the grower for seventy centimes the litre. This famous Provençal wine is sold neither in bottles nor in casks, but in those huge, round, glass vessels with the straw envelopes which go by the name of a 'Dame Jeanne.' The *dame* in question must really have been one of the most 'merry wives' of Provence, for her namesake holds from ten to forty litres!

The country which produces this good wine is also rich in flowers. If your visit be not too early in the spring, you will find the milk-wort, the flower of Rogation Days; and if it is later you can gather the Hypericum, that charms away thunderstorms, and that the monks called *fuga dæmonum*. There is in the fields plenty of that pink saintfoin which they esteemed as the 'Holy Hay of the Manger of Bethlehem,' while in the vine-drills grow the white, and the more uncommon yellow 'Stars of Bethlehem,' which the peasants call *la dame de onze heures*, as the petals remain closed till within an hour of noon. On the walls grow quantities of the small, purple Muscari, the grape-hyacinth that smells like a baby's mouth, and in the fields you find the other kind, the one which has no perfume, but a large, feathery tuft. The little woods are blue with hepaticas, primroses linger about their edges, while on the sunny banks the Urospermum shows its globe of light, and the bee-orchis the velvet of its lips. The peach-coloured cistus—the *fleur de St. Jean* —flowers on the rocky ledges; the sword-lilies push bravely through the corn; the large periwinkle, and the lesser one (the flower of Jean-Jacques Rousseau) trail beside the stems of the oak trees; Euphorbias of the most brilliant green spring up among the very stones of the road; the tulips lure you down into the damper fields; and you can fill your hands with allium looking like snowdrifts, or with the pink convolvulus, the blue flax, and the aromatic, purple thyme.

At the bottom of the valley which we have now entered, the Malvans runs, showing by its pale greenish tint that its waters have been fed from the snows on the Cheiron range. St. Paul now appears to your left; but to the right, and nearer to St. Jeannet, opens the gorge of Bufflé. That romantic spot was the lair, or favourite hiding-place of the celebrated highway robber —the Robin Hood of Provence—Gaspard de Besse.[1] When not engaged in waylaying the jewellers and packmen who passed through the Esterels on their way to the fairs of Grasse and Nice, or in frightening the retinue of a vicar-general at the fords of the Var, Gaspard was wont to retire to this place, and from it to plan fresh exploits and fresh hairbreadth escapes. But 'tant va la cruche à l'eau' that it ends in getting broken, and perhaps Gaspard de Besse, when the day of reckoning came for him at last, and he passed through the dark streets of Aix to the place of execution, remembered with a sigh St. Jeannet's glorious cliff, with the free air blowing about its head, and the happy orchards at its feet.

But here is St. Paul. Turning sharply round a screen of tall cypresses, we find ourselves on the esplanade and before the frowning gate of this little 'fenced city.'

After the campaign of Marignano, and after that disastrous raid of Charles V., when he crossed the Var, sacked Antibes, and lit in the forest of the Esterel a conflagration that blazed for fourteen days and nights,[2] Francis I. bethought himself that the passage of the Var ought to be better defended for the future. Some coign of vantage must be selected to act as a post of observation, a depôt for provisions, and a base of operations

---

[1] Besse, the fief from which the robber took his name, is a hamlet near Carnoules.

[2] There is a curious burlesque poem on the advance and retreat of Charles V. into Provence. The *Meygra Entrepriza Catoliqui Imperatoris*, per A. Arenam, was published at Avignon, 1537.

for an army planted on the frontiers of Provence. He heard that in Arles there lived a noted military engineer of the name of Mandon. Those who have seen the sketch-books of Lionardo da Vinci will have realised how, at the beginning of the sixteenth century, the most cunning heads and hands in Europe occupied themselves with the science of fortification. The invention of fire-arms had revolutionised the old Roman, and the older Celtic systems of entrenched camps, and *oppida*; but as the new guns did not carry far, there was scope given in the plans of every fortress for the *mêlée* and the scaling-ladder. 'Noble Mandon,' who was supposed to be master of all these secrets, came at the king's summons. Francis then bade him go over the district, and choose the town, or the spot, most suitable for the combined purposes of observation and of defence.

The engineer selected St. Paul-lès-Vence, as it was then called—a rich little town, with a royal charter that dated from 1391, and which in the thirteenth century had been, first the *chef-lieu* of a *viguerie*, and later the residence of the seneschals of Provence. It occupied a position of great beauty and, what was more, of great strength on a *mamelon*, or rocky parcel of a lateral spur of the hills that is driven boldly down into the Malvans valley, and from which the ground falls away sharply on every side but one. Its continuous wall (the work of Mandon) has such foundations in the natural rock that it would be hard to break, and harder still to scale, and this circle of masonry can only be entered on one side—namely, by the gate.

The esplanade sweeps up to it in a direction from

north-east to south-west, but the gateway does not stand fair to the esplanade, and any besieging force was prevented in this way from approaching the gate in numbers, or in solid array of battle. Moreover, this esplanade has two great flanking towers or bastions, which serve to mask the embrasures from which two culverines could pour a cross-fire, and so rake and scatter the enemy when prepared to wheel and form in front of the portal. Arrived there, the enemy stays perhaps to parley for a moment. He summons the place to surrender 'to the most noble, the most puissant prince,' &c. The reply comes in the form of a shower of molten lead, poured through the machicolations of the tall gate-tower. A strong portcullis, studded with iron, and well secured by bolts and bars, has already dropped into its groove just inside that gate. This would seem to bar the way indeed; but we will imagine that it has yielded to force or fire, and then, in such numbers, and in such order as is possible for him, the invader presses on, through a space that is not more than eight feet wide. The lead showers continue to fall on his rear, and, worst of all, this gateway turns out to be really a long, covered passage, and to have an opening to the right which communicates with the western ramparts of the town. Thence rushes in a contingent of troops. A hand-to-hand *mêlée* now begins; but the enemy is strong enough to hold on, and to attempt both the second archway and the second bolted portcullis, through the bars of which he is able to see that there is a third and last archway, and beyond that a glimpse of a narrow, sloping street,

THE GATE OF ST. PAUL-DU-VAR.

which is densely lined with heads and javelins, and which communicates (on the left) with the long lines of musketeers and bowmen who man both the ramparts and the north-eastern towers. They are in numbers sufficient to overpower the few and sorely pressed men who may have been rash enough to push through the first portcullis. Not one of them escapes. The attempt had been a hopeless one, for the place is, as 'noble Mandon' promised it should be, unassailable by any of the engines of war of the sixteenth century. By guns of long range it could of course now be destroyed in an hour, but those risks did not exist when St. Paul was built to defend the passage of the Var, and the masonry of its walls stands as Mandon left them—not a bastion cracked, not a stone amissing.

Such was the art of fortification in France exactly a hundred years before Vauban was born. Tradition says that the king was delighted with the work, but that, for fear Mandon should ever turn skill so consummate against France, he ordered the great engineer to be hung! Fortunately for the memory of a king who nursed the dying hours of Lionardo da Vinci, this cruel story is a myth: made on the lines of the tale which says how the Tzar Ivan-Véliki put out the eyes of the Italian architect who built his great cathedral for him. 'Noble Mandon,' so far from having been hung from his own ramparts, returned to Arles, and lived there happily in the society of some of the Du Ports of St. Paul, with whom he had allied himself in 1536.

The parish church of St. Paul is well worth a visit, with its crypts and family vaults, and its carved *ciborium*, a piece of workmanship which the Hôtel Cluny might be proud to have in its museum. But, in truth, all the chapels of this curious town are rich in carvings, for in the fifteenth and sixteenth centuries the chisels of Henri Palambaca, of Pierre Tassone, of Jacques Bellot, and of Jean Etienne were busy, and native talent was rife in the Maritime Alps. The patron saint of this place was St. George, but the church, being dedicated on the Feast of the Conversion of St. Paul, had a picture of the Conversion presented to it by the family of Villeneuve-Thorenc. The house of Panisse-Pacy gave one of the processional crosses, and though the Revolution swept off much of the so-called 'treasure' bearing the arms of Guise and Joyeuse, Prosper Mérimée could still find reliquaries and small silver statuettes enough to excite the admiration of an experienced archæologist.

Beautiful as St. Paul is, it is very difficult to get a good sketch of it, because one that does justice to its outlines can give no idea of the esplanade or of the gateway, which are both, so to speak, hidden away on its northern side.

The whole country is one great fruit-garden. The oranges are famous in the local markets; peach and almond trees stand, all rose and silver, above beds of violets; bright carnations glow beside a little shrine, over which the stiff and hoary cypresses tower like sentinels; and down in the ravine, where the Malvans laughs and runs, you see the peasant pruning his olive-trees. Till I had seen this done in Provence, I never realised the promise that in the Kingdom of Peace men 'shall turn their spears into pruning-hooks.' The only hooks I knew were the sickles of the Scottish harvest-fields, and *never*, I thought, could any spearhead be beaten out into a long, thin hook like that! But the 'pruning-hook' in question is really a short and hooked knife set obliquely on the top of a long, slender reed—just such as might have previously served to carry a javelin.

St. Paul had always a royal governor. Nothing can be more rural, however, than its present aspect. Its solitary cannon, a long, narrow, sixteenth-century piece, of the kind one meets with in the designs of Renaissance monuments, lies rusting above the gate, and through that gate no longer comes a clattering company of gallants, with his Excellency the Governor, all ermine and steel. The main street is quite as dark and narrow as the others, but I should advise a visitor who wishes to see some of the vestiges of past greatness to follow it beyond the draw-well, to a *café* on the right hand. The *café* itself I found well worth a visit. It is a big, vaulted place, coloured by centuries of wood fires to a rich amber colour; in the outer half of it there are chairs and tables, but the inner half serves as the dwelling-place of mine host and his wife. Both are well stricken in years, and the husband has the strongly marked Celtic type which may be noticed in this district under the hills. A cuckoo-clock ticks from the wall, and near a fine large 'Queen Anne' window, which lights up the whole place, there sits a very old woman. She is so old that she takes no heed of strangers; she sees only the blonde mass at the top of her distaff, and, as her spindle twirls and falls, the thread forms itself mechanically under her lean fingers. Perhaps she thinks that it is her beads she is telling, for with sunk mouth and pallid lips she says over to herself the psalms that she has known for more than eighty years. '*Secundum magnam misericordiam tuam*,' she is whispering, and you feel that before many months are past she will be gone over to the silent majority, to waken no more till the long night has departed, and the shadows fled away.

From mine host you can get permission to see the old townhouses of the Du Ports, the De Hondis, and the Barcillons.

The last named, like many of the great families of this coast, came from Spain: a certain Arnold de Barcillon, an Aragonese, having been made Bishop of Vence by Robert of Anjou, Count of Provence (father to *la reino Jeanno*), in 1337. The Barcillons, once planted, took care to grow. They were ever known as ' nobles et égrèges chevaliers,' and they made good alliances among the Castellane, Glaudèves, Espitalier, and the like. Claude de Barcillon, judge for the king in St. Paul, married Lucrèce de Grasse-Brianson, and lived here in a very handsome house. Its staircase of honour is low, with shallow steps. On the plinths there are pheasants and vases, and mermaids and flowers, while at each angle there crawls and grins an heraldic monster about two feet high. Halfway up the landing there is a pretty, five-sided *entresol*, a room evidently used by the present proprietors of the house. The first floor is mainly occupied by a handsome ball-room with a

IN AN OLD HOUSE.

carved mantelpiece, and out of which opens a smaller 'withdrawing room' with a still finer fireplace. These apartments are lit by four noble windows, through which the western sun pours. They command first a view of the hanging gardens of oranges and lemons, through which vines scramble, and among which the tall *Campanettes* (Abutilon) toss their orange and scarlet bells. Lower down come the ramparts with their groove-like *banquettes* and passages, and far below lies the valley, with its paths and its rosy trees, and a background of the wooded hills that border the rapid Loup. Eighty couples could easily have stood up to tread a measure in this great hall. But how are the mighty fallen! The mantelpieces have classical subjects: the siege of Troy is there, with the parting of Achilles and Briseis, the death of Hector, and the piety of Æneas: but what terrible squalor in these stately rooms! There, in one embrasure, stands an old couch. No doubt it once had damask cushions on which the Judge's wife leaned, while the Governor whispered compliments to her. Now the rats and the mice play in the ball-room, and the mistral sweeps and whistles through each deserted chamber. Some of the rooms are now in common, very common! use, and the pen of a Zola would be required to do justice to the unmade beds, the *désordre achevé* of their owners. One must know Provence well to believe it, even if it were all catalogued by me. Suffice it to say that here is no rustic plenty or poverty, but that the modern inhabitant of St. Paul keeps his old clothes, his warming-pans, his boots, his ledgers, his mouldy apples, his rags, and his nuts, along with his dirty plates, and with the straw on which his grapes repose—'*Guarda e passa!*' The gentry are all gone from the town. You look in vain for the De Hondis, who used to send so many canons to the Chapter of Vence; for the Courmis, whose veteran, Raphaël, fought for France when he was more than eighty years of age; for the Aymon and the Malvans, with their many branches and their wide kinships; for the Baudoin, one of whom planted the French flag on the walls of St. Jean d'Acre; even for the *haute bourgeoisie*, like the Tombarel: they have left not a wreck behind. Their great, echoing rooms, their chapels, their carved balustrades, their vast cellars, their coats-of-arms, and their broken lutes remain, but with the easy classes a whole civilisation has perished.

What has the country gained?

Personal independence, freedom from the terrible burdens of which Vauban described the pressure, the representation of the people in the Chamber, primary schools, and numberless chances, such as provoke to spontaneous action through the establishment of a new social system.

In it we find too truly the dearth of much that ennobles society, and the multiplication of a narrow and envious *bourgeoisie*, to say nothing of the bitter sense of the inequality of happiness which devours the more brutalised proletariat. But in looking at the small life of small towns it must not be forgotten that these narrow-minded people, who are *bourgeois* but not *citizens*, have every possibility in their future, and that we have here a hierarchy of men placed above want, and above every form of injustice, except those which they take an extreme pleasure in practising on each other.

It may be that, starting from this platform of personal liberty and of the vast multiplication of careers, the lower and the lower-middle classes may yet achieve a civilisation of their own. Of this no one ought to despair, for the incidents in the great drama of Life and Country are never really allowed to flag. It may be that, though ignorant of history, they will become sensible to patriotism : and that, though sceptically impatient of the claims of religion upon reasonable men, they will recognise some moral law that can restrain desire ; that God will stir the air from above, and fling over a land too much disposed to deny Him, a new light and a better destiny. But at present the social aspects promise badly. True secular progress has ever been seen to come far more from high spiritual aims than from that physical well-being which presages rather the decline than the rise of a national greatness, and of all the combinations in the world, that which is now most despised, as an archaic mistake, has had the greatest tenacity and the strongest life—I mean the Christian Church. But the French lower orders can see no form or shapeliness in the old, pale images of sorrow and sacrifice, and they have but two ruling passions—Enjoyment and Equality.

How joyless and graceless home life is let these tattered and unsavoury rooms speak, and it is in vain to reply that true Provençals ask for only simple pleasures —love, oranges, sunshine, a ripe melon, and the like. It is true that if their climate were a more severe one they could not endure the bareness and the gauntness of a home from which one only wonders that fever and cholera should ever be absent, but the true reason for this extreme nastiness must be found in the absence of real refinement, and perhaps even in the presence of extreme stinginess. In the meantime I know nothing more depressing than the dead level of such lives and the narrow round of such pleasures. Yes; there is one thing still more grievous: their incessant lawsuits, and the harshness of their dealings with all whom they think they may safely injure, or overreach.

The absence of manufactured articles in a town of over eight hundred inhabitants is another curious sign. These townsfolk are not positively primitive, like the peasant who makes his lantern of a bit of oiled paper, but their *paillasses* are made of the sheaths of the maize, and in their mattresses of wool there lurks many a burr. They have none of the wants of their lordly predecessors. No armourer's shop is needed here for the vant-braces of a knight; no one puts a saddle upon anything but a beast of burthen; there are no fans, or gloves, or ruffles, no viols or mandolines, no carpets or torches, no printing press, and no looms. Shops are only needed for coffee, boots, and knives, because the wine and the oil, the flour and the figs, all belong to the man who consumes them, and whose riches consist in having a few baskets of lemons to sell. Animal food is much more freely eaten than it used to be, but still the fastidious appetite has to choose between the cow that died too late, and the calf that perished too soon. The market held in St. Paul twice a week shows how few are the expenses of a population that is not in want, though it seldom has any money. What they have they do not spend; they only quarrel over it, and marry, and make wills so as to tie it up securely. Life has been stagnating here for the last sixty years, and nothing flourishes now but Litigation, the eldest-born of Avarice. Before the nineteenth century expires, however, it will be generally noticed in France that Avarice has a younger and a more fascinating child. Her name is Speculation.

CHAPTER XIV.

VILLENEUVE-LOUBET.

'E dentro alla presente margherita
   Luce la luce di *Romeo*, di cui
   Fu l' opra grande e bella mal gradita.

Ma i Provenzali che fer contra lui
   Non hanno riso, e però mal cammina
   Qual si fa danno del ben fare altrui.

Quattro figlie ebbe, e ciascuna reina,
   Ramondo Berlinghieri, e ciò gli fece
   Romeo, persona umile e peregrina.

E poi il mosser le parole bieco
   A dimandar ragione a questo giusto,
   Che gli assegnò sette e cinque per diece.

Indi partissi povero e vetusto:
   E se il Mondo sapesse il cuor ch' egli ebbe
   Mendicando sua vita a frusto a frusto,
Assai lo loda, e più lo loderebbe.'
                         Paradiso, Canto vi.

WHEN Nice belonged to the House of Savoy you always heard this castle called 'Villeneuve-in-France.' That was, no doubt, what Charles V. called it in his own mind, when, on sitting down to supper here, he rubbed his hands and exclaimed, 'Poco à poco, rè di Francia!'

To be master of Villeneuve-on-the-Loup was to hold already one castle in France, for it lies beyond the Var, and it owes its real name of Villeneuve-Loubet to the fact that the Loup runs under its bastions. In the eleventh century the Villeneuves bore as a cognisance a castle *azur* on the banks of a river *argent*, identifying themselves thus with the mountain stream which swept round their towers, and turned their mills.

The castle is about four kilomètres distant from the station of Cagnes, from which it can be easily reached on foot. If you drive to it from Cannes, you must allow a couple of hours for the drive, and you can bait your horses at a little inn (in the village of Villeneuve) between the parish church and the river. A friend of ours, on sketching bent, once slept at that small hostelry for a couple of nights, and he can recommend this as a certain method of getting a very sharp attack of rheumatism!

The Antibes road which you must follow from Cannes is so well known that we will pass along it to-day without a word. No! I am wrong; it is impossible to pass the Tour Bellevue without a cry of joy. The panorama of the Alps, from the Cheiron to the Col de Tende, and from the glacier de Mercantour to Bordighera, is unrolled before us, while by looking back you may catch an exquisite vignette of the roadstead of Golfe Jouan, with two ironclads framed, as it were, at the end of a vista of trees. And what shall we say of this bit of foreground? The ivy-leaved geranium trails over a garden wall: under this oak-stump some dark blue periwinkles lurk, and there rises a great *aigrette* of vegetation. There is the aloe, with its grey-green sheaths, and its towering flower-stem, a true *candelabre dou bon Diou*, as the peasants say, and close to it is a bush of pale pink china roses, through which the iris, the *fleur de St. Joseph*, pushes its great flags, and its pure white flowers.

After Antibes you get down on to the cold, draughty plain of the Brague, and reach the stream itself. The road to Biot turns off here to the left, and the meadows that lie between it and the river are a happy hunting-ground for botanists. Most delicate grasses and orchids are to be found here; there are tangles of the single pea, flaunting beds of scarlet tulips, pale grey flax, and daisies with stems nine inches long, while everywhere, to right and to left of you, spread the daffodils of Enna, that Narcissus—*tazzette*—which in the days of Proserpine loved the brackish meadows of the Sicilian shore, and loves such meadows still. Of these pale straw-coloured flowers you might reap sheaves. The fields seem to dance with them. It would be easy in the course of half an hour to fill the carriage. But I would not advise anyone to do so. In the first place you cannot be long in discovering that these *tazzettes* have a scent[1] only less powerful than that of the white Narcissus-of-the-poets, the one which causes the shepherds of Dauphiny to swoon sometimes in the fields.

[1] The best Jewish critics hold, as does Canon Tristram, that, to be scientifically correct, this Narcissus (*tazzette*) is the *Chavatzeleth Hasharon*, the 'Rose of Sharon' of the Song of Songs.

In the second place this flower always has its feet in cold, brackish water, so to the invalid who shall persist in playing at Proserpine along with them in a damp meadow, *Dis* (in the shape of the doctor!) will not be long of appearing.

The road to Villeneuve turns off to the left as soon as you leave the shore. It looks unpromising at first, as if it would grow narrower and narrower, and end by going up a tree, but it really is a very fair road, and takes you through a pretty country, past rocks and ruins, and little homesteads, till you come to the crossing of the Loup. Here a beautiful sketch may be got. A long, wooden bridge, over which the white poplars droop, now replaces a former one in stone which the river carried away in one of those fits of rage that earn for it the name of the *wolf*. Of this older bridge the crumbling piers compose a charming foreground, as the greenish stream sweeps away under their shadow. Just in front of them is the village with its church, and above that is the great portal in the outer wall of the castle of Villeneuve-Loubet. Through that arched gateway, and up that steep paved road, kings came and went: Charles V. when he crossed the Var as an invader, and lay here before going up to attack Grasse; Pope Paul III. when he came here as a pacificator; and Francis I., who lived for three weeks under the tower of Romée de Villeneuve, when that tower was already three hundred years old.

The vegetation of the castle slopes is tropical. Palms and palmettoes flourish; the Barbary aloes throw up their flame-coloured spikes; the veronicas

Q

and the damask roses grow in thickets; and the white spirea trails along the foundations of the ramparts. You can take a walk not only round these massive walls but also inside them, for a narrow, flagged passage runs, like a groove, in the thickness of the walls which surround what seems to be a modern dwelling-house. The castle is really an ugly, quadrangular affair, with plenty of yellow plaster, and the most commonplace-looking windows, of which the green shutters are a serious blow to a tourist in search of a sketch! I never saw anything so ugly or so meagre, except, indeed, the old Government House at Aix in Provence, in which the Grignans used to hold their court. That is as hideous as this plastered front of Villeneuve-Loubet, but then it only proves that both are eyesores! The inner quadrangle, which is paved, has a few coats-of-arms on the walls, and there you may still trace the lances of Villeneuve, and the star of the terrible barons of Baux. There is a ruinous chapel, and the rooms upstairs have some old books and furniture, which, however, you cannot see without getting a permission from the owners. But you need not regret it, for the rooms have all been modernised, and there is nothing to recall the visit of Francis I. or the days of Dante's noble 'Romeo.' The place has changed hands many times since that great seneschal of Provence built the spur-shaped tower beside the fast-running Loup. Tradition, which has been so busy about Romée's birth and career, avers that he had it built by his Moorish slaves, and it is certain that its spur-shape, and the small, square stones employed, with the rows of flat ornamentation near the top, all point to a Saracenic taste, and prove that it is certainly not the work of the Pisan builders who constructed the watch-towers of Antibes, Cannes, and Grasse. This *vigié* of Villeneuve—ninety feet in height and visible for miles—was for long one of the wonders of the country. A local rhyme says:

> Casteou di Cagno,
> Tourri di Villanovo,
> Et gran jardin di Venço,
> Soun chacun bello caouso
> Que l'on ves in Prouvenço.

The view from it is very fine. You not only see the coast, but you can follow the windings of the Loup, the mills at his mouth, the wooded gorges, and the tower of La Trinité. Of this ruin the peasants will tell you without hesitation that it belonged to the Templars. It is probable that it once did, but as after the ruin of their Order their lands were divided and granted to other religious bodies, the very name of this ruin would seem to connect it with the Order of the Trinity, with monks who are known to have had estates in Provence, as in the case of their foundations at St. Étienne-aux-Monts. Those Mathurins, or red friars, who had for their founders St. Jean-de-Matha and Félix de Valois, professed for their special object the relief of prisoners. They were bound to devote one-third of their revenues to this purpose, and in all their chapels to say masses for the souls of the men who lay among the Moors.

But it is time for us to come down from the watch-tower. No Moorish galleys sweep the seas to-day;

there is nothing in sight more threatening than the tall masts of the 'Chazalie' going round to coal at Nice, so we may descend, and choose a shady spot in which to eat our luncheon. Nor when luncheon is finished will we forget to take some scraps to *Clairon* and *Trompette*, two beautiful, yellow dogs whom M. de la Panisse-Pacy keeps chained in his stable-court. After having fed those good dogs we can lie on the grass, and as we watch the oranges falling with a heavy thud from the trees, one can try to discover why Villeneuve-Loubet has had so many owners, and why it now belongs to the Comte de la Panisse-Pacy.

The truth is that, beautiful as it may be, this castle is a '*porte-malheur.*' To begin with the legend of Dante's 'Romeo.' Good and wise as the seneschal was, he is represented as having been traduced by enemies, and obliged to vindicate himself from the most odious charges. He was not, however, the poor and wandering pilgrim (*romieu*) of which the legend tells, but the husband of Delphine Grimaldi, and a cadet of the noble house of Villeneuve-Trans. He was, along with Raymond, bishop of Fréjus, and two other ministers of Raymond-Berenger, the compiler of those *Statuts de Fréjus* which were for many centuries the written code of Provençal laws, and of which a copy (probably the original, 1235) still exists in the archives of St. Paul-du-Var. Dante is correct, however, when he speaks of the royal master of his 'Romeo,' of Raymond-Berenger IV., last of the counts of Barcelona, lords of Forcalquier and of Provence, and of the four daughters of this count, who all made royal marriages. It was from this alliance of

Beatrix, the youngest, with the brother of St. Louis that sprang all those events which unite the history of Provence with that of France and of Naples. The celebrated Queen Jeanne, of whom we shall have to speak in the next chapter, was the great-granddaughter of this little Princess Beatrix, to whom old Romée de Villeneuve acted as guardian after the death of her father, the last of the Berengers. Here, in this castle by the Loup, the seneschal pondered over the marriage and the fortunes of his ward, and then took the little girl to Lyons to give her to her proud, dark-browed bridegroom; here he corresponded with the Grand Master of Rhodes, and here he died in 1250, lord of Loubet, of Cagnes, of Thorenc, of La Gaude, of Coursegoules, of Malvans, and of Vence, which his family retained for so long, and where his last will and testament are preserved to this day. The branch of Villeneuve-Vence which descended from him intermarried in the eighteenth century with the Simiane family, and thus mingled with their own the blood of Madame de Sévigné. They became extinct only recently in the person of Hélion, twenty-sixth lord of Vence, whose heiresses sold the estates of Vence and Tourrêtes in 1862.

Just two hundred years after great Romée's death his castle passed out of the hands of the Villeneuve, who had possessed it during those two centuries so full of romance and incident, and rendered so eventful in Provence through the wars of the Countesses, and the career of Queen Jeanne. It was sold to Pierre de Lascaris, count of Tende and of Ventimiglia. That descendant of the emperors of Constantinople was the very type of the semi-royal despot of the fifteenth century. The Lascaris were masters of Nice as well as of that country beyond it which the peasants describe generically as *la Mountagna*: just as we speak of the Perthshire Highlands. Pierre's mother was a Grimaldi, and from her he learned a vaulting ambition, so that no prouder despot ever lorded it over his neighbours near the Var. He had the misfortune to lose his heir, and on his death a granddaughter carried the estates into the house of Savoy-Sommariva, an illegitimate branch of the ducal house of Savoy. A certain Claude de Sommariva was the landlord of Villeneuve-Loubet who was asked to lend his castle to Francis I. The election of Paul III. had obliged that king to suspend for a little both his operations in Italy, and those further demonstrations against his great enemy the emperor on which his mind was fully set. So hostile was his policy, that any reconciliation between the august rivals seemed to be a task even beyond the powers or the tact of Alexander Farnese. Yet this new pope had, during the reign of four pontiffs, watched all the fatal consequences of those intrigues and quarrels which not only drenched Europe with blood and drained her of treasures, but also left her open to the inroads of the Turks. Paul III., therefore, not only proposed an interview between Charles and Francis, but offered to come himself to Nice to arrange a peace which he considered essential for the best interests of Christendom. Such an offer could hardly be rejected. It is true that from the stupendous edifice of the

Papal power many stones had been already pulled out. Its supremacy was rejected already by England, Denmark, Sweden, and more than the half of Germany, as by a part of Switzerland; but the belief of Paul III. in his own prestige and influence was unshaken, and he so far prevailed over the French king as to persuade him to come to Villeneuve-Loubet, and there to await the arrival of Charles V.

May was smiling with all her roses, and the fields were growing white already for the harvest. The coast seemed alive with shipping, and the roads with messengers and *estafettes*. The handsome Valois king arrived at the castle. With him came his son (Henri II.) and his wife Eléanor: besides the Cardinal of Lorraine, uncle to Mary Stuart, and Antoine de Bourbon, the father of the kings to be. This goodly company lived within the ramparts; the companies of *lansquenets* were lodged at Vence, and the country, by no means rich since the disastrous inroads of Charles V., was scoured to find capons, and *fraises de Mai*, for such a host of guests. Local artists, who had decorated the castle for his reception, hastened to offer their respects to a king who was popular in this the sunniest, if the most insecure, province of his fair France. Then a messenger came riding out from Nice to say that the galleys of the emperor were in sight. He was followed by another, who trotted sharply through the fords of the Var to say that the emperor had landed at Villefranche; and then the Provençals, remembering how the forest of the Esterel had blazed at his last coming, and how the road from Aix to Cannes had been strewn with dying men in his last retreat to the coast, trembled at his very name. In the mind of Francis it stirred such bitter memories that he refused to see his rival. Charles, it seemed, had precisely the same antipathy to seeing the king, or to revisiting Villeneuve, which he had entered last as a conqueror. So the Pope had to make himself the intermediary, while Francis found in a visit to him at Nice the opportunity for one of those displays which his picturesque vanity so dearly loved. Imagine the narrow, dirty Rue de France thronged with this amazing procession:

  80 *lansquenets* of Würtemberg,
  400 nobles on horseback,
  400 lancers,
  115 rows of pikemen, seven abreast,
  37 rows of pikemen with corselets,
  21 rows of halberdiers,
  9 banners,
  150 rows of pikemen,
  70 rows of bowmen,
  The Count of Nassau, with 250 gendarmes,
  600 caparisoned horses,
  The Duke of Lorraine, with 100 horses,

and an infinite number of nobles, and lastly, the Dauphin, the Duke of Orleans, the Archbishop of Milan, Cardinal Contarini, and Jerome Ghinucci of Siena. In this state did the king cross the Var and the Magnan, and salute the Pope.

His Holiness soon after announced a return visit to Francis in the castle on the Loup. No man ought to have known the road thither better than His Holiness. As

Alexander Farnese, he had been bishop of Vence, and more familiar to him than to anyone else in the castle should have been this green valley of the Loup. He was now an old man; how he looked his portrait shows to this day, and we can fancy those piercing eyes gleaming from his litter, as with his purple train of prelates and followers he was borne up the paved road and through the gate of Villeneuve-Loubet, recognising now and again some half-forgotten face, and blessing the crowd which had collected to see him pass.

The Pope, who had to go now to the one, now to the other, promising, reproaching, and entreating them to abandon their incompatible pretensions to the possession of the Milanese, at last prevailed on the rivals to make a peace of ten years. It is the peace commemorated by the *Croix de Marbre* at Nice, and which, though often called the 'Treaty of Nice,' really received the signature of the king in this Castle of Villeneuve-Loubet, June 25, 1538.

A few words more about this curious historical house, and the estate which was soon again to have another owner.

During the wars of religion Villeneuve belonged to the great leaguer and antagonist of Henri IV., the Duc de Mayenne. He had obtained it with the hand of Henriette de Lascaris, but presently the Lascaris disappear from the castle walls, just as the Villeneuve had done, and in the days of the Jansenist controversy we find that the place belonged to the Bouthillier. One member of that family was governor of Antibes, and, Provençals themselves, these Bouthillier were connected by marriage with the Mesgrigny of Troyes, one of whom was the celebrated bishop of Grasse, and the other (the well-known engineer) was son-in-law to Vauban. One likes to fancy that prince of all engineers during his visit (1680) to this coast, pacing the ram-

ARABS AT WORK.

parts and admiring this five-sided tower, from which he could judge of the whole aspect of the country that lies between the mountains and the sea.

The next owner was the Marquis de Thomas, who acquired the estate by purchase; but here again it soon changed hands, and passed (by marriage contract) into the possession of the family of Panisse-Pacy, to whom it now belongs.

But Villeneuve-Loubet keeps up its reputation of being a *porte-malheur*. Its owner has recently had the sorrow of losing two children here by diphtheria, and since his great loss he has never returned to his castle.

Clairon and Trompette are all alone in the stable court. They are overjoyed to see a visitor, and will lick your hands rapturously. But at nights, and when the moon is high over the great tower of Romée de Villeneuve, these good dogs howl. Perhaps they see under the palm trees the gliding shadows of his Saracen prisoners, of the dusky builders who were all slaves.

CHAPTER XV.

JEANNE, QUEEN OF NAPLES, AND COUNTESS OF PROVENCE.

'Cette princesse intéressante et malheureuse est toujours vivante dans le souvenir des Provençaux, malgré ses fautes et ses grandes erreurs.'—GARCIN.

'Jeanne avait une intelligence très cultivée, des habitudes d'élégance et de raffinement semblables à celles qu'on rencontrait dans les cours italiennes.'— Marquise DE FORBIN D'OPPÈDE.

> 'Mid gods of Greece and warriors of romance,
> See Boccace sits, unfolding on his knees
> The new-found roll of old Mæonides:
> But from his mantle's fold, and near the heart,
> Peers Ovid's "*holy book*" of "Love's sweet smart."'—COLERIDGE.

IN the history of a country we sometimes meet a man or a woman whom we recognise to be not only a personage but a type. Cæsar was the embodiment of Roman power and capacity, as St. Louis was of medieval piety, while Henri IV. is felt to have been a typical Frenchman, and Lincoln a representative New Englander. Bismarck as undeniably illustrates the Prussian ideal, in its commanding intellect, its physical grossness, and in all the harshness of its self-will.

To personify Provence what should we require? Extreme beauty, youth that does not fade, red hair that holds the sunlight in its tangles, a sweet voice, poetic gifts, cruel passions, regal peremptoriness, a Gallic wit, lavish hands, genuine magnanimity, and rhapsodical piety, with strange indecorum and bluntness of feeling under the extremes of both splendour and misery. Just such a lovely, perverse, and bewildering woman was 'la reino Jeanno,' the great-granddaughter of Raymond-Berenger IV., the pupil of Boccaccio, the friend of Petrarch,[1] the enemy of St. Catherine of Siena, the most dangerous and the most dazzling woman of the fourteenth century.

So typically Provençal was this Queen's nature that had she lived some centuries later she might have been Mirabeau's sister. She had the same terrible 'gift of familiarity,' the same talent for finding favour and for swaying popular assemblies, while the same generosity, and the same shamelessness, along with great sensuousness and the boldest courage, were to be found in this early orphaned, thrice-widowed heiress of Provence, in this large-thinking, eclectic, beautiful, but terrible Jeanne. Like Mirabeau, she seemed to hold the keys of a coming era. Behind her reign in Provence lay the more chivalrous thirteenth century, with its *chiuso parlar*, its discreet fictions, and all the mysticism that inspired the *Commedia* of Dante, and the *Summa* of St. Thomas Aquinas. But before her was unrolled that learning of the classics which was as the twilight of the gods. She was born among the strife of antagonistic principles, when the *Monarchia* of Dante contended that the ideal

[1] '. . . ti dirò brevemente che in quanto a codesta nobil Regina, io mi chiamo sodisfatto, e pienamente contento; conciossiachè, se io non m' inganno credo che l' anima sua generosa, benefica, et serenissima, nulla che di lui o di me fosse degno avrebbe saputo di sua spontanea volontà negarmi giammai.'—*Lettere di Petrarca*, vol. v. lett. 17.

of unity and order rests in the Empire, but when St. Thomas declared that Christian society marches towards eternal salvation under the guidance of the Pope, in whom is vested the authority of the universal Church. Yet in this fourteenth century all civil and social institutions, not omitting the Church itself, showed symptoms of decay, and contemporary with Jeanne lived Cola Rienzi, the tribune, the embodiment of a new political ideal, the emblem of something like popular opinion in Rome. If Delphine de Sabran was inculcating the merits of virginity and poverty, and if St. Catherine was pleading for moral reforms, there was Boccaccio on the other hand, to form the judgment and imagination of Jeanne on a semi-pagan pattern, while Petrarch was the almoner of a queen who certainly preferred Ovid to the Golden Legend.

Jeanne with her small head, and her red hair, does even now, through her smile, remind us of the sunshine of a fine day, and on her tomb her face looks as if she had never known a care. It would be more true to say of her that she had never known a blush:

> Yet he who saw that Geraldine
> Had deemed her sure a thing divine,

and to this day the memory of the *reino Jeanno* lives in her native land, associated with a number of towers and fortresses which do by the style of their architecture really attest their origin under her reign. As that was in many ways a disastrous time in Provence, it says a great deal for her personal fascinations that, so far from being either cursed or blamed, she is still remembered and praised. The ruins of Grimaud, of the Tour Drammont, of Guillaumes, and of a castle near Roccaspervera all bear her name; at Draguignan they will tell you that her canal has supplied the town with water for generations: at Flayosc it is the same tale, and in the Esterels the peasants, who got free grants of land, still invoke their benefactress; while at St. Vallier she is blessed because she protected the hamlets above the Siagne from the vexations of the Chapters of Grasse and of the Lérins. At Aix and at Avignon her fame is undying because she dispelled some bands of robbers, while at Marseilles she became popular through a legislation that modified the local government, and settled the jurisdictions of the vicomtes and the bishops. Go up to Grasse, and in the big square where the trees throw a flickering shadow over the traders of the streets, you will see built into a vaulted passage a flight of stone steps, and there is not a barefoot child but can tell you that those steps belonged to the palace of *la reino Jeanno*. The walls have been altered, the gates have disappeared, but down those time-worn steps once paced the liege lady of Provence, the heiress of the Berengers, the incomparable 'fair mischief,' whose guilt, both as a wife and a queen, must ever remain one of the enigmas of history.

To realise Jeanne's relations with Provence we must remember how before he came to die, and by the advice of old Romée de Villeneuve, Raymond-Berenger IV. betrothed his youngest daughter Beatrix to Charles of Anjou. She was five years of age when she was taken away by the old Seneschal to be betrothed to the stern brother of St. Louis, to the prince whose statue at Hyères says that he was 'le gran roy qui conquit Sicile,' and who was a haughty and a bigoted man. His conquest of the Two Sicilies, and the deaths of Manfred and Conradin are all well-known features of Italian story, all the better known because the struggle thus begun, and the questions then raised, continued to vex Europe till the close of the Middle Ages.

Charles and Beatrix were succeeded by that Charles II. who surrendered the Templars in Provence to the cruel will of Philippe le Bel, and whose marriage with Marie of Hungary opened a new and tragical chapter in the history of the house of Anjou-Sicily. He had two sons, Charles-Martel, King of Hungary (father of Andrew), and Robert, King of Naples, father of the celebrated Jeanne. Petrarch praised this king under the name of the 'buon rè Roberto.' He certainly was a cultivated man, but not an able one, for he said of himself that he loved letters dearer than his crown, and Dante says of him that he was more fit to preach than to reign.[1] It was certainly no proof of wisdom to have surrounded his heiress with baseborn favourites, who in their schemes for power perverted the instincts and lowered the morality of a child who was to be brought up for the throne. By such training Jeanne was assuredly ill-prepared for the 'heritage of woe' to which she succeeded at seventeen, and that after a childhood compared with which the youth of Mary Stuart might be considered to be fortunate, since the Guises, with all their faults, ought not to be named

[1] 'E fate rè di tal che è da sermone.'—*Paradiso*, viii.

along with the Catanese woman who misguided King Robert's grandchild.

Betrothed at seven years of age to her cousin Andrew, Jeanne's affections seem to have lain dormant. Andrew was unattractive to her, and the so-called Neapolitan party,[1] with the Catanese and Louis of Tarento at its head, were jealous of a youth whom some historians declare to have been ' as a lily among princes.' They worked on Jeanne to postpone his coronation, but Andrew prevailed on her at last to yield to him in a matter which would give him at least a better standing as *le mari de sa femme*. A day was fixed. Jeanne was pregnant for the first time, but the enemies of Andrew contrived to inveigle the royal pair to a lonely castle near Aversa (September 1345). There Andrew was murdered; foully and cruelly done to death in the presence of his young wife, who, while he was being hung from the balcony of her bedroom, never stirred from her pillow. Fear of the Catanese may well have kept her passive that night, but her speedy union with Louis of Tarento, one of the party implicated in the murder, has inflicted a lasting stigma on her name. The King of Hungary instantly set forth to avenge Andrew, and Jeanne, who had nothing to say for herself or for her new husband, thought it best to retire to her kingdom of Provence.

It is now that we behold Jeanne and her Provençals

[1] 'E perchè Andrea più giovane della moglie stato sarebbe disadatto a reggere il freno del regno, nè avrebbe voluto prendere il governo la vedova Regina Sancia d'Aragona, nominò Roberto un consiglio di Reggenza, di cui pose alla testa Filippo di Cabassoles, vescovo di Cavaillon.'—*Lettere di Petrarca*, vol. ii., note to lett. 1.

in a characteristic light. They cared little for her guilt or her innocence. She was their own; she was a woman, and a beautiful one, so the crowd cheered her, and the great barons who like Baux and d'Agoult were her kinsmen, made use of her. She landed at Nice, at the Ponchettes, and the consuls came out to assure her of their devotion. 'I am come,' replied the heiress, to whom her wit always suggested a happy phrase, 'to ask you for your hearts, and for nothing but your hearts.' She did not

MOUGINS.

allude to her debts, so the populace threw up their caps; the Prince of Monaco, just cured of the wound got in Crecy's hard-won field, put his sword at her service, and the Baron de Beuil, red-handed from the cruel murder of one of the Caïs of Nice, besought her patronage; which, perhaps, out of a fellow-feeling for homicides, she promised him with great alacrity.

She travelled by the old 'route d'Italie,' behind Antibes, Clausonne, Vallauris, and Mougins to Grasse. There she won all hearts, and made many promises. These southern cities, being already full of aspirations for the liberty without which trade could not be carried on, had favours to ask from their Queen. Part Jew, part Greek, and part Italian, the *tiers-état* of maritime Provence lived in these semi-Moorish cities, in constant jealousy of their neighbours the feudal barons. Jeanne, suffering at that moment from the power of her barons, was lavish of charters to the cities, and she was so evidently capable of governing that the Provençal municipalities looked for a period of prosperity.[1]

The goal of the Queen's journey was Avignon. There she could not only rejoin her husband, but get her marriage recognised by a pontiff in whom she discerned a protector. Pope Clement VI.[2] was really well disposed to her, yet morality actually obliged him to ask Jeanne to vindicate her conduct, and to explain her recent change of husbands. The queen pleaded her own cause before the three cardinals he appointed to be her judges. Not a blush tinged her cheek, and no tremor altered the pitch of that melodious voice, as Jeanne stood before

[1] The consuls of Grasse had already made a grant to the Berengers of ground in the city on which to build a palace 'dans l'endroit qui sera le plus à sa convenance,' and Raymond-Berenger, after having the ground valued by an expert, paid for the site of a house which he was never destined to build, or to inhabit. But Jeanne, eager for popularity, and anxious to feel at home among her Provençals, instantly set to work, and had the palace built which filled the upper part of the present Place des Aires. Till the invasion of Charles V. this edifice remained, and till the seventeenth century the property continued to stand on the list of royal demesnes. It was sold, and all that now remains of the palace is the kitchen-stair, and a few mouldings that testify to the antiquity of a property which is held by one of the many families of Isnards of Grasse.

[2] Pierre-Roger de Maumont, a Limousin.

the red-robed princes of the Church, and narrated, in fluent Latin, the murder of Andrew, the death of her baby (a girl), and her subsequent marriage with Louis of Tarento. While she spoke Louis stood by her side, and the wily Pope noted behind them some proud Provençal nobles, like the Villeneuve, come to meet the descendant of Beatrix-Berenger. The D'Agoult were there in the person of her Seneschal, Foulques d'Agoult, Comte de Sault;[1] with the Baux, and the Lascaris, bringing promises of fealty from the hill country above Nice, and Roustan de Courmis come down from St. Paul-du-Var, with neighbours like the Barcillon, all well worth cultivating. Jeanne, on her way to Avignon, when eager to be acquitted, and to make sure of the barons, had sworn to them 'that she would never alienate or wrong her royal and loyal estates of Provence,' and not a hint did she then drop to the effect that, being deeply in debt, and having already sold her jewels to the Jews, she was at that very moment covenanting with the Pope to sell him Avignon, the fairest inheritance of the Berengers, for 80,000 pieces of gold.

The trial having run its length, the pontiff declared the Queen to be blameless. This was satisfactory as far as it went, but when the barons discovered the price that their Queen had really paid for the verdict they were aghast. Remembering her recent oath to them at Aix they declared the sale illegal. Jeanne explained that she and Louis were penniless, and the Pope maintained his bargain, so Avignon was sold, and Clement began to

[1] Seneschal of Provence, 1355 : Chancellor, and Chamberlain of Sicily, 1360 : married, 1325, to Alix des Baux.

build that palace of the Popes which still looms so grandly across the Rhone. Jeanne quitted Provence almost immediately, but the palace well served to remind the Provençals how their sovereign had betrayed them, and, as they never forgave her, Jeanne had reason to regret her lost popularity when, on a later occasion, she had to embark at Agay in haste, and in unpitied tribulation.

If it be true, as the poet sings, that

> The wind that beats the mountain blows
> More softly round the open wold,
> And gently comes the world to those
> Who are cast in gentle mould,

then it must be conceded that Jeanne was not formed to pass quietly through the changes and chances of royal life in the fourteenth century. Her orphanhood, the deaths of three of her husbands, and of her child, would alone have sufficed to fit her for the heroine of a tragedy, while every circumstance seemed intended to enhance the lights and deepen the shadows of her strange career. In her reign occurred the great Plague of Florence. So terrible was the disease that neither summer heat nor winter cold, nor mountain ranges could stop it. It spread from the coast. Marseilles was decimated, Cannes was in mourning, Biot was stricken, and the streets of Nice were only less full of the dying and the dead than were those of Avignon. In her reign happened the great flood of the Durance, when the river, no longer the 'pallid stream' about which Petrarch wrote, swept over leagues of country, and left famine along its banks. In her reign Rienzi roused the passions of the Roman populace; and, finally, the life of Jeanne was complicated with the so-called Great Schism of the West, when during thirty years, Christendom, doubting whether he who filled St. Peter's chair were the true Pope or not, gave a divided allegiance now to Urban VI. and his successor, and now to the Antipopes. In that way, though the concept of the papacy remained unaltered, the Christian populations saw the Pope divided from the papacy; and every European prince deliberately sought his or her advantage in siding with the one or with the other. Jeanne, true to her Provençal instincts, upheld in Clement VII. a subject of her own, and by so doing she stirred to deeper wrath St. Catherine of Siena. That saint supported Urban with all the passion of her elect and fervent soul, and the correspondence between the two women is extraordinarily curious. The saint began by addressing the Queen in the terms of the highest respect, praised her supposed intention to go to Palestine, and advised a sovereign so ready to 'dar sangue per sangue,' to continue 'permanente nella santa e dolce religione di Dio.' It is hard to imagine that Jeanne read such letters without a suppressed smile, for worlds are not more asunder than were the minds and temperaments of two women whose interests were soon to clash. Catherine's tone then changed. She wrote that she hoped to go to Rome to admonish 'la reino,' but, when unable to do this, she wrote again, reproaching her with the vices of the Antipope, and threatening the laughter-loving Queen with dark days to come. 'You will be,' cried the prophetess, 'set as a beacon to terrify all who rebel.' Considering the many difficulties and the very unstable policy of Jeanne, it was unlucky for the 'femmina Napolitana,' as the saint called her, that she should have such antagonists. Urban undoubtedly had the largest share in her reverses. It must be added, however, that here, as ever, Jeanne had herself to thank for the great dilemma in which she found herself. She had first constituted Charles of Durazzo, her niece's husband, her heir, and then, withdrawing her promise to him, she put forward Louis of Anjou, a French prince, and a supporter, like herself, of the Trans-Alpine Pope in Avignon. Urban, on the other hand, supported the pretensions of Charles, so that Jeanne's position, weak in the Two Sicilies, was only strong in Provence. It would be more correct to say that it ought to have been strong there; but, alas! broad lands had been sold, and oaths disregarded, and Jeanne had too often broken a promise that positions of trust in Provence should only be given to Provençals. Her Seneschal could no longer keep order. The cruel civil war called of Les Baux devastated the country. Corn in Nice was at famine price, and Draguignan was ruined, having to buy indemnity from the companies of Armagnacs and Ecorcheurs at the price of ten thousand florins, and two thousand sheep. In short, Jeanne's popularity was lost. She might and she did plead that necessity has no law, but then the necessitous must expect to have few friends. Finding the Angevine party altogether too weak for reliance, the Queen was rash enough to sail suddenly from Agay, and to trust herself in a city that could only be fatal to her. Charles of Durazzo asked nothing better than to see her run into the very jaws open to devour her. In Naples she became virtually his prisoner, yet, as she was clever enough as to be formidable even in weakness, he felt her presence there to be a menace. The Angevine party might rally, and Provençal galleys might anchor some day in the bay. A company of Hungarian soldiers was forthwith sent to despatch Jeanne in the lonely castle of Muro in the Basilicata. Some historians say that the Queen was smothered, others that she was strangled when at her prayers; but about the deed itself there can be no doubt, and so on the morning of May 12, 1382, perished that Countess of Provence whom Boccaccio used to call the 'singular pride of Italy.'

Unless it might be her restless and bankrupt cousin, Humbert, the last of the Dauphins of the Viennois, no creature was ever more curiously compounded than was this perverse child of genius. Opinions and evidence will always differ as to her gallantries. Every man of note of the day has been credited with having been her lover, and with having enjoyed the favours of a woman who at fifty years of age was allowed to have still been beautiful. Yet it hardly seems as if this Jeanne of the four husbands had leaned to the soft side of the heart. Her habits of sensuality, like her strong intellectual bias, rendered her a sceptic even as regarded pleasure; there was no tenderness in her nature, and quite as much of policy as of passion in her conduct. Love was only the crown of that supremely Epicurean conception which she formed of life: the groves and laughter of the *Decamerone* having replaced any antique belief in love's fatality. That she allowed the episodes of Alaciel's career to be copied from her own shows an indifference to shame, and we blame her all the more because there is no instance of genuine infatuation on her part that can at all compare with the ruinous passion of Mary for Bothwell. Jeanne thoroughly enjoyed existence. For her the troubadours Vidal, and Sordello, and Castelnau sang: for her Giotto painted, for her Petrarch spoke, and for her, 'constrained,' as he says, 'by the authority of a superior,' Boccaccio wrote the more indecorous of his pages: to regret them bitterly in later years. When this jocund Queen went to Rome, Petrarch did the honours of the Holy City to a scholar well able to understand all its charm, and, after the procession of the fourth Sunday in Lent, the Pope gave her the Golden Rose, 'that type of cheerfulness, joy, and contentment;' a gift perfumed with musk and balm, a thing to be coveted by kings, and granted but to very few.

Perhaps because of her cheerfulness this Queen, who ate in her peasants' houses, has still a charm for the Provençals.[1] I asked a man once what had been the merits of her person or of her reign, because, to the best of my recollection, the wars and civil wars of those years had wrought most cruel evils for her kingdom. He replied that he did not know; but that when Jeanne was queen, 'on avait le temps que l'on voulait!' I doubt if seed-time and harvest were different then; but it is quite certain that many of the charters and statutes of this great Countess of Provence remained in force for centuries, and that her influence has been an undying one. If the pious aspirations of St. Catherine of Siena were destined

[1] The street in Nice called *de la Reine Jeanne* is a modern one.

to receive a future gratification in the movement which we call the Reformation, it must be said that the classical and artistic sensibilities of Jeanne were also destined to live on in that other movement which we term the Renaissance. When she began to reign real learning resided only with Arabic and Jewish scholars, and the 'twilight of the gods' had not dawned upon Provence. Thanks to her reign, and above all to her personal character, energy, and culture, Provence came to enjoy a premature and an intensified knowledge, not only of European politics, but also of the revival of classical learning so soon as it was felt in Italy.

CHAPTER XVI.

THE TEMPLARS IN MARITIME PROVENCE.

> I almost saw the armour glance
>   In every chance sun-ray,
> And feathers move and horses prance
>   Amid the cataract spray—
>
> When swift within me rose the thought
>   Of some chivalrous forms
> Who boldly here had dwelt and fought
>   With worse than Nature's storms—
>
> The warriors of the Sacred Grave
>   Who looked to Christ for laws,
> And perished for the faith they gave
>   Their comrades and their cause.
>
> They perished in one fate, alike
>   The veteran and the boy,
> Where'er the regal arm could strike,
>   To torture and destroy.
>
> While darkly down the stream of time,
>   Devised by evil fame,
> Float murmurs of mysterious crime,
>   And tales of secret shame.
>
> And still the earth has many a knight
>   By high vocation bound,
> To conquer in enduring fight
>   The spirit's holy ground.
>
> And manhood's pride and hopes of youth
>   Still meet the Templar's doom:
> Crusaders of the Ascended Truth,
>   Not of the empty Tomb.—R. M. MILNES.

To realise the pathos of these verses from Lord Houghton's graceful pen, I invite the reader to go up to Vence, and to view the ruined Castle of St. Martin-lès-

Vence. It was the home of Hugonin de Capitou, Lord of Mandelieu, and last Commander of the Temple in Provence. Seen in the early morning, when the shadow of its hollow walls is flung over the russet woods, it is a study for a painter—it is at all times a theme for a poet. The bosky dell at its feet, so full of blue hepaticas and morning songs of birds, is fit for an idyl of Theocritus, and it is hard to associate such sylvan beauty with the black-and-white banners of the Templars in their noonday of pride and ferocity, still less with the dark deeds of their evil fame, or with the horrors of their fiery fate. In Provence they are regretted, even though tradition does not spare them. Take, for example, the legend of Ste. Croix-de-Pennafort. The Templars of Vence had a grange there. The place, now often called Roquefort and Castelleraz, lies on the Loup, on the road between Grasse and La Colle. The knights must have been pleased when they first got it, which they did, as a gift, from the monks of the Lérins in 1137, for it is an enchanting spot. The Loup, forgetting the rapidity of its earlier course, here creeps over sandy shallows. Above a clump of osiers rises a little hamlet. There are red roofs, and a white gable, and pools full of dappled shadows; goats browse among the honeysuckles, and the air is perfumed by a dozen scents, for the buds of the cherry and the chestnut trees, and the resinous firs on the Pennafort hill, like the myrtles and the tufted grasses, all give out their breaths —all assure us that Nature is ever hopeful, because she is for ever young. Yet over Pennafort a shadow broods. The path up to the ruins is on the opposite side of the high road, and is so steep that it must be followed on hands and knees. Over this brow the legend tells that François de Roustan, the Commander, flung that golden goat which was the object of the secret and obscene rites of the Templars, and which he thought it most politic to destroy when the dark days of 1307–8 began in Provence. There are but few vestiges of this house remaining, only the gable of a chapel, which was once forty-five feet long, by twenty feet wide, and which was dedicated to St. Michael. It is noteworthy how this warlike Order generally chose warrior patrons, like St. Martin, St. Michael, and St. Dalmas: never, as far as I can charge my memory, putting its buildings under the 'vocable' of a patron of the feminine gender. Here, in this valley, the grange is called Ste. Croix, but from this dedication I am inclined to suspect that it was only so named by the Knights Hospitallers, when they had fallen heirs to the estates of the Templars, and they wished to celebrate the Cross on their own shield.

Founded in 1118, by a Provençal, the Order of the Temple was always strong in Provence, and rendered more than usually popular there at once by the constant piracy of the Moors, and by the connection of the Berengers with those kingdoms of Aragon and Castile, where military knights were highly honoured, and often needed to hold the frontiers against the Caliphs. Apt expression of an age even more mystical than martial, the Templars were the bravest of the brave. They have been called the Turcos of the Middle Ages, and though this epithet describes their appearance, as they spurred about on their small and fiery barbs, it is one that is unjust to their culture. They were forbidden to give quarter, or to ask for it, even when they were as one to three, and their oath forbade them to yield, even in that unequal death-struggle, 'one inch of their territory, or one stone of their fortress.' With their 40,000 *honors* (manors), their immense wealth, their conquest of the Balearic Islands (1229), or their sieges of Acre and Damietta, we have not to do in this place, but rather to see how much of Eastern and Maritime Provence belonged to the Temple.

To begin near the shore, there was the great Commanderie of St. Martin-lès-Vence on the road to Coursegoules, and from it depended the granges of St. Raphael-de-Vence (destroyed by the Croats) and of Ste. Croix-de-Pennafort, which I have just described, with the castle in the valley of the Grande Valette, now called 'La Trinité.' Farther off, and on the right hand of the departmental road, about one kilomètre out of Tourrêtes, and nearer to the bridge of the Loup, was Tourrêtes-lès-Vence, and the house known as St. Martin-de-la-Pelotte. There is also St. Dalmas-les-Tourrêtes, of which the bell still exists, St. Jeannet (or St. Jean), and, to the south of Gattières, the great house of La Gaude, with ruins still sufficient to identify its sometime size and strength. Nearer the sea, but with only some walls left on a little mound, is La Cros-de-Cagnes. Beyond Grasse we have another group of manors belonging to them. There is St. Martin-de-St. Vallier, built by an architect of the name of Magnico, the granges and *cuves* of Tignet at the passage of the Siagne (near the Col noir), and a great commanderie at Clans, of which the portion of ruins still remaining can be identified as having been used for housing the *Caslans*, or free labourers, of the Knights. The fine castle of Thorenc continues to possess memorials of them, though it has had many changes of masters since the catastrophes of 1307-8. Their secularised lands were finally divided in 1520, between the Villeneuve of Gréolières and the family of Raissan, by consent of a certain Jean de Grasse, in whose castle of Calian this deed of partition was executed.[1]

In the valley of the Esteron the Templars possessed Collinges: behind Antibes they held Clausonne, and thus approached very near to the monks of the Lérins in their summer quarters at Vallauris, but in Nice I have failed to find any vestiges of them, except the fountain called 'of the Temple,' on the Genoa road. At Sospello they had a commanderie and a really magnificent house, which after their ruin was given to their rivals, the Johannite Knights. Higher up in the hills, and in the valley of the Tinée, they held Isola, St. Dalmas (*il selvatico*), and, far beyond the reach of even modern roads, the granges of St. Dalmas-le-plan, where their flocks grazed in summer. St. Martin-de-Lantosque was also the seat of a commanderie; at Utelle they had a store of salt, while the houses of Beuil and of St. Martin-d'Entreaunes (on the Upper Var) bring us up to the most northern commanderie of Puget-Theniers, with its farm of La Croix, to the lead mines, and to the foundation at Glandevès.

Anyone who chooses to look out these places on the

[1] The deed is preserved in Grasse to this day, and is in the possession of M. Frederic Pérolle, whose family have had for four hundred years a notary's business in Grasse.

map of Provence may realise the territorial importance of the Templars, and can understand how many enemies such importance gained for them. Professionally, the Hospitallers were their rivals, and theologically, the Dominicans suspected them; but here, and in Western Provence, they had also given umbrage to the great barons, and to such Chapters as those of the Lérins and of St. Victor of Marseilles. Overgrowth has dangers, and to be rich is sometimes to be hated; yet the pride which was the great feature of the Order, led the Templars to suppose themselves invulnerable.

When the fourteenth century opened, the Temple consisted of 15,000 knights all told, with 40,000 manors, and a treasure such as no king could reckon on. Philippe le Bel, when once sheltered in the Temple, noted that theirs was a bank in which lay gold enough to set him at his ease, even after his disastrous campaigns. He first proposed that he should be made a member of the Order, but finding that idea unacceptable he then hinted that, for the future, Templars and Hospitallers should no longer have separate Houses, but be merged in one. The Master of the Hospital was frightened, and Foulques de Villant, opining that such a suggestion from such a quarter could bode no good, even to Johannite knights, fled, and so put seas between himself and the cruel, fair-faced king. The Grand Master of the Temple, less prudent, was only angry. All that '*superbe*' of which Cœur de Lion used to complain was roused. 'Tell the king,' cried Jacques de Molay, 'that the *religion* is rich enough and strong enough to defend itself against the world.' No man and no institution is really strong enough to stand against malice, and the Templars, so far from being blameless, were brutalised by power, wealth, and impunity. They owned no lay and no clerical superior, their Grand Master's style was '*Par la grâce de Dieu*,' and they could confess and absolve each other. It is probably false that in the Canon of the Mass they omitted the terms of consecration, the '*Hoc est enim corpus meum*;' but it is certain that peculiar rules of their own had come to supersede the rule of St. Benedict to which they had first been subject. They were said to wear as an amulet a string which recalled the string of the Brahmins, and they were reported to worship a goat, a toad, and a cat, to say nothing of a mysterious wooden idol adored in their secret rites. Their guilt or innocence of the crimes imputed to them must ever remain an enigma, as enigmatical as was the creed of these superstitious and voluptuous men who, from long residence in the East, had been led to modify their own faith. Those developments of Islamism which gave birth afterwards to the sect of the Druses, probably left their mark on the Templars, while in Southern France they would be tempted to add the Manichean doctrines of the semi-Gnostic Albigeois to their own half-digested Mahometanism. Fierce and self-willed they refused to take warning from any of the signs of the times. The great Albigeois crusade began in 1209. The Lombards were persecuted in 1291; Arnaud de Villeneuve,[1] denounced by the Dominicans, had to fly

[1] We have seen how retentive is the Provençal memory with regard to its *reino Jeanno*; it is equally so with regard to Arnaud

from France; and the Jews of Languedoc were in 1306 driven from the homes and counting houses which they had possessed through seven centuries of commercial and intellectual life. What if the turn of the Templars was now come? In 1272, and again in 1289, they had received warnings, and Boniface VIII. thundered against them in a bull (1298-9), which told them that in the Holy Land their future presence would be undesirable.

Yet the storm when it burst found them incredulous of danger.

When Philippe le Bel first supported the election of the Archbishop of Bordeaux for the papacy, it is said that he made his candidate promise him six favours in return. The nature of the first five was soon disclosed, but the sixth remained *in petto* till the moment came (1307) when the king was ready to spring a mine on the Templars. He has been specially blamed because of his descent from the crusading king St. Louis of France, but if conduct like that of Philippe le Bel can admit of any excuse, perhaps one might be urged, when we recall the facts of the battle of Mansoura in

---

de Villeneuve. Born 1238, there seems to be a doubt whether he was really a scion of the great Provençal house of Villeneuve. The discoverer of sulphuric, muriatic, and nitric acid, of alcohol, and of the medicinal qualities of turpentine, he was held to be part alchemist, part astrologer, and part wizard. The peasants about Grasse will still say of some remedy that it is like

> L'onguent de Mestré Arnaud,
> Que ne fa ne ben ne mau.

Pope Clement V., so far from sharing this opinion of his prescriptions, summoned to Avignon the doctor already banished and condemned for heresies. *Mestré Arnaud* sailed from Italy to go to the Papal Court, but was drowned on the voyage.

Egypt, and the subsequent refusal of the Templars to pay 30,000 livres for the rescue of St. Louis. At all events, the king was determined to ruin the Order; it remained to have the help of the Pope, of the Dominicans, and of the Count of Provence so as to effect it.

The Grand Master, Jacques de Molay, with a hundred and forty knights, was suddenly summoned to Paris to be present at a royal baptism. Few royal events were in those days ungraced by the presence of the proud Templars, and Jacques de Molay, if he remembered how Guillen de Montredon had once brought up an infant king for Aragon, can have seen nothing novel or threatening in an invitation to act as sponsor to the child of Philippe le Bel.

On Friday, October 13, he and his knights were haled and flung into prison.[1] Then from out fair France there rang a cry which was as a blast from the trumpets of the Day of Wrath and Mourning. It was the time of vintage, but of the wine of their grapes the Templars were fated never to drink: rather to tread alone in a Gehenna of faggots and coals of fire. Sixty knights were seized at Beaucaire, and nine in Sens; the alarm spread to Poitiers, to Troyes, to Caen, to Pont de l'Arche, to Bayonne, to Béziers, to Carcassonne and to Cahors. The majority of the Templars fled to the mountains of Dauphiny, and called on the Alps to cover them, for their Grand Master was in the grip of a king who

---

[1] Furent les Templiers sans doutance,
Tous pris par le royaume de France,
Au mois d'Octobre, *au point du jour*,
Et un Vendredi fut le jour !—*Old Ballad.*

never spared, and who had secured the participation of the Pope.

Clement, willing to make some show of hesitation or legality, proposed to summon a Council; but the king made him feel that such a course was much too dilatory. A pontifical commission was formed, and the trial of the great and self-governed community of the Temple before this court of inquiry was the longest, as it was also the strangest, and the most important legal proceeding of the fourteenth century. It lasted for months. Two hundred and thirty-two witnesses were examined, of whom not six gave testimony exonerative of the accused. The allegations made were horrible, but not quite strange to a generation that had heard of the crimes imputed to Boniface VIII., that believed in sorcery, and that had some reason to fear lest in two hundred years of life, a proud and austere Order, which St. Bernard had once hailed as a permanent crusade, might have undergone painful changes for the worse. The Church had, however, the grace to be ashamed of the matter, if not of the manner, of the trial, and only two copies of the *procès verbal* were allowed to be taken. Of these, one was till last year preserved under triple lock and key in the Vatican, and the duplicate, which remained in France, has recently been printed and edited by Michelet.

The result of the trial was the Bull '*Faciens Misericordiam*' (August 12, 1308), and the condemnation of the Order, not as guilty, but as 'Suspect.' It was accordingly canonically suspended; but the murder of Jacques de Molay and of his companions had nothing whatever to do either with this stupendous trial, or with its verdict. It was the personal and irresponsible crime of Philippe le Bel. By tortures too dreadful to be described the king wrung from the Grand Master and his knights confessions of mysterious guilt. But Jacques de Molay and his fellow-sufferers afterwards withdrew all their self-accusations, and they died bravely in the streets of Paris at fifty-four stakes. While they were being racked, tormented, and murdered, the papal tribunal was still sitting at Avignon, and its *procès verbal* contains this short but pithy notice of the day on which their fiery death was intimated to the commissioners:

In ista pagina nihil est scriptum.

Many pages have, on the other hand, been filled, and by many hands, with discussions as to the guilt of the Templars. Voltaire vindicated them, but Napoleon confessed that he had not been able to make up his mind. Theiner expresses a very adverse opinion, while Raynouard's is on the whole a favourable one, and Milman pleads strongly in their behalf. Sismondi says that the quantity of truth in the accusations can never be known, but that presumption ought to be in favour of men whom both a king and a pope agreed in 1307 to condemn; and it is certain that if the century was one of depraved morals it was also one of Manichean tendencies, and one of still greater injustice in all judicial matters. Though torture was used by the Spanish Dominicans, *no confessions of any kind were got from any knight except in France*, and the guilt of the Pope lies especially in this, that he did not insist on being sole judge and sole referee in the case of knights who had no lay superior. This duty devolved on him as of right, and it is hard to suppose that he was either ignorant or indifferent to his position as Supreme Head of the Church. Had he been so, the University of Paris had just pressed the matter on him, for Philippe had referred to them, and they declined, till the Pope had spoken, to give any sentence for or against the Temple. What the University would not assume Clement was base enough to forego, and Jacques de Molay estimated the pusillanimous crime at its true worth. When bound to the stake he declared his innocence, and with his last hoarse accents summoned to the tribunal of God both the Pope and the king.[1] They were to meet him there within the year. Clement was the first to obey the call: dying at Roquemaure on the Rhone, in April 1314. The cruel king carried about the dying Templar's curse for seven long months. He was but sixty-four years of age, and, says De Nangis, 'his face was still fair when it began to pale from some nameless disease.' Philippe le Bel had 'neither fever nor visible malady,' but none the less, and to the astonishment of leeches and courtiers, the king departed, to meet his victim at the judgment-seat of the most just God. He died at Fontainebleau, November 1314. By 1328, and through the deaths of his three sons, the direct line of his house had become extinct, and the crown of France was worn for the next two centuries by princes of the house of Valois.

[1] In 1824, and during the episcopate of Monseigneur de Quélen, a Mass was celebrated at St.-Germain-l'Auxerrois for the souls of Jacques de Molay and his companions.

How fared it meanwhile with our Templars of Provence, with the Commanders of Vence and Sospello, and Puget-Theniers, all subjects of Charles II., the Lame, King of Naples and Sicily?

The cruel arm of Philippe le Bel stretched beyond the Rhone to the Maritime Alps. He made Charles II. believe that the Order would give him trouble in Cyprus, and, by promising territorial wealth to be gained by its ruin, he bought the connivance and assistance of his kinsman. The secret of the plot, first hatched in 1307, was ill-kept, the letters-patent made out by Charles not coming into immediate use, so that the Templars had in many cases time to escape. Bouche says that forty-eight in all were netted. The papers relating to their seizure are now at Marseilles. The order runs thus, that 'à ce jour que je vous marque, *avant qu'il soit clair*, voire plustost en pleine nuict vous les ouvrirez.' ... The knights were to be committed to 'prisons les plus fortes et dures,' and all this 'surtant que vous craignez de perdre vos corps et biens.' The goods of the Temple were, on the other hand, to be carefully inventoried. The inventory of Puget-Theniers goes to prove that, so far as life was concerned, this cruel measure caused more cry than damage. In the castle of Rigaud, the usual residence of the administrator of the Order, only the Bailli, and one young layman, named Michel de Roquette, were seized.[1] Local tradition at Vence maintains, however, that the Commander of St. Martin was

[1] *Reg. Templarium*, vol. iii. A.D. 1308 : vide *Archives du Département des Bouches-du-Rhône.*

less fortunate, and that at midnight Hugonin, the last of its Templars, was seized, and—by way of Castellane and Pertuis—carried to prison at Tarascon. The archives now at Marseilles do not contain a notice of the death of this Hugonin de Capitou, so we may hope that he was not, as the legend goes on to tell, one of the forty-five knights burnt to death at Beaucaire: 'Qui eurent moult à soufrir, et *furent ars.*' Still there is an entry by Du Puy which does look ominous for him, as it says, 'all the Provençal knights were condemned to death *and executed*, their goods being confiscated to Duke Charles of Provence, who made over some part to the Pope, but presented to the Hospitallers their lands and buildings.' The benefit to the Johannite knights was enormous. Here on the coast they settled themselves at St. Jeannet-du-Var, the Mathurins succeeding them at La Trinité, and the Carthusians at La Celle-Roubaud, while they divided the ground at Nice with the Dominicans.

As for the refugee Templars, all who escaped the arm of the king made the best of their way over the mountains into the northern provinces of Spain. There they found in Catalonia and Aragon almost the same Occitanian speech, and on the frontier lands of the Crescent and the Cross they met with a welcome from princes to whom the power of Islam was not a memory, but a stern and an ever-present reality. Many of them enrolled themselves in the Orders of Calatrava and of Mendoça,[1] and others took advantage

[1] For an account of their reception in Spain the reader should consult *Histoire des Chevaliers Templiers, et de leurs Prétendus Successeurs*, by E. de Montagnac. Paris, 1864.

of the protection of the sovereign to enter the Order of Christ, founded in Portugal by that King Denis who was called 'The father of his country.' Thus enrolled, the '*Christi Milites*' enjoyed a sort of second life, and it is pleasant to think that over Vasco di Gama there floated the black-and-white banner with its legend of '*Non nobis*,' which had once fluttered before the proud knights of the long since ruined Order of the Temple.

CHAPTER XVII.

OF SOME NOBLE FAMILIES.

'L'aristocratie ne peut d'ailleurs improviser un noble, puisque la noblesse est fille du temps.'—CHATEAUBRIAND.

SHALL I be thought singular if I say that at fourteen years of age I had a fixed and familiar ideal of a French *Marquis*? He was a person not to be confounded in any way with such of his English equivalents in rank as I had the honour of seeing. No: all rural matters were beneath the notice of that *Marquis*, of a man who wore a sword and buckles, and who carried a snuff-box set in diamonds, which was the gift of his sovereign. My *Marquis* was a man who took pains to please, and to be pleased. He sang little songs, with a little, cracked voice, took snuff, and made incomparable bows. His talk was of courts and camps, and though parents, as a rule, did look askance on all foreigners, still no one could have helped being charmed with that *Marquis*. Of course his name was to be found in the Mémoires de Sully and in the Lettres de Sévigné (the only French books I had read), and had he but visited our lonely castle by the sea, in the remote province of Sutherland, he must have proved an acquisition.

I have never yet seen that *Marquis*, but in France

I have met with his likeness, once or twice in a picture, and also I think on a tomb! And then the Frenchmen I *have* seen are so unlike him! Some of the *gommeux* are (Poole *regnante*) more like Englishmen than my fancy at fourteen could possibly have admitted. Some have titles that go back to the Germanic Empire; some date from the Second Empire of the Buonapartes; and some have no titles at all. They belong to the frigates that swing in the roadstead, or perhaps to the magistracy, *debout* or *assise*; or else to the great, provincial world of doctors, artists, and notaries. Not one of them resembles that pattern on my nail, that charming *Marquis*; and the French nobility in 1884 is just as unlike the French *noblesse* before 1787. The gentlemen who now represent, more or less well, the Crusaders, Templars, Leaguers, and courtiers of France differ essentially from their ancestors in this, that they no longer possess a vested, and nearly exclusive interest in the soil. It is no longer a question of pit and gallows, of *droits de chasse*, of pigeon-house or warren, of the *four banal* for the bread, or of the winepress for the grapes of the poor. The Revolution deprived them of all those feudal rights; exile and bankruptcy have caused their *hôtels* to change hands; a great many families are positively obliterated, while those that remain have no Court at which to shine. Neither do they any longer raise or command regiments, every soldier of which is now supposed to carry in his knapsack the legendary *bâton*.

In Provence, where the territorial importance of the barons was great, feudal princes first held land on a grant from the Emperor. To the titular kings of Arles succeeded the Bozons and the Berengers, and the counts of Anjou. These were quasi-royal, or wholly royal houses, and such rulers, who had seneschals and prothonotaries, both coined money with their own image and superscription, and made peace or war as best they pleased. Marriages took place between them and other crowned heads, but also among their great *leudes*, and thus the families of D'Agoult, Caraman, Simiane, Grimaldi, and Villeneuve, to say nothing of Les Baux, became closely allied with reigning dynasties, and threw their weight now into one scale, and now into the other. For such barons it was thought a creditable item to have a Pope, a Grand Master of the Temple, or a Bailli of Malta, in their genealogy, to say nothing of suitable alliances, and of a shield well known in battle. The heraldic tree was always carefully preserved, and for this reason, as an old compiler of peerages pithily observes, 'That the Gospel opens with a genealogy, and that the oldest authors, Moses, Homer, Pausanias, and Plutarch, like Josephus, gave pedigrees to their heroes.'

The same writer, M. Barcilon de Mauvans, goes on to argue that genuine nobility ought not to be confounded with the titles of the *novi homines*, and he enumerates the distinctions to be recognised. First, there are the '*nobles de sang, d'armes, et de nom*,' descendants of those *braves* by whose help the kings first reigned. Such were companions of princes, their parentage being lost in the mists of antiquity. On their shields and mottoes our author dwells with delight, and he waxes ironical over the way in which, in a degenerate age, the word 'noble' came to be misapplied. It was given to individuals who, like the engineer of St. Paul-du-Var, excelled in any way; 'we have,' he says, 'noble merchants, we shall probably soon have noble potters!' M. de Barcilon liked not the *tiers état*, and was jealous of a class which, had it but had fair play given to it in the seventeenth and eighteenth centuries, might have secured a broad and national basis for social life in France. But to our local peerage-maker it seemed best that nobility should be a caste and not an institution, and he passes on rather contemptuously from the *nobles de race* to the third category of nobles, that of the '*anoblis*.' He pauses to admit that their existence is a proof of great power in a king who 'is able by letters patent to create that which did not previously exist.' To the fourth rank he relegates the *nobles de robe*.

All these distinctions did in their time give rise to mighty pretty quarrels, and Nostradamus, D'Hozier, Robert de Brianson, and Anselme lost many friends by entries in their histories and peerages. Robert de Brianson gravely says that ' many have lost their lives in pursuit of the knowledge of the peerage of Provence.' I should not like to imperil those of my readers by such a course of study. They may pass over this chapter if they have no taste for it, but some of them may like to turn over the leaves of De Brianson's book. The copy I use is in three small volumes, and it originally belonged to the monastery on the Lérins, where it was in truth composed; for De Brianson was a monk, and one who, to avoid quarrels with his neighbours, inscribed them all in his peerage in alphabetical order only. Of precedence he would not allow it to be a question; but even as it was, his pages must have had many a curious and many a quarrelsome reader. They are dedicated to that strange, old Marquis de Mirabeau, Jean-Antoine de Riquety, better known in Provence, after his wound, by his *sobriquet* of '*col d'argent.*' Married to a Castellane, he had none the less a good deal to fear from a peerage-maker, because his family, though of ancient Tuscan extraction, belonged for long after their arrival in France simply to the *roture* of Marseilles. De Brianson treats this fact mercifully, and seems to have been anxious to speak well of all his neighbours. For this reason M. de Barcilon de Mauvans contradicts him frequently, and launches forth into invectives or innuendoes against his own greatest neighbours, the Counts of Grasse.

How those descendants of Rhodoard prince of Antibes acquired the title of Counts of Grasse, and forty fiefs in Maritime Provence, I have already had occasion to tell, so I need not refer to them here, but go on to the consideration of some of the other powerful landowners on this coast.

The best patent of nobility which any of them can show is the Red Book of good King René.[1] His nobles

---

[1] Twenty-two Provençal families still exist whose names occur in the Red Book, and their *Dîner du Roi René* has become a feature of the Parisian season. At the one which took place on May 28, 1884, forty-eight representatives of these houses were present. The Honorary President is always the General Marquis de Galliffet, and on that occasion the President was the Marquis de Forbin. The Prince de Valori-Rustichelli read a poem descriptive of many historic sites in Provence, and the *menu* was ornamented by the shields of the families. Some of their *blasons* are of the old punning sort, the *armes parlantes* of the heralds—for example, a castle for Castellane, and a grasshopper for Grille. The dinner took place at the Grand

were all well known to him, and the story goes that after his death (1480) a list of them was found in the king's handwriting. The same royal hand had appended to each name a qualification distinctive of the character which the house bore, or had long borne. The continuous inheritance of certain qualities in historical houses is not quite a fancy, and though King René sometimes dipped his pen in gall, still the notices are on the whole so far flattering that the present owners of the names can well afford to smile. To have had a history during four hundred years may console anyone who reads of the '*simplicité de Sabran.*' '*Sottise de Grasse*' is less soothing; but who knows? Authors, even royal ones, are at best an irritable race, and perhaps the Comte de Grasse had mistaken King René's last chaunt for 'something he had heard before:' or had just been detected yawning during a long extract from the royal poem of '*La très doulce Mercy!*'

The most powerful families of Maritime Provence were the Grimaldi, the Lascaris, and the Villeneuve. Of the first I shall speak when we meet them in their rock-bound little kingdom of Monaco, so I pass at once to the Lascaris. Greatly feared were they in Nice and in the hill county. Theirs is that grim town house in the dark street behind the Préfecture; and when you have looked at its balustrades, I beg of you not to forget

Hotel: one of the guests told me that they had passed a charming evening: yet the last lines of the poem recited have an echo of sadness:

> Rêvons, mes bons amis, à cet âge prospère,
> Où deux époux royaux, l'amour et la prière,
> Gouvernaient tour à tour un peuple chevalier,
> Gentilshommes, rêvons! Rêver, c'est oublier!

that these despots once lorded it, not only among the avalanches of Tende, but also at Villeneuve-Loubet, and in the lemon-groves of Gorbio. They once possessed Cypières, in the valley of the Loup, but having let it go to the D'Agoult by marriage, they kept themselves for the future rather to the eastern side of the Var. Their villa of the Piol still exists, just outside Nice, in the suburb of St. Etienne. Like the castle of Gorbio, the Piol is a huge, unshapely mass, part fortress, part granary, with an *escalier d'honneur* of countless steps, and with many echoing rooms, now inhabited by peasants. Peasants also crop the vast garden, a place in which, till quite lately, you might dream away many a sunny hour. I have spent long days in it, sketching under the wych elm, or fancying 'Beatrice di Tenda,' hapless daughter of the despots, gliding under the cyprus trees. There are broken fountains, all fringed with delicate maidenhair ferns, and red arbutus berries lying by hundreds on the grass, but the kings of Cyprus and Jerusalem are forgotten, and the mistral sighs, and the tall reeds rustle where the Lascaris used to give laws to their vassals, or plan a campaign against the Turks. Paul Lascaris de Castellane, Bailli de Manosque, was named Grand Master of the Order of Malta in 1636; his brother, Don Pierre Lascaris de Ventimille, occupying a secondary place in the same noble 'auberge de Provence,' and in an Order possessed of enormous wealth as well as credit. Pope Urban VIII. regarded it with eyes as unfriendly as those with which we have seen Philippe le Bel counting the treasure in the Temple at Paris. But the seventeenth century not lending itself to such summary methods of destruction as could be employed in the fourteenth century, Urban only undertook to revolutionise the Order without consulting its Grand Master. He gave to the commanders power to test, or bequeath by will. This had ere long the effect of emptying the treasure; fewer galleys could be equipped, and the hands of Lascaris were pretty well bound. But he was not easily subdued. He endowed a commanderie at Nice out of affection for the auberge de Provence, and sought to be long remembered near his palace of the Piol. But, in truth, his rule was very fatal to the '*religion*.' European wars prevented money from coming in from Germany, Venice, or Poland, and many sovereigns seized the opportunity for alienating from the Order manors and rights which it was never able to recover. Nor was Innocent X. more friendly than his predecessor had been. In vain did Lascaris represent to the crowned heads of Europe that he could not struggle with the Turks if his hands were tied by the Spiritual Head of Christendom. Then came a famine in Malta, galley slaves were lacking, and, in 1654, Lascaris found himself embroiled with France on a question of pratique. Louis threatened, in consequence, to appropriate all the goods of the Order in his kingdom. This luckless Grand Master died in 1657, aged ninety-seven, in the middle of a war with the Turks, and when Tenedos had just been surprised by the infidels.

Between the years 1551 and 1676, thirteen men of the house of Lascaris entered this military Order. There is not now one male descendant of the despots of

Nice, Tende, and Ventimille, and their line became extinct quite recently in the person of the Comtesse de Gréffuhle.

To Eastern Provence belonged the Blacas, with their estates at Carros, on the lower valley of the Var; the Pontevès, who sent forty-four knights to the Order of Malta, and who had a castle near Le Bar; the Pisani of La Gaude (who gave the last bishop to Vence), the Crisp of St. Césaire (now extinct), the Roustan of Cannes, and the Montgrand of Napoule.

Napoule always attracts the eyes of visitors, and they ask immediately if it had not a history of its own. It had. The monks of Lérins kept an eye upon it, the Villeneuve-Trans possessed it, and the Leaguers burnt it with as little pity as the Barbary corsairs had pillaged it; finally, the Montgrand bought it, in 1719. They were liked as landlords, and having been brave soldiers, it is a pity that their name and fame should both have disappeared from the tall ruin and from the rocky bay. The last of the family, Joseph de Montgrand, was created a marshal by Louis XVI., but he lived little at Napoule, preferring the castle of Cannes, the same which in its present ruinous state belongs to M. Hibert. The lands of Napoule were sold in 1876, and the name of Montgrand-de-Mazade is no longer heard in the Maritime Alps.

The Lombard of Gourdon made great marriages. Thus we find among the brides of that house a Lascaris of Tende, a Grasse-Cabris, a Villeneuve-Tourrètes, a Gilette of Nice, a Glandevès, a Grimaldi, and a Castellane. For their dwelling-place they had a real eyrie

—a desolate heritage at the expense of which a local rhyme makes merry:

> Auribeau sur Siagne,
> Bandol dans les bois,
> Gourdon sur le Loup,
> Sont trois mauvais endroits.

Till quite lately the village and castle could only be reached by a mule-path of countless zigzags, but now you can drive from Grasse to Gourdon by an excellent road, and both visit the native camps and look at the portraits in the castle. A certain François de Lombard was *Lieutenant du roy* during the siege of Grasse; Annibal was a Knight of Malta, and one regrets that their names should be forgotten in Provence. The Lombard are now extinct, and by their last representative the estate was bequeathed to a Villeneuve.

The Durand of Mouans-Sartoux are an exception to the disappearance of its local gentry from the old *viguerie de Grasse*. When counting the towers, and admiring the pines of that old-fashioned *bosquet* at Mouans, it is pleasant to remember that though Mouans was originally a fief of the Villeneuve, these Durand go back to the reign of King René, and many Knights of Malta belonged to their house.

At St. Paul-du-Var lived the Courmis, who enrolled five knights under banner of St. John of Jerusalem, the De Hondis, the Barcilon, the Mauvans, and the Baudoin. High up in the hills we find the Lescheraine, and the Gubernatis of St. Martin-de-Lantosque, whose name is commemorated by a street in Nice. Below them were the Caïs, with the Espitalier-de-Cessoles, D'Orestis of Conte, and the like—to say nothing of Del-Borgo, Constantin, Beuil, and Aspromonte, all relations of the great house of Grimaldi, as settled in Monaco and in Cagnes. Neither ought we to forget the Roubion, whose town house exists in the Rue St. François-de-Paule, or the Massengy, whose estate is now covered with princely villas, or the Château-neuf, intermarried with the Fayères of Cannes. But the native aristocracy of Nice had been, as was inevitable, recruited from Piedmontese families, for a Piedmontese sovereign brought with him thither now a D'Ossac, a D'Oncieux, a Caudia, or a De Sonnaz, according as he required, or rewarded, their services. Nice is now essentially cosmopolitan. Its families are but as a drop in the bucket in a society which has no local 'cachet.' The battle of life there is no longer to the strong, but to the rich; the Templars and Johannites are all forgotten, and the 'chevaliers' to be seen in Nice are not 'de Malte,' but only 'd'industrie.'

I have kept the tree of Villeneuve till the last, because it requires and deserves the most careful investigation of its rich, varied, and historic past. There is a good plan for commencing an acquaintance with the heroes, seneschals, saints, beauties, worthies, and authors of this race—viz. by reading an historical romance called '*Lyonel, ou la Provence au treizième siècle.*' This is the work of a Vicomte de Villeneuve; the plot is not exciting, but the notes are exceedingly curious. I found the book doubly interesting when it was perused, in the dusk of an autumn evening, in the beautiful library of the Marquis de Forbin-d'Oppède. I was at St. Marcel, and under the roof of one of the most accomplished of Frenchwomen,[1] herself a daughter of the house of Villeneuve, who in her distinction of mind and holiness of spirit was no unmeet representative of her great ancestresses, St. Roseleyne de Villeneuve and Delphine de Sabran. The hour was late; I was working, as it were, against time, and the charming young secretary, a niece of Dr. Döllinger, smiled as she handed down now another and another volume. The firelight glistened on the balustrades of the gallery of the library, the house was fragrant with the late roses and fruits from the slopes of St. Marcel, yet when our host appeared at length to summon me to a place beside him at table, I felt as if I had been living out of this work-a-day world. I was not within an hour's drive of Marseilles, but, with Raymond de Villeneuve, I had just seen Charles of Anjou start for Sicily, and with Mabille de Villeneuve-Vence I had beheld in the court of Love, that Queen of Beauty crowned at Aix.

The *Villanova* came originally from Aragon. King James I. of Aragon mentions them[2] honourably in his Chronicle, in the same '*Mémoires pour servir à l'histoire de son temps*' in which he tells how he went one spring to Lérida, and there met his kinsman Raymond-Berenger, Count of Barcelona and of Forcalquier, and Count of Provence. To these Berengers the semi-Spanish extraction of the Villeneuve, so far from seeming to render them aliens, helped them to favour and fortune. They

[1] Marie-Aglaé-Roselyne de Villeneuve-Bargemon, Marquise de Forbin-d'Oppède, died at St.-Marcel, 1884.

[2] A Villanova goes into battle with King James: *Chronicle*, cccxxviii.; and of Bertrand de Villanova he says, 'My own born subject, a man whom I knew and loved well.' *Chronicle*, cccxxix.

held estates from the Var to Toulon: from Esclapon, on the hilly ledges under Mont Lachen, down to Napoule's yellow sands. This great and powerful house soon split up into branches. The eldest was that of Trans-Arcs-Barrême, which by virtue of the fief of Trans was able to arrogate to itself the place of the senior marquisate of France. The second was that of Vence. The great features of this line were its descent from the Seneschal Romée, and its intermarriage, in the eighteenth century, with a great-granddaughter of Madame de Sévigné. The third was that of Tourrêtes-Fayence, from which descends the present family of Villeneuve-Bargemon.

Time and space would fail were we to enumerate the *honors* (fiefs) which at one time or another were held by the Villeneuve, or to trace all the ramifications of their house. I will only draw from the roll of the Knights of Malta a list of the Villeneuve who took its vows. They were ninety-one all told, but even my short list will give a notion of their possessions, which can be looked out in the map of Provence. There are enumerated knights of the houses of—

Villeneuve of Trans,
Villeneuve of Gréolières,
Villeneuve of Vence,
Villeneuve of Tourrêtes-Fayence † (of *Bargemon*),
Villeneuve of La Berlière,
Villeneuve of Barrême,†
Villeneuve of La Carisette,
Villeneuve of La Villevielle,
Villeneuve of Rebaut,
Villeneuve of Croisille,
Villeneuve of Clemensaux,

Villeneuve of Esclapon,†
Villeneuve of Mons,
Villeneuve of Thorenc,
Villeneuve of Flayosc,†
Villeneuve of Mouans,
Villeneuve of Napoule,
Villeneuve of Flamarens,
Villeneuve of St. Eulalie,†
Villeneuve of Maurens,
Villeneuve of Clumassens,
Villeneuve of Cananilles.

The fiefs marked with a cross still belong to branches of this illustrious house. Gourdon on the Loup, and Le Rouret, have been recently left to them, while to his lands of Beauregard the Vicomte of Villeneuve-Barrême has lately added a new estate near Avignon, to say nothing of the villa in the Rue de France, of Nice, which his amiable father inhabited for so many years. In the valley above Les Arcs is the village of Bargemon, which was the birthplace of Moreri. It has a ruined castle, and a church with a fine flamboyant doorway. Old, feudal Bargemon stood here—on a hill: but it is down in the meadows that the modern dwelling-house of the family nestles. Everything there is simple, yet neither grace, nor patriotism, nor laughter of children are lacking in that pleasant home. The public life of the Marquis and Marquise de Villeneuve-Bargemon, while at the prefecture of Nice, gave an example of virtues which are rare in that pleasure-loving city, and which have no doubt been fostered in them by the examples and by '*la grande tradition*' of their race.

If one begins to speak of the Villeneuve of history one is puzzled where to begin, and, above all, where to stop. Of Romée, the seneschal. much has already been said. Shall I rather speak to-day of Louis de Villeneuve-Trans, surnamed '*Riche d'honneur*,' who was the friend of Bayard, and who first obtained from Charles VIII. the right to quarter the lilies of France along with the lances of the Villanova of Aragon; or shall I pass from Raymond de Villeneuve, Bishop of Grasse, and Abbot of the Lérins (1251), to Sanche de Villeneuve, Queen of Beauty; or, leaving jousts and songs, betake myself to the cloister of Ste. Roseleyne de Villeneuve, the Carthusian Abbess of La Celle-Roubaud? There is a pretty legend which tells how the loaves in Roseleyne's apron turned to roses when her avaricious father was about to blame her for her charity; but the legend of her death is prettier still. Her brother, Hélion de Villeneuve, Grand Master of Rhodes, was the bravest man who ever led the Johannite knights. History says that he was three times victorious over the Moors, but the legend goes on to affirm that, defeated at last, he was taken prisoner by the King of Morocco. A great ransom was naturally asked for such a captive, and till its payment Hélion languished and laboured—a captive and a slave. One night, after praying for a speedy return to freedom and to Christendom, he fell asleep. He dreamt that by his sister Roseleyne his fetters were struck off, and his prison opened. When he came to himself he found that the dream was so far a reality. He was unfettered, he was free, but he stood in the moonlight alone! Making his way to Provence he learned that Roseleyne was dead. She had rendered her pious soul to God on the very evening of his release. The only part of this tale which is historical is the death of the Abbess on January 17, 1329. She was alone with one of her nieces, when she suddenly said: '*Adieu! pour la dernière fois, adieu!*' The time of her death corresponded, says the legend, with the hour of Hélion's deliverance, for the free spirit of Provence's fairest saint went forth that night to liberate the brother she so dearly loved.

Roseleyne was ever a passionate Crusader at heart. At this time Islamism, not content with possessing those old and glorious strongholds of Christianity—Palestine, Egypt, Syria, Asia Minor, and Carthage—had a firm grasp of Spain, and constantly menaced Provence. Moreover, Aquitaine was leavened with Arabic and Jewish ideas; the Albigeois heresy there defied the authority of the Church during more than a hundred years, and the Italian system of repressing thought was hardly sufficiently successful, even after the crusade, in maintaining orthodoxy in the South. The great religious Orders arose to assist it. Dominicans and Franciscans were founding their houses, while Crusaders kept their armour bright. Roseleyne the Carthusian had thirty-one years of active life. In constant correspondence with all the most distinguished men of her day, she founded over twenty convents, and she contributed not a little to the development of that monasticism which was intended to make head against free thought and heresy. The conquests of orthodoxy occupied all her powers, and she died accordingly in the odour of sanctity. Miracles are said to have been worked at her grave, and to a miracle it was ascribed that in the reign of Louis XIV. her corpse was found so unaltered that the king ordered one of the eyeballs to be pierced, to see if it was made in glass? This buried saint 'still sheds perfume,' and even in this age of progress the memory of Hélion de Villeneuve's little, red-haired sister is still beloved. The railway from Les Arcs to Draguignan runs within a few yards of her conventual home of La Celle-Roubaud; but in 1882, a casket containing her relics was ordered to be carried to a chapel on the hill above Bargemon. The Bishop of Fréjus, who promised to be present, fully expected an unfavourable demonstration on the part of the populace, for the Var is by no means a *bien pensant* department, and radical mayors have in several towns forbidden the yearly procession of Corpus-Christi Day. But Roseleyne maintains her popularity; crowds followed the procession of her relics, and nothing but goodwill was expressed for the saintly lady whose piety and courage have certainly been hereditary in her house. The tomb of her brother Hélion is at Malta. His name is associated with the division of the Knights of St. John into seven divisions, or *tongues*. Out of compliment to their then Grand Master, Hélion de Villeneuve, the precedence was accorded to the '*langue de Provence*,' a compliment certainly merited then and later by the Villeneuve, who, when Vertot closed his list, had sent more knights into the Order than any other house in Provence.

Let me next draw attention to a certain Christophe de Villeneuve who lived in the end of the sixteenth century, and who, had he been born in the legendary ages of Christendom, would certainly have been praised as the slayer of a dragon, or some such '*laidly wyrm.*' When he received the order to make an example of the Huguenots in Provence, he simply refused to obey, and his correspondence with the king through that period of religio-political strife would do credit to any statesman. I would fain linger over the pedigrees of the Villeneuve, and tell how Sophie de Villeneuve-Vence was one of the few good influences of Mirabeau's life, but I must hurry on to the man who fought at Trafalgar.

Vice-Admiral Jean-Baptiste de Villeneuve-Flayosc

was born at Valensoles, in 1763. He served with distinction in what French seamen term both 'the seas of Ponant and Levant,' and belonged to the golden age of the French navy, when she had so many great captains, and when so many of those were Provençals. He fought as second rear-admiral at the Nile (1798), but was able to cut his cables, and to take his ship, the Guillaume Tell, safely to Malta. After his return to Europe that vessel fell into the hands of the English, striking to Captain Dixon, and De Villeneuve's flag was flying on the Bucentaure, when, in the autumn of 1804, he sailed from Toulon. Of the vast and indefinite plans formed by Napoleon to damage the power of England, he said afterwards that he had meant to entrust the greatest share to De Villeneuve. That officer was to have effected the invasion of England, and yet it is certain that, unlike his predecessor La Touche-Tréville, he never was a favourite with the Emperor. The Duc d'Otrante says truly in his memoirs, that Napoleon was sensitive 'about his naval honour, *though he never had any*,' and that this made him difficult to please, but De Villeneuve had really given him serious cause for displeasure. His indecisive action with the English virtually led to the failure of the famous Boulogne expedition, for De Villeneuve did not score a victory in the battle of Ferrol, and after it he retired to Cadiz instead of pushing on to Brest at a moment when the expedition only waited for his appearance. Napoleon exclaimed peevishly, '*Quel Amiral!*' and yet De Villeneuve was both a brave and an able man. Critics like Clerk and Eken have said of his tactics at Trafalgar, that they were showy rather than sagacious, but his orders were precise, and both by precept and example he did his duty nobly. His saying 'Celui qui ne serait pas dans le feu ne serait pas à son poste' is not very different from the celebrated message telegraphed to his ships by the one-armed sailor, who, as a child, had once asked, 'But what *is* fear?' The truth is that, at Trafalgar, De Villeneuve had too formidable an antagonist. In the stern-cabin of the 'Victory' sat the patient and ever anxious guardian of England's honour watching off Cape St. Mary for the first sight of the combined French and Spanish fleets, and determined that they should not give him the slip: 'not if it is in the power of Nelson and Bronte to prevent it.'

Nelson loved a plan. He would cover sheets of paper with what he called 'flocks of wild geese,' and he prepared the sketch for this action with consummate care. As written out by him, the memorable document now fills only sixty-eight lines of print in a quarto page. Yet nothing is omitted, and as little as might be is left to those chances of wind and surprise, of all of which Nelson knew so well how to take advantage.

The morning was fine, the wind light and from the west, with nothing to warn an eye less experienced than his of the tempest likely to arise before night. De Villeneuve's fleet was, says an eyewitness, distinctly seen to leeward, 'standing to the southward under easy sail.' But later ' the enemy's fleet changed their position, and having wore together formed their line on the starboard tack.' The wind shifted a few points to southward of west, and their rear ships were thrown far to windward of their centre and van. This was unlucky for De Villeneuve, as the wind being light, many of them were unable to gain their proper stations before the battle began. The first shot was fired about noon. Nelson, in full dress, with the four stars on his breast, and his coffin ready in his cabin, was in the highest spirits, and remarked that it was 'the 21st of October, the happiest day in the year in his family.' His attacks were generally of a novel and unprecedented sort, and to-day he bore down in two columns, hoping for a victory before the French van could succour the rear. Admiral Collingwood said afterwards of De Villeneuve's line, that it had been 'close and correct, and that both he and Gravina displayed great passive courage,' though there had been 'no nautical management, and only the Intrépide showed active bravery.' The first three English broadsides proved a great shock. Nelson then began what he called 'close work,' and in that the French admiral was no match for him. How the battle raged, how Nelson fell, and in falling bade Collingwood anchor the fleet, is an oft-told tale, though it is one that never tires, and Lady Londonderry was right when she wrote about his death, that 'his health would never have been equal to another great effort; therefore in such a death there is no sting, and in such a grave there is an everlasting victory.'

Admiral de Villeneuve's heart was broken by his defeat. Before his Bucentaure struck to the Conqueror he got into a boat, but being recognised, he was picked up and taken on board the Mars, where he remained till the 24th. Transferred thence to the

Neptune, he was treated by Captain Fremantle with the greatest kindness and respect. But there are no wounds like those in the hearts of brave men. He would not risk a meeting with Napoleon, a master never partial to him, and who had once sent him as a piece of advice the startling recommendation to 'give battle, and lose half of the fleet if necessary.' Alas! more than half the fleet was lost on this day, for only thirteen vessels escaped, and those only for a time. They were all taken, some at Cadiz and some by Calder, so that of the Admiral's fleet not one single ship returned to France. De Villeneuve, soon after landing, committed suicide at Rennes. A ghastly tale circulated among the enemies of the Emperor, that Napoleon had desired De Villeneuve to take his own life before entering Paris. There is no proof of this. The cold cruelty of the Emperor was quite capable of such a message, and on hearing of the tragic close of the Admiral's career he only remarked with a sneer, that 'De Villeneuve had apparently studied anatomy in order to find his heart.' Yet in St. Helena he said to O'Meara, when discussing these events, that 'the Admiral need not have done it. He was a brave man, though he never had any talent.' The portrait of De Villeneuve gives this idea, that of a brave and amiable man, and a most pathetic interest attaches to some sketches of his frigates, which I have seen on the walls of the children's school-room at Bargemon. They were done by the Admiral's own hand, with loving touches given now to elaborate a piece of rigging, or now to render the horizon of the sea on which the good ship floats.

I began this list of worthies by speaking of a book written by one of the Villeneuve to illustrate life in the thirteenth century. A book by yet another Villeneuve, the Vicomte Alban, is more in tone with our own age. It handles the social problems of life in the nineteenth century. If Madame Aglaé-Rosaleyne de Forbin inherited the temperament of Sainte Rosaleyne, Alban de Villeneuve inherited at once the sagacity of Romée and the humanity of Christophe de Villeneuve. He was neither prothonotary nor seneschal, only prefect of a French town (Lille), where he discovered a sixth of the population to be paupers, and that at a moment of perilous and precarious experiments. It was necessary in the best interests of liberty to reconcile the new *régime* of France with that ancient and glorious monarchy which still boasted of such memories as place it beyond competition, and which might be sufficiently great to be able to meet liberal movements without fear. 'Old governments,' said Benjamin Constant, 'are more favourable to liberty than new ones.' Alban de Villeneuve was convinced of this, and he belonged to a family of which Charles X. said that he wished he had one of them in every prefecture in France; but most assuredly his was no easy task: to consolidate the liberties gained, to treat prejudices leniently, and to abstain from aggravating hostilities which existed, and could not but exist, all around him. His book, evidently that of a Christian socialist, was the result of personal observations. The Revolution, intended to level distinctions, had only brought into greater prominence the inequality between capital and labour, and the Vicomte Alban felt that there was danger in the new and often fraudulent nostrums offered to the workpeople. He travelled a great deal, he familiarised himself with the arguments of Malthus, Sismondi, Mathieu de Dombasle, Droz, De Gérando, and Charles Dupin. He saw that all these arguments 'gave to Frenchmen neither work nor bread.' Wearied and disappointed, he would have been still more disappointed could he have known that, fifty years later, the same difficulties would not only exist, but that they still continue to be regarded with the same bitterness which he deprecated.

Quoting Lamartine one day, he cries, 'Elevons souvent les regards des hommes, notre pensée et notre voix, vers cette puissance régulatrice d'où découlent, selon Platon, comme selon notre Evangile, les lois et la liberté. Confions-nous à cette Providence dont l'œil n'oublie aucun siècle et aucun jour. Faisons le bien, disons le vrai, cherchons le juste, et *attendons*!'

CHAPTER XVIII.

THE GRIMALDI OF MONACO.

'In the morning we were hastened away, having no time permitted us by our avaricious master to go up and see this strong and considerable place, which now belongs to a Prince of the family of Grimaldi of Genoa, who has put both it and himself under the protection of the French. The situation is on a promontory of solid stone and rock. The town walls are very fayre. We were told that within was an ample court, with a palace furnished with the most rich and princely movables, and a collection of statues, pictures, and massive plate to an immense amount.'—EVELYN'S *Memoirs,* vol. i. (1644).

'Que de ruines, et quel cimetière que l'histoire ! . . . Singulier mélange de passion dramatique, de philosophie douloureuse, d'observation exacte, de trivialité maladroite et d'une puissance pittoresque.'—H. TAINE.

THE principality of Monaco, which used to include Mentone and La Roquebrune, now consists of four districts. First of all there is Monaco proper, on its 'promontory of solid stone,' with its palace and courts, still so full of mediæval beauty and of artistic riches. Next comes the port, or bathing station, a land-locked little bay where the *tartanes* and the English yachts ride in smooth water of the most wonderful hues. After this comes the Condamine, with its new world of white villas; and, finally, there is Monte Carlo.

The last-named spot is of course the point of attraction for strangers. The casino is the thing that all Europe, Asia, and America talk of, that all moralists decry, and that all pleasure-seekers declare to be a paradise. It is the casino that gives wealth and fashion to this section of the coast. It is the casino that causes a dozen trains to stop daily at Monte Carlo; that keeps up the palace, the army, the roads, the opera-house, and the Hôtel de Paris. It is the green table that keeps the gardens green and the violins in tune; that has brought 3,000 residents and so many hundred prostitutes to the town; that gives work to 1,000 servants, and causes the annual issue of about 335,000 tickets. When we consider these facts, the fabulous beauty of the site, the mildness of the climate, the good dinners, the better music, the pigeon-shooting, and the many exciting chances, can we wonder that 'Monte Carlo' is in every mouth? The subject is so hackneyed, and in some respects so repulsive, that I prefer to leave it to other pencils and to other pens. Its sovereign has to avoid the place. Weary of scandals, of newspaper articles, of sensational letters, of indignation meetings, suicides, painted women, and worry, he now sees the capital of his principality as little as may be. Monaco has its governor, and his papers have an *archiviste*, and for his own part he usually resides in the north of France, where he possesses (by long inheritance) a much larger, if a much less remarkable estate. The evil of the gambling tables seems to be for the present almost beyond his control, for the land is let on long lease, and the lessees are no longer only the sons-in-law and heirs of the late M. Blanc, but a number of sagacious persons, who will soon form a real *Société anonyme*. Their voices represent all that modern greed, and modern luxury, and modern vice can suggest. What irritates them most is any remonstrance. The anti-Monaco meeting held in Nice was interrupted by howls, and quite recently a respectable Parisian paper, which told the truth, was forbidden to enter the territory, though during the cholera panic of last autumn, visitors to Monte Carlo might pass free of restrictions. At intervals the French Government makes a show of wishing to suppress the gambling tables; but considering the position of the Prince, as independent ruler of his little dominion, the right of France to interfere with the lease of a part of his estate for a Casino, may be legally questioned. Nor are the shareholders likely to be less tenacious of their rights. Who are the owners of shares made *payable to bearer*, can never be known. They may be men in buckram, put forward to plead beggary if the lease is cancelled; at best they are the acute inventors of the new issue of 60,000 shares (of 500 francs), announced on the Paris Bourse in August 1884. Their objects are to prevent pressure being put on their landlord, the hope of getting an indemnity, and the wish to make it be believed that there is a vast host of respectable (?) shareholders interested in maintaining the gambling tables. The monstrous evil threatens to be long-lived, and I do not propose to weary my readers further with the subject, but rather to carry their attention back for many generations.

Once upon a time, when neither gamblers, nor croupiers, nor *souteneurs de filles*, nor hotel-keepers, nor railway trains, nor baths, nor yachts, nor Jesuit colleges were to be found here, there were Grimaldi in Monaco. They were bold men, in spite of King René's saying that they were to be known for their *finesse*, and they mated.

with the Spinola, the Lascaris, and the Trivulzi; sent Doges and admirals to Genoa, and abbots to the Lérins; parleyed with Andrea Doria as with an equal; made treaties with kings, and traced back their lineage for twelve centuries. Their good fortune dates from the exploits of a certain Gébelin de Grimoald, son of Pépin l'Ancien, and uncle to that greater Pépin, who made the office of Mayor-of-the-palace hereditary. It is said that Gébelin did himself fill that position, but he is better known as the paladin, who along with Isarn, Bishop of Grenoble, succeeded, early in the eleventh century, in expelling the Saracens from Provence, Dauphiny, and the Lower Alps. The district of wooded hills, still called, from their hundred years of occupation, Les Maures, lies between Toulon and Fréjus. The Garde-Fraxinet was the Moorish capital or stronghold; the bay of Grimaud was their harbour, and as they held a strong position on the other side of Nice, their presence in Maritime Provence was a perpetual menace. Looked at from the point of view of modern science, it is doubtful whether their expulsion from Provence really was the benefit which it then appeared to the national and Catholic party, as personified by Gébelin and Isarn. To them the Semitic element was simply hateful, though, in truth, Europe could in those dark and early days but ill afford to lose her Arabs. They had, it must be confessed, a higher culture than the Christian paladins who withstood them, and they brought Jewish traders in their wake, so much so that to this day the '*rue des Juifs*' in Grimaud reminds us of the counting-houses of the Hebrews who grew rich there under the wing of the

A STREET IN COGOLIN.

Moors. When the Saracens were finally driven out, they left behind them their system of irrigation, their Bushra roses, their pumps, their *norias,* and their porous water-jars. Rice, sugar, cotton, flax, silk, saffron, and cork were all brought into use by sheiks who have left us the words 'chemise' and 'sarsanet.' The palm and the peach grew in their gardens, and they bequeathed to Christendom their 'syrups, juleps, and elixirs.' If in botany, surgery, and medicine they, and their Jewish friends, were in advance of all Christian leeches, poets also learned from them to rhyme, astronomers got 'the use of the globes,' and barons, even such as Gébelin de Grimoald, learnt hunting and falconry. The Moors paved their streets, while Western civilisation waded foot deep in mud; and to this day the towns and villages of Les Maures bear the stamp of an architecture intended to defy the heat of the sun. Look at this street in Cogolin. It is really a passage, for the houses cross the so-called street, and the first floor on the one side is continued into that of the opposite side, where the masses of dark walls have but few windows. Something like this looked the towns which Gébelin de Grimoald got for an heritage when his stout right arm had driven away the dusky invaders. After his death (656), the family, as it increased in wealth and importance, split up into branches, with a tendency to enlarge its borders on the eastern side—viz. in the direction of the strong place of Monaco which they were to acquire in 968. Antibes accrued to them in 1237; but that the Grimaldi did not at once abandon the western district is evident from the great prosperity of the branch settled near La Ciotat. To this day the phrase 'the purse of M. de Raguse' is used to express a fortune as exceptional as that of Grimaldi, Marquis de Raguse. Cagnes belonged to the Grimaldi, Marquis de Courbon, and it remained with them till the close of the eighteenth century. In what state they lived there may be judged from the castle at the top of the hill, with its *escalier d'honneur*, and its ceiling painted by Carlone, the Genoese. One of these Courbon-Grimaldi, while governor for the king, and for the Prince of Monaco, received a letter signed by Loménie de Brienne, and countersigned by Louis, bidding him beware of Spanish intrigues, and of a certain Spanish agent disguised as a monk, whose presence was dangerous for the coasts of Provence.

To the Grimaldi, Counts of Beuil, fell a much wilder heritage than any of these seaboard places. If Cagne feared Moorish pirates, and Monaco dreaded Spanish ships, the uplands of the county of Nice had wolves, and avalanches and late frosts. Local histories tell how cruel and bold were these hard-living Counts of Beuil, and they were especially formidable to Nice in the early reign of Jeanne, in that era of civil wars and mortal feuds, when battle and murder and sudden death had so hardened men's minds and manners that morality had fallen to quite as low an ebb as it now has at Monte Carlo, from very different causes.

All the branches I have enumerated were of much less account than the reigning House of Monaco. The earliest records of its '*faicts et gestes*' are a little fabulous, but royal charters of 1237, 1267, 1411, and 1438, bear witness to its importance, and we certainly touch firm ground in 1218, with the Grimaldi who commanded, in the harbour of Damietta, the fleet of the Crusaders which was to carry the town in 1219. From him descended the lines of Grimaldi, Marquis of Mandinio, in Naples, and that of the Grimaldi of Seville. His successor was the first to assume the leading position in the Guelf party which we shall find proper to the princes of Monaco. It was this Admiral Charles who bought the lordships of Mentone, Roquebrune, and Castillon, while his son, the friend of Queen Jeanne, governed in Provence as her lieutenant. The friend of princes, his enemies seem to have been those of his own household, for he was kept out of his castle of Monaco for seven long years by his fierce kinsman the Grimaldi of Beuil. The tale of their exploits reads like a page in Sir Walter Scott's 'Tales of a Grandfather,' from the early history of Scotland. In fact, wherever hard blows were going, a Grimaldi was generally to be found, at Crecy, at Lepanto in 1571, and at the battle of the Texel, 1666; but the boldest of them all was Augustine, that abbot of the Lérins who sided with Charles V. in wars so fatal to Maritime Provence.

Evelyn in his Diary speaks of the Grimaldi as of a Genoese house, and the list of the Doges of that republic would incline one to agree with him. Neither is it till 1622, that we find French brides asked in marriage by the princes of Monaco, for they had wed with Genoese and with Milanese ladies. The language of the principality points to Italian rather than to French relations. It was, and it remains to this day, a curious dialect; being, like some of the other *patois* of this Ligurian shore, a corruption of the 'vulgar tongue' of Genoa. Even where the words seem in their spelling to assimilate themselves with French rules, the peculiar pronunciation of the vowels preserves to the language an essentially Italian character. Take the following specimens:

> Nostro païre che sei in celŏ, che ŏ vostro nome sia santificao, che 'ŏ vostro regno arrive, che *ra* vostra volonta scia fà, sei *ra* terà, couma a *ro* celo. Dène anchei *ro* nostro pan di ciacea giorno. . . .
> Santa Maria! Maïre de Diŏ, preghè per noi, poveri peccatoi aora, e a *ro* ponto de *ra* nostra morte. Cosei scia.

It will be seen that the Monegasque speech still preserves the forms *ro*, *ra*, and *ri* for the articles *le*, *la*, and *les*, a corruption renounced by modern writers and speakers of the Genoese dialect, though—as late as the beginning of this century—they might still be caught on the lips of the old-fashioned, local Genoese nobility.

But I must return to the Grimaldi. After seven hundred years of possession, the male line threatened to become extinct. Like many races of despots, the lords of Monaco lacked an heir male. Antoine X., by his marriage with a princess of Lorraine, had only two daughters, and his brother the abbot was in orders. It therefore behoved Antoine to choose among the suitors of Louise-Hippolyte a family eligible for grafting on it her name and quarterings. This was a matter requiring much personal thought, and which also warranted royal interference. The hand of Mademoiselle de Monaco could not be assigned to the first comer. Even if King Louis might forget for a moment the centuries of sovereignty enjoyed by the Grimaldi at Monaco, he could not forget that Richelieu had only recently conferred on those princes the titles of Duke de Valentinois and Marquis des Baux, with grants of land in Provence and in Auvergne. Moreover, Honoré II. had put the sovereignty and independence of his estates under the protectorate of France. That act had been effected by the Treaty of Péronne, September 14, 1644. Its first article stipulated 'a garrison shall enter into the said fortress of Monaco, composed of five hundred effective soldiers, all Frenchmen born, and not of any other nation, to keep the fortress, to remain there, and to serve in four companies. . . . The said prince shall be captain and governor for the king, and after him his heirs and successors in the said principality.' These conditions had been proposed by Honoré II. because, as the treaty states in its preamble, ' the Spaniards had, so to speak, appropriated the place of arms and fortress of Monaco, *which he holds as sovereign*, usurping so much power that it is no longer at the disposal of its prince.' The benefit seemed to be all on his side, since he obtained along with the protection of Louis XIII. a garrison of five hundred men, the prince being also left '*liberty and sovereignty within his own dominions*,' but, on the other hand, the place of arms over which he ruled barred the only road of communication between Italy and Provence. Its importance was all the more felt by Louis because the Spanish fleet had only a few years earlier assembled in front of it, before giving battle to a French squadron off Mentone. The permanent occupation of Monaco being taken into consideration, no slight interest naturally attached to the betrothal of its heiress. Dangeau writes:

'Wednesday, March 20, 1715.

'The marriage of Mademoiselle de Monaco with M. de Thorigny is arranged.[1] M. de Monaco cedes the duchy of Valentinois to his daughter; the Abbé, to whom the duchy would revert, renounces in favour of his niece; and the king not only consents but adds a *pairie* to the duchy, since—though the lands are a duchy—they would only carry the *pairie* for heirs male.'

Portraits of this bride and bridegroom are not wanting. They sat to Carl Vanloo, and he painted them surrounded by their six children. Fortunate in her wedded life, and the founder of a new line of princes, Louise-Hippolyte can never be reproached by her descendants for having derogated from the pretensions of her birth. Since the junction of the line of Grimaldi to that of Matignon the following titles have been added to the family roll: 'Sire de Matignon, Comte de Thorigny, Baron de Saint-Lo, Baron de la Lathumière, Duc d'Estourville, Duc de Mazarin, Duc de la Meilleraye, Duc de Mayenne, Prince de Château-Porcien, Comte de Ferrette, de Belfort, de Thann, and de Rosemont, Baron d'Altkirch, Seigneur d'Isenheim, Marquis de Chilly, Comte de Lonjumeau, Baron de Massy, Marquis de Guiscard,' &c. &c.

The archives of the family are rich and most interesting, and if H.S.H. the Prince of Monaco could be prevailed on to print some of his treasures, the world of historians and archæologists might revel in a vast number of original letters illustrative of the records and

---

[1] Jacques-Léonor de Goyon-Matignon, Comte de Thorigny. Madame de Sévigné possessed, and eventually sold, a house in the *Rue de Thorigny* at Rennes.

friendships of the house, first as princes of the family of Grimaldi, then as Matignon, and, finally, as representing the house of Mazarin.[1] I have seen forty-six volumes of the correspondence of Joinville, of Henri III., of Catherine de Medicis, and of Henry IV. M. Saïge, the archivist of the palace, brings to the classification of the family papers both great care and great historical knowledge. One may spend most delightful hours in his company, and quite forget the neighbourhood of the Casino; in fact, be carried back in imagination to a totally different age of the world. I remember laughing when we recalled there the attempt made by the Duchesse de Mazarin and her sister Marie, wife of the Constable Colonna, to land at Monaco. The husbands of those beautiful Mancini exercised at all times but little marital control over them. However, that little was felt to be too much, and they determined to escape from it. They took ship at Civita Vecchia. Their skipper asked an exorbitant fee, but necessity has no law; Marie Mancini was horribly frightened, and still more horribly sick, so she ended by offering him one hundred pistoles over and above the sum agreed on, if he would, without more delay, land them in France. It blew a tempest, and they hoped to land at Monaco, but there was no *pratique* for vessels coming from Civita Vecchia, so these heroines, travelling, as Madame de Grignan, the Governess of Provence, said of them, with 'many jewels and no clean linen,' had to spend their money on buying a permission to land. They had to continue to wear men's attire lest their identity should be suspected, but they finally did

---

[1] Honoré IV. married Louise F. V. d'Aumont, only child of the Duc de Duras, and great-grandchild of Charlotte de Mazarin.

get safely into France (from La Ciotat) in spite of all the galleys of Tuscany which the Constable Colonna had sent out to track his fugitive wife.

Even more conspicuous among ' *les grandes amoureuses*' of that *siècle Louis XIV.*, was Charlotte de Gramont, Princesse de Monaco. She was the daughter of Richelieu's friend, the Maréchal de Gramont, and a haughty, witty, unscrupulous beauty who would have been out of place on any soberer stage than that of the court of Versailles. Her intrigue with the King, her passion for her cruel, cunning, and ambitious cousin Lauzun, her consequent rivalry with the Grande Mademoiselle, and the jealousy of the Prince of Monaco of a wife who never even aspired to fidelity, would fill a volume, as they have furnished Saint Simon with some of his least edifying pages. The Prince lived at Monaco while Charlotte amused herself in Paris. He cannot have had much sense of humour when he invented a new way of revenging himself on his rivals. His principality is small, but he made it look very small when he caused gibbets to be erected at intervals all along its frontiers. From them he hung the effigies of all the courtiers on whom he believed that his Princess had smiled. 'Not only,' wrote Madame de Sévigné, 'is this measure retrospective, but people divert themselves by telling him of things that go on now. The result is that the gibbets are obliged to be put closer together, and more than half the gentlemen of the court are now hanging along the frontiers of Monaco. I assure you I have had many a laugh at this, and others with me. The King himself laughs at it. It is a frenzy of *hangings* that passes all belief.'

Another legend connected with the Palace of Monaco is of a graver character than this: I mean the death there of the Duke of York, who was also Duke of Albany. Horace Walpole's letters reflect the popular emotion when it was known in England that the poor, good-humoured prince had ended his life at Monaco. He died of a chill caught after a ball, by travelling when he ought to have rested, and changed his linen. Though the cause of so much suffering and distress was childish enough, the Duke, when he saw his end approaching, met his fate with the greatest courage and serenity (September 17, 1767). He had the gift of sincerely attaching to his person all who served him; his servants could hardly listen with composure to his last orders, and the equerry, Mr. Wrottesley, who brought home the tidings, broke down completely. His host at Monaco did everything that a kind heart and a liberal hand could suggest, but the blow was not to be averted; and to this day a stately room, with heavy draperies and some good pictures, is known in the palace as 'the Duke of York's room.'

The direct line of the princes of Monaco hangs at present on the life of the one male heir, of the infant son of the Hereditary Prince by his marriage (since dissolved) with Lady Mary Hamilton. Should this line fail, the succession will again, as in the days of Louise-Hippolyte, Mademoiselle de Monaco, pass to an heiress: to H.S.H. the Princess Florestine, widow of the Duc d'Urach-Würtemberg.

CHAPTER XIX.

TWO FRENCH ADMIRALS.

'Fuimus Troes.'

THE baronies of St. Tropèz and of Briançon, from which the Bailli Suffren and the Comte Joseph de Grasse-Briançon took their titles, are both within a day's journey of Cannes. The first, so well known by its lighthouse, forms one of the headlands of the Bay of Grimaud; the second, in the mountains beyond Grasse, is a place of resort for its citizens during the great heat of summer. Both fiefs were in the fifteenth century, by an odd coincidence, appanages of the family of Grasse, but, in the eighteenth century, they belonged to the two best seamen of the best period of the French navy, to admirals who were found formidable antagonists by Hughes and Howe, Hood and Rodney.

The war of American Independence must be admitted to have been little less serious for the mother country than for her Transatlantic colonists, busied as they were in forming themselves into a confederacy of thirteen free states. It was perhaps the most dangerous war in which England ever engaged, for it forced great sacrifices upon her, and exposed her to the greatest perils by sea as well as by land. The European powers, according to their different instincts and interests, drew off into new affinities, but the attitude of France was, from the first, one of cordial sympathy with the rebels, as afterwards with the young republic of the West. New tactics were everywhere discussed. England had to change her old and received systems of commerce and of policy, and few perhaps suspected how the mutual relations of mankind were all so far involved as to be preparing everywhere for that far greater revolution that was soon to follow. Nowhere were the consequences of American democracy to be so fateful as in France; yet, in the first blush of the novelty, the Cabinet of Versailles was blind to the danger of influences imported from the West, and likely to cause its own overthrow. The French realised nothing in the dawn of American liberty but that pleasure which their ancient rivalry made them experience in any misfortune befalling the English. They were moreover eager to efface the stain which the Treaty of Paris (1763) had left on their own reputation as a great maritime power.

It has been argued that the Cabinet of Versailles ought, on the first hint of hostilities, to have forestalled the attack of the English, and this omission has been blamed. If it really was an error, it is certain that the omission was atoned for in those campaigns which lasted in both hemispheres from 1773–1783, when war was waged on us in the West as well as in the East Indies. Suffren's attack was all the more formidable because our position in India was already imperilled. Pondicherry had been wrested, it is true, from the French, but their troops had assisted Hyder Ali, and that tyrant had brought about a confederacy of native princes well calculated to annihilate British interests in India. The siege of Arcot, like Sir Eyre Coote's march on Vellore, shows how British energy and British strategy were both tasked by the enemy. Sir Edward Hughes was off the Coromandel coast with a fine fleet, but he was already opposed by the frigates of M. d'Orves, and it now only needed the appearance of a second French squadron to render the situation very threatening in the southern part of the peninsula.

That was what happened.

In March 1781, two French fleets cleared out of Brest. The one, commanded by the Comte Joseph de Grasse, was bound for the West Indian station, and would supplement the seven line-of-battle ships, which M. de Ternay had twelve months before taken across the Atlantic to raise the young courage of the United States of America. The other, commanded by Admiral Suffren, sailed to reinforce our enemies in India. It was also understood that a Spanish fleet should attack us at Gibraltar.

As Suffren's sails dip beneath the verge, let me pause for a moment to say a word about the sailor and the ships.

Pierre-André de Suffren, Baron of St. Tropèz, and Bailli of the Order of Malta, was a Provençal. If there be anything 'in a name,' this great sailor was destined to prove an exception to the rule which would see in the derivation of the word 'Suffren' a man predestined to reverses. The family belonged essentially to the *noblesse de robe*. It had had representatives in many parliaments of Aix, and it could boast of a certain Conseiller de Suffren greatly trusted by Henri IV., who appointed another Suffren confessor to his queen, Marie de Medicis. In spite of the legal traditions of this family, it was, in 1749, represented by two brothers, who had abjured both the bar and bench; by Jerome, afterwards Bishop of Sisteron, and by Pierre, who, choosing the navy for his profession, sailed with La Galissonière. At twenty years of age he entered the Order of St. John-of-Jerusalem, and enrolled himself as a member of that *Auberge de Provence* which had during centuries comprised members of every noble Provençal house. Suffren entered where a D'Agoult, a Caraman, a Forbin, and a Villeneuve had passed before him, and where a Mirabeau was to follow him. He knew all the recorded great names among the Commanders and *baillis* of Malta, and he was probably familiar with that Church of St. John which was appropriated in Aix to the devotions of the Knights of the *Auberge de Provence*. It remained for him to make his own name worthy of such companions, and we shall see how he contrived to shine as a star of the first magnitude.

His first brush with the English was at Port Mahon. In 1778 he sailed with D'Estaing, and distinguished himself off Rhode Island. His courage and sagacity were remarked, and it would have been better for D'Estaing if he had confided more in the advice then given him by the Marquis de Bouillé, and by this young Suffren, who then commanded the *Fantasque*. Off Grenada the bold Provençal also showed his mettle, and so gratified his admiral that he was recommended to the king for a pension of 1,500 *livres*, which was accordingly settled upon him. Suffren was a seaman of exceptional character, as brave as Nelson, and as rough as Benbow, and so popular with his sailors that to this day his quaint Provençal humour is remembered, and his sayings are repeated. A broadside became in his vocabulary ' a basket of Antibes figs,' and, in arranging an attack, he used to tell his boarding party ' to rub these English well with Aix oil.' These jokes were very popular, and it was assuredly with every wish to treat the English to both dainties that he cleared out of Brest in the spring of 1781. His men were as eager as he was himself, and it mattered not whether the enemy were Commodore Johnstone, with his convoy, in the chops of the Channel, or Sir Edward Hughes, far in the Indian Ocean. His own flag was flying on board the *Héros*, that 74-gun ship which he loved, which came to be considered as a synonym for himself, and on which, so full of years and of adventures, he ultimately returned to Toulon.

He fell in with Commodore Johnstone off Porto Praya, and, after a sudden attack and desperate fight, he was obliged, by an equally sudden retreat, to confess that he had undervalued his enemy and overrated the advantages of a surprise. Suffren's chief business was to watch the Cape of Good Hope, and, bearing this his paramount duty in mind, he sailed for False Bay, where his timely arrival preserved the Cape and its dependencies for Holland.

Sir Edward Hughes he did not meet till February 1782, and then in Madras Roads, when Suffren lost five prizes, a great deal of ammunition, and three hundred men of the regiment of Lausanne, taken on board the transport *Lauriston*. Eight of his best ships gave battle, and it was fortunate for the English that this overmastering force drew off after a change of wind. The next adventure of Suffren's came to him through no blows struck by himself. M. d'Orves died, and Suffren suddenly found himself in sole command of the French fleet. His course now lay to Babacolo, on the coast of Coromandel, and thence to Cuddalore, where he seemed able to grasp the realisation of Hyder Ali's dream. Might it not be possible for him to crush the English squadron, and to besiege Madras from the sea while the tyrant beleaguered it by land? One struggle succeeded to the other, for Sir Edward Hughes took the offensive, and pursued Suffren, till the latter, finding the wind in his favour, threw his whole force on the centre and rear of the English line. Bold as this measure seemed, it was not decisive. It was, however, so severe, that after it the two commanders were glad to lie for several days within sight of each other, repairing vessels that made a landsman speculate how crafts so damaged could possibly remain afloat. Hyder Ali owned to a great disappointment, for had Suffren only been able to sweep the English off the seas, he had hoped to reduce the whole of the Carnatic.

The English fleet had been in the meantime so thinned by sickness, that it is hardly possible to overrate the courage with which Sir Edward Hughes gave battle after battle to his great antagonist. They fought again in Pondicherry Roads, and from that engagement the

French admiral hoped for great things. Hughes, painfully aware that his seventeen ships were undermanned, was grateful to find that Suffren did not come into closer action, and so render their fifth battle more sanguinary. In truth, Suffren was not very well supported, and no man was ever less able to bear disappointment calmly. Was it for this that the *Héros* had worked her way across the infinite ocean, and exposed herself and her convoy to British shot and shell? He wrote home, 'My heart is broken by the most general desertion, so that I have lost my chance of destroying the British squadron. I had fourteen line-of-battle ships and the *Consolante*, but I assure you that only the *Héros*, the *Illustre*, and the *Ajax* fought close and in line. All, I say *all*, might have come close, but none did so. Yet several of these very men having fought bravely in other battles, I can only attribute this " *horror* " (*sic*) to a wish to close the campaign, or to ill-will, or to ignorance: for I cannot suppose anything worse! The result has been terrible. . . . Never, Monseigneur, could you imagine the tricks that have been tried here to get rid of me. I may have made mistakes—in war *who* does not make mistakes?—but I do not deserve those which have been imputed to me.'

Neither in truth did the subordinates of the bold Bailli de Suffren deserve all the blame that in his angry pain he heaped upon them. Some of the ships, being becalmed, could not, with the best will in the world, have taken up the posts which he would fain have seen them occupy. Among the officers who fought that day were men like La Pallière, the very flower of the French navy, seamen incapable of any baseness. But Suffren was inconsolable, and he remained so till, in June, he was able, between Novo and Gondelour, to score such a victory that Hughes had to withdraw. The situation of the British was so much altered for the worse by this last battle that Suffren felt as if he had now really fulfilled his task, and accomplished that result which had been for so many months both his morning prayer and his evensong. He was named lieutenant-general for the king; his name passed from mouth to mouth, and when he appeared at Port Louis the French colonists received him with alternate cries of '*Vive le roy!*' and '*Vive Suffren!*' The brave old man was gratified, but he was also cautious enough to exclaim, '*Gare les revers!*' So much popularity made him tremble for a reverse, yet it was with a pleasurable sense of labour rewarded that he dropped the anchor of the *Héros* once more in the roadstead of Toulon.

This Indian campaign had been, so to speak, the Bailli's personal work. The great distance between himself and Versailles had given such ample scope for his initiative genius, that he repeatedly acted in the teeth of the instructions sent out to him. Taking for his guide the circumstances which, as they arose, sufficed to suggest a policy to him, he had carried on the war with passion. As was but too certain to be the case, his subordinates, weary of so much zeal and enterprise, were sometimes laggard in carrying out his most brilliant conceptions. He himself never knew either fear or fatigue. Huge of stature, strong of sinew, full of passion and of a peremptoriness that was not without a tinge of brutality, he was also rash of speech, as became a Provençal, and he carried in his heart, along with the warmest patriotism, that love of glory which ought surely to be distinguished from the mere love of fame. Then jealousy springs so naturally in the human breast that Suffren, if unapproachable by rivals, yet came to have enemies. Nor can it be denied that when he was irritable he often confounded want of good will with that want of ability which is so common, but which is also quite unselfconscious, and of which he unavoidably met with examples in officers of mediocre talents.

His reception in Paris was of a nature to gratify him. He had truly deserved well of both king and country; and French vanity, wounded as it was by the defeat of the Comte de Grasse, was both able and willing to rejoice over the hero of Trincomalee. Suffren, already a Commander, and a Bailli of the Order of St. John-of-Jerusalem, was named the fourth vice-admiral of France, and he never had cause to complain of one of those reverses of public favour which his sagacity had anticipated. Only his old sailors did complain that their bold captain was lost to them, for he remained in Paris till his death, in 1788, when he was buried, as became a Bailli of Malta, in the Temple. To his man-of-war's-men, to his *pichoun* (children), as he had been wont to call them, Pierre de Suffren had for long been a gallant figure, filling at once the eye, the imagination, and the heart. There was in his character a something both pleasant and terrible which was fascinating for Provençal sailors. The result of this has been that to this day the ballads of the Provençal seaports sing his praises. They bewail that bold '*Baile Suffren*,' who was so terrible to the King of England, and who, after such a fine *chapladis* (carnage), most unfortunately

> Parti per Paris,
> E se vie marin jamai l'an piu revist—

His old seamen have never seen him more.

With Suffren there sailed many Provençals of noble birth. The navy was rich in them, and the Bailli had under him at different times a Forbin, a Villeneuve, a D'Adhémar, a Glandèves, a Castellane, a De Gazan, and a Coriolis-d'Espinouse. But of all French captains the one who, next to Suffren, centred in himself the hopes of the Cabinet, and the good wishes of the fleet, was the Comte de Grasse.

Joseph de Grasse-Briançon was six years younger than the Bailli. He belonged (through its fourth branch) to that great family of Grasse which Rhodoard, prince of Antibes, had founded about 950, but which had been extinct in the main line since 1725. His filiation to the original house of Grasse was in this wise:

> Jean de Grasse, 1499, married Catharine de Villeneuve,
> Antoine de Grasse, 1546, married Nicaise de Rassan,
> Jérôme de Grasse, 1597, married Jeanne de Calvi,
> Charles de Grasse, married Marie de Gucci,
> François de Grasse-Briançon, married Marguerite de Brun,
> François René de Grasse-Briançon, married Marie de Chailan,
> Admiral Joseph Paul de Grasse-Briançon, married in 1750 to Catharine de Castellane-de St. Juérs.

Many centuries of noble breeding, of intercourse with Italy, and of experience in the ranks of the Knights of Malta had served to form in Joseph de Grasse a proud and graceful man of the world. When he left

Brest in March 1781, though really only the *chef d'escadre*, he held the provisional commission of lieutenant-general for the king. His flag was carried by the *Ville de Paris*, that splendid 104-gun ship-of-the-line which the city of Paris, at a cost of 4,400,000 *livres*, built and gave to Louis XV., and which was for long considered to be the finest specimen of naval architecture in the world.

It is impossible to overrate the assistance which the Americans received at this juncture both from the troops of Rochambeau, and from the ships of the Comte de Grasse. A monument in York Town commemorates to this day, and in language which is not exaggerated, the repulse of Lord Cornwallis, and the exploits of the French fleet off the Chesapeake. Space would not allow me here to follow De Grasse through all the labours of that campaign to his attack on St. Kitts, and to his return to Martinique. We must pass at once to those preparations for the reduction of Jamaica which led to the appearance of Sir George Rodney, and to the great engagement off the north end of Dominica.

At seven o'clock on April 12, 1782, the hostile fleets met on opposite tacks, and the first French shot was fired into the *Marlborough* (Captain Penny).

The tale is one of extreme gallantry on both sides, but De Grasse made some mistakes which allowed Rodney to give him battle at very close quarters and thus to ruin the French ships by the fire of his carronades. Those short pieces, manufactured and invented by a private firm near Carron on the Forth, threw shot of 24 lbs. or 68 lbs. weight. In fact, the whole English broadside was to be feared, since its fire had lately become more sure and more rapid, thanks to some improvements in side-tackle, cartridges, and locks, to all of which Rodney and Sir Charles Douglas had devoted their attention.[1] The first shots, as I have said, were fired by the French, and from their seventh ship. Then the signal for close action was thrown out by Rodney, and the English ships ranged closely and slowly along the enemy's line, under their lee. The English flagship, the *Formidable*, fixed on the tenth ship, and kept edging in on their line, with a full sail. Drake's division did wonders, and the fire from the *Duke* and the *Canada*, along with the work of his own well-directed and really insupportable broadside, all enabled Rodney, after passing the *Ville de Paris*, to cut the French line between the second and third ships astern of De Grasse's flag. This bold manœuvre made victory secure for the inventor of it. Not content now with raking the four next French ships astern, the *Formidable* wore suddenly round on her heel, our whole van tacked, and our fleet was brought to windward of the enemy, on the same tack.

About a quarter past two the whole French fleet seemed to be disabled. But the Frenchmen would not yield. The *César* fought till her captain was killed, till her foremast was gone, and till there was not a yard of canvas on her that had not a shot-hole. The *Diadème* went down next, then the *Hector* struck,

---

[1] French ships, 34 ; English, 36 ; weight of French broadside, 28,191 lbs. ; weight of English, 22,163 lbs., not to speak of the carronades.

and next the *Ardent*, but at a quarter to six the *Barfleur* (Sir S. Hood) stood on to the *Ville de Paris*. The Comte de Grasse, not less brave than his captains, had been already nearly wrecked by the fire of the *Canada*, and he had endured for four hours the anguish of seeing the rout and ruin of his matchless fleet. He seemed only to have waited to have the honour of yielding to the flag of a rear-admiral, and after ten minutes more of the carronades he struck.

When Lord Cranstown was sent on board with a complimentary message he found the Admiral of the fleet, a tall, pale man, standing between the two other men who were left alive on the quarter-deck. Heaps of dead and dying lay around them, and the English officer, as he stepped up to receive De Grasse's sword, noticed that he walked over his own shoe-buckles in blood, for only the setting of the sun closed a battle which for more than eleven hours had raged with unremitting fury.

It was calculated that the French lost not less than a quarter of their total numbers; but, desperate as the action had been for them, the English only lost seventy-three men, and Lord Robert Manners, who died of his wounds, was perhaps the greatest loss Rodney had to deplore. And now the far-famed *Ville de Paris*, with her Admiral, her standard of France, and her treasure-chest of 500,000 *livres*, was in the hands of a seaman who had known how to convert the advantages under which he undoubtedly went into action into this decisive victory. His splendid prize, the finest that was ever taken from an enemy, could not carry a stitch of canvas on her shattered spars. She had eighty-four shots in her hull, but she was towed into Jamaica, where the sailors of Hood and Rodney joyed over her; though, after they had visited her, they reported the celebrated prize as dirty, ill-disciplined, and lumbered. Her Admiral came on board the English flagship on the morning after the battle. An eyewitness, who breakfasted with him, described the Comte de Grasse as 'affable and fairly communicative.' His victor-host, Sir George Rodney, who had spent some years of his life in France, and had once been offered service by the French king, spoke French fluently, and the Comte de Grasse made him the confidant of his grievances. He even told how he fired into one or two of his own ships during the engagement, because their captains provoked him by their apparent pusillanimity and mismanagement. By them, he added, he had been prevented, '*comme vous voyez*,' from completing his career in the West Indies by the reduction of Jamaica.

If De Grasse had contented himself with blaming his subordinates at the breakfast-table of the *Formidable*, it would have been better for him. But facts came to be sifted before a royal commission (appointed to sit at Orient on the officers under his command), and there many of the accusations formally lodged by the Admiral were ordered to be erased. Nine-tenths of his complaints proved to be without foundation, while they were especially calumnious of the brave De Vaudreuil. The Admiral never returned to his Provençal home, yet the two years of his absence from France might have been quietly spent in England, where his gallantry and his high-breeding rendered him a most acceptable guest, had De Grasse not unfortunately preferred to spend them in futile recriminations, and in demands for a fresh appeal before new judges. The Government, having once closed the subject, declined to reopen it, and the naval authorities hoped that the vanquished Admiral would end in accepting the facts, and therefore cease from pamphlets which could neither soothe his own sorrows, nor yet restore the beautiful *Ville de Paris* to her place in the navies of France. The king at last, weary of the unpalatable topic, sent to tell De Grasse that, though willing to suppose the Admiral had done his best at Dominica, he was not disposed to extend his royal indulgence to those complaints which had been lodged against the officers of his navy, and that he should therefore forbid the Comte de Grasse to appear at his court. This sentence, and the laurels of Suffren, must have been great trials to a man of De Grasse's temper. He died in Paris in 1788, not much regretted by his comrades, and nowhere better remembered than in the country where he was once a prisoner, and where his conduct on the quarter-deck of his fine flagship is still one of the classical incidents of naval history. Rodney's sailors were for years wont to discuss how it had been possible for an officer so far above the ordinary height to fit himself into the cabin of a ship, even into the stern-cabin of the splendid *Ville de Paris*.

CHAPTER XX.

CANNES AS IT WAS.

'We lay at Cañes, which is a small port in the Mediterranean. . . . The soil about the country is rocky, full of pines, and rare simples. . . . Here we agreed with a seaman to carry us to Genoa.'—EVELYN'S *Memoirs*, vol. i. A.D. 1644.

'The heavenly blue sea, stretching so far and wide, is in accordance with one's feelings, and the beauties of Nature have always something comforting and soothing.'—*Letter of Alice, Grand Duchess of Hesse*, Cannes, Dec. 14, 1869.

IT is difficult for me to describe the place in which I habitually live, where the winters succeed each other, but do not resemble each other, either in their weather or in their social pleasures. Here everything changes from day to day; and if the dying come here to live, the living, alas! come to die. Here four Piedmontese workmen will in four weeks make a rock disappear, while twenty-four such labourers will in four months build a barrack four storeys high. Here the valleys get filled up, and the eucalyptus tree grows ten feet in the year; here the poor suddenly grow rich by speculation, and the rich grow poor, thanks not only to speculation, but to the excessive cost of living.

Everyone will find in Cannes what he looks for, or puts into it. The visitor may live in a boat, or through a succession of morning visits. He may either go to picnics, or lie in a balcony; he may explore the mountains, or hire a studio; drive a team of miniature ponies, or ride on a donkey. He may dance cotillons, or sing psalms, or look for trapdoor spiders; he may live on the shore, or among the resinous firs on the hill; he may learn languages, and play on divers instruments; he may flirt and quarrel; or he may, which is far more difficult, seek peace and ensue it. In short, Cannes has so many aspects, that I will not describe the winter city which everyone visits, but rather leave it to the guide-books to tell you its latitude and its longitude, and to the medical works to reassure you as to its mean winter temperature.

Let us rather try to reconstruct old Cannes.

The best way to see its real outlines is to take a boat, and go a couple of kilomètres out to sea. Then the little bay, and the group of masonry and towers on the Mont Chevalier, are sharply defined, and we can see that old Cannes, which never quite filled the space between the Riou[1] and the Foux, was crowned by a castle that was as nearly as possible square.

The fief of Cannes belonged, as I have already had occasion to mention, to the Abbots of the Lérins, whose castle occupied the site of a Roman encampment. In classical records the place was called Egitna, and when the inhabitants were frightened away by the barbarians, they removed to a hill which is still called *Mons-Egitna* (Mougins), and where till quite recently the beauty of the men and women was supposed to have descended to them from the primitive type. In mediæval records the place was called *Castrum-*

---

[1] The word '*Riou*' means a stream or rivulet; on the other side of Fréjus it becomes '*Réal.*' Is this the same as our 'rill'?

Francum, and as such the Berengers, counts of Provence and of Barcelona, spoke of it when Edward the Confessor was king of England. A certain abbot, Adelbert II., was moved in 1070, to begin the great, square tower which still commemorates his prudence : for all beaches were insecure in those days, and from the very Arabs whom they dreaded, the Provençals (like the Genoese) had learned to build such an *Al Menàra*, to serve as fire-beacon, watch-tower, and stronghold in time of siege. Its foundations were laid in 1070, but the Abbot did not live to complete it, and his successors, either less rich or less spirited, neglected a work which both the Pope and the Berengers encouraged. It was not finished for more than two centuries, when the Abbot Jean Tournefort completed it in 1393. Evidently from its masonry, the work of Italian, probably of Pisan builders, it was originally (like many of the towers at Albenga and other places of the Ligurian coast) crenelated, and till 1829, when the lightning split it, it retained its ornaments. The tower of the castle, which now forms the belfry of the parish church, is of later workmanship, and there was at one time another tower, called La Béronde, which was lower, and nearer to the beach. The destruction of the villages of Arluc (Mont St. Cassien) and Mandelieu favoured the early growth of Cannes ; but the monks, in return for the protection afforded by their towers, drew heavy dues from the Cannois. Every time a bit of land changed hands the Abbot exacted a *fisc*. The peasants might gather acorns for their pigs, but flour must be ground at the convent mills, and wine, oil, figs, tunny, and hemp were all taxed. The population consisted of peasants, fisherwomen, pilgrims, and pirates; the procession on St. Honorat's Day was apt to end in a fight, and the citizens had leave to wear swords, '*comme il est d'usage dans les lieux maritimes suspects.*'

Till the close of the Middle Ages the history of Cannes is that of its Abbots, and though the town, ever since 1447, possessed a municipality, that was quite overshadowed by the Superior who wore the Benedictine habit. Of its sufferings during the wars of Francis I. I have had occasion to speak in another place. Charles V. came here twice, and the inn in the Suquet where he lay was only removed a few years ago to make room for the present Hospice de la Ville.

The most fatal year that ever passed over Cannes was 1580. It is three hundred years since a woman was landed there from a levantine. She died of the plague, but not before she had propagated an infection which spread from town to town, and which cost Marseilles more than twenty thousand lives. The burial grounds of the Great Plague are still spoken of in Cannes, and when the huge boulevards of the Société Foncière were cut, there were old men who shook their heads and hoped that no harm might come of stirring ground which had not been turned since 1580.

The League was the union formed by the Catholic party to defend their own interests, and those of Catholicism, against the pretensions of the Huguenots, the incapacity of Henry III., and the claims of his heir, Henry of Navarre. The *parlement* of Provence declared for the League, and, to clench the matter, named as its future king, Charles de Bourbon, then Abbot-commendatory of the Lérins.

In the war that followed, Cannes was successively occupied by the troops of the royalists and by the Leaguers, and also by those of that Duke of Savoy, to whom the Leaguers, on the death of Henry III., had actually offered the kingdom. We know how at last the sword of Lesdiguières turned the balance in favour of the royalist party; but many brave Provençals bit the ground, and many a soul left the body, and many a wife became a widow, ere Henri IV. was duly acknowledged; and Cannes, in particular, was so sacked by the Duke of Savoy, that there was little left in it worth preserving.

'*A quelque chose tout malheur est bon*,' says the proverb; and the Cannois, to test the truth of the saying, thought this time of war and tumult an auspicious moment for trying to free themselves from the monks. They were only partially successful, but the town and its trade revived, the big parish church was built, and men hoped for a time of prosperity. It never came. At the close of the Thirty Years' War the Spaniards invested Ste. Marguerite, and had to be repulsed; all the '*noblesse et milice de Provence*' being assembled round Cannes: their leader, M. de Harcourt, having his headquarters in the district of Montfleury. This is what Evelyn refers to: 'We touched at the islands of Ste. Marguerite and St. Honoré, so lately taken from the Spaniards with great bravery by the Prince of Harcourt.'

During the war of the Spanish Succession, the army

Y

of Prince Eugene marched on Cannes. Auribeau was invested, a camp formed at Biot, and Grasse was sacked. Next came the war with Maria-Theresa, when, in 1746, Hungarian troops appeared at Antibes, and struck terror into every heart. As General Brown made his headquarters first at Vence and then at Biot, legends of his Croats long lingered in all the villages on the Loup. The inhabitants of Cannes fled to the islands, but were driven back to the mainland by some English ships. The town, according to a curious MS. account of it which exists, then held 3,000 inhabitants, and it had a hospital, worked by Capucin monks, on a site where the street called 'of the Capucins' now stands. Monseigneur Mesgrigny, the then Bishop of Vence, belonging himself to that Order, gave the friars leave to establish themselves, and M. de Vendôme, Abbot-commendatory of the Lérins, sanctioned their presence. The document which treats of this, and of other local and contemporary matters, adds, '*Cannes deviendra dans la suite une ville considérable,*' and the words were prophetic, though a century had to elapse before the prophecy was justified by events.

The churches at that time existing were the parish church on the Mont Chevalier, the twelfth-century chapel of Ste. Anne, which is next to the great tower, the chapel of St. Pierre, from which the quay takes its name, and Notre Dame-de-Bon-Voyage, standing among the sandy *dunes*, rather to the eastward of a town which was then bounded by the Grasse road. On the farther side of that road was the chapel of St. Esprit, and the Hospital. Above the town was the chapel of St. Nicholas, and off

ST. CLAUDE DU CANNET.

the Cannet road that of St.-Claude, afterwards turned into an oil mill. Cannet was a hamlet, or rather a group of hamlets, built by the Italian colonists whom the monks put in to till their lands. A rough road led across the hills from it to Vallauris, which was the summer residence of the monks, and where they had fine vineyards.

The families belonging to Cannes had the names which the Berengers knew, and with which we are ourselves now familiar. There were Rostan, Arluc, and Calvi, and Bertrand, and Ardisson, and Isnard, and Jordany, and with all this a bold spirit among the seafaring folk.

Such was Cannes when Masséna knew it, and there the son of the Jewish shopkeeper, the future Duc de Rivoli, Prince d'Essling, wooed his first love, Mademoiselle Lamar, the chemist's daughter. Such was Cannes when Pius VII. passed through it as a prisoner, and when Buonaparte, as a general of brigade, cut the best oaks on Mont St. Cassien to make gun-carriages. The Cannois must have seen with disgust that destruction of their 'holy shade;' in fact, the commerce of the place was ruined by the wars of the Empire, so that Napoleon was unpopular both before and after his appearance in Cannes in 1815.

Notwithstanding that unpopularity, Murat, when driven out of Naples by the Austrians, was not afraid to land and to live here for some weeks. Marshal Brune came here to confer with him, and there are men still alive who can remember those two ill-fated soldiers pacing the quay together, and talking of many things, unconscious of the tragic fate which awaited the one in Italy and the other at Avignon. I have also heard how Murat gave a moonlight ball to the fishers of Cannes, on the beach before the Hôtel Penchinat, where he lodged. He noticed that a young girl was crying, and on asking her what was the cause of her tears, she said that her engagement ring had fallen off her hand in dancing, and was now lost in the sand. Murat drew a diamond ring off his own finger, and placed it on hers. It was his last kingly act, for Murat sailed from Cannes next day, and landing at Pizzo on the Calabrian coast, was apprehended and shot.

Modern Cannes is justly grateful to Lord Brougham. He was the first to buy land here, and to suggest to delicate women, and to men grown old in public life, that life might be prolonged, and death made less dreary on this beautiful shore. That was in 1836; but, in truth, Cannes owes nearly as much to the persons who followed his example so promptly, to Sir Herbert Taylor (1837), to Mr. Leader (1838), and, above all, to Mr. Woolfield. His practical good sense and liberality have made a new world grow out of a bed of flowers. But these constructions all lay to the westward of the old town, and M. Tripét-Skrypetzine was the first (1850) to recognise the charms of the quarter that now slopes, laden with mimosas, from the hills to the eastern bay.

The fortune of Cannes had risen above the horizon, but it could not be complete till a railway and a supply of excellent water came to secure its prosperity and its health. Cannes is now a place of more than 14,000 inhabitants; it has its hotels, its pleasure-boats, its

CANNES AT SUNSET.

studios, its potteries, its club, its gardens, and, above all, its beautiful villas. The villa Dognin is a *chef-d'œuvre*, but the excessive price of land in Cannes is the reason why none of the houses, except the Châteaux de Thorenc and de St.-Michel, have very extensive grounds. There is nothing here like the parks of Baron Derveis or of the late Mr. Edward Cazalet at Brancolar, or like the terraces of Baron Haussmann on the Villefranche road. The three most extensive gardens in Cannes are those of the Château St.-George, of the Villa Victoria (with its splendid *Bougainvillia*), and of Villa Montfleuri, where on a day in March I counted sixty-three different kinds of plants in full flower. These, like the gardens of the Duchesse de Luynes, are always kept in the most exquisite order. Not a leaf here is out of place, while round the Château Leader there stretches a wild, rough piece of ground, part garden, part jessamine farm, redolent of perfumes, and also of a truly Provençal neglect. As to the Villa Vallombrosa, I have never made up my mind which of its aspects pleases most—its gorgeous flower-beds on a May morning, or its appearance by lamplight. The palms then throw their fantastic and multitudinous shadows on the sward, a fountain lifts its tall, white column into the moonlight, and as the roses fling themselves from tree to tree you expect to see, dancing among their ropes of flowers, the elves of some 'Midsummer Night's Dream.' I speak only of the exteriors of these villas. Of what is to be found inside them it would be a breach of good manners if I were to speak, or to discuss here some of the kindest of my friends. Suffice it to say that Cannes has the best, the most varied and the most cosmopolitan society in Europe. If the place has been spoiled it is only owing to the number of its admirers, who, so to speak, kill it with kindness, since they cause the overgrowth of what was once a primitive little place. Yet even this defect has its good side. Cannes is so big that you can now live in it where you please, and as you please. If there are fewer lanes, and woods, and country walks, the dairies and the shops have improved, drainage has made some progress, and a body of medical men of the highest character and ability has been attracted by this vast concourse of patients, who are of all classes, as they are of all kindreds and tongues.

CHAPTER XXI.

NAPOLEON AT CANNES, March 1815.

> 'He either fears his fate too much
> Or his deserts are small,
> Who fears to put it to the touch
> To win or venture all.'—THE MARQUIS OF MONTROSE.

> 'Si Napoléon n'eût écouté que l'intérêt de l'humanité, la voix de la France, et son devoir envers elle, il eût sans doute reculé devant l'affreuse pensée de la précipiter dans les horreurs d'une nouvelle guerre. Mais cette fois encore l'intérêt personnel et l'ambition endurcirent son cœur, mirent un voile sur ses yeux et sur sa conscience.'—E. DE BONNECHOSE.

THE Golfe Jouan is one of the best roadsteads on the French coast. I have seen as many as eleven ironclads lying within musket-range of the shore. It is said that the Roman galleys trusted themselves to its deep and land-locked waters, and that the ruins called *Les Crottons* indicate the existence of some maritime station now sanded up and forgotten.

Between Antibes and Leghorn, in the spring of 1815, an English ship of war was supposed to watch the station, and to control the movements of the exile in Elba. But it is always the unexpected that happens. Napoleon, in Porto Ferrajo, was wont to complain that the annual subsidy of two millions assigned to him by the treaty of last April, was not fairly paid. However that may have been, he was not without friends and assuredly not without funds. Money and letters reached him in parcels of gloves, a trade which Dumoulin of

Grenoble had recently started with a view to the Emperor's interests, and to the convenience of Eméry, the Emperor's doctor, a Dauphinois of some influence in his native province. The money thus supplied furnished three brigs, some volunteers, and a small military chest, and thus equipped the Emperor sailed from Porto Ferrajo at a moment when he had reason to know that the English cruiser was lying at Leghorn, and that the commanding officer was amusing himself in Florence.

The sun of the 1st of March, 1815, had passed the meridian when the *Inconstant* and her convoy dropped their anchors in the roadstead of Golfe Jouan. A low range of pine-clad hills encircles the bay, and a hedge of roses and aloes runs down almost to meet the little wooden jetty. There, with a few charcoal burners and fisher-folk, and a couple of coastguardsmen to stare at him, Napoleon landed: to test the popularity of his person and of his dynasty in France. Without an hour's delay Eméry started off by the Vallauris road, despatched alone and on foot to make his way to Grenoble. In nearly as short a time a picket of men was marched to Antibes, and commanded to order the allegiance of General Corsin; which he refused. Meanwhile Cambronne, with twenty-five men of the Old Guard, were on their way to Cannes. He had orders to ask for a printing press, and to requisition both food and horses. The Emperor himself remained under the olive trees, and spreading his maps on the ground, he abandoned himself to some hours of silent meditation, till the red light of sunset had begun to glow on that white mountain range which here seems to mount guard over the coast of France.

I have said that it is always the unexpected that happens, yet, in very truth, this escape from Elba was not a surprise to every Frenchman. An enigmatical saying had been passing freely from mouth to mouth in Paris, 'that the *violet* would return with the spring.' The Imperialist party had its correspondents in Chambéry and in Grenoble, Miollis, who commanded at Aix in Provence, was warmly attached to his old leader, and many good judges like Savary prophesied, ' we shall see Buonaparte again.' Talleyrand was at Vienna, but Jaucourt, the acting minister of foreign affairs, wrote to him from Paris, ' Everything is in a false and unfortunate position, and *there is much to fear from the man.*' The hour had come, and the man!

In 1815, Cannes consisted of the few dark streets that clustered under the Mont Chevalier. It had its little port, and behind that, in the bay looking to the Esterels, the one small inn there called of ' Saint Pierre,' from a chapel on the quay.

The *Mairie* was in the middle of the Cours, now called the Rue Centrale, and next door to the *Mairie* was the public, or Communal School. The space in front of these houses was planted with elm trees, the last of which only disappeared five years ago. On a bench, close to the window of that school, a boy sat, slate in hand. It was Master Sardou, now the most genial and charming of Provençals, and the father of Victorien Sardou, but then a boy ten years of age. He was supposed to be following the arguments of a teacher who, at the farther end of the schoolroom, and with his back to his scholars, was working a sum in simple division on a black board.

The 'malady of not marking,' from which all schoolboys suffer, does not of course affect sights and sounds outside the temple of learning; so Master Sardou became aware first of a strange noise, and then of a stranger sight. Five-and-twenty grenadiers, with *queues* and tall fur caps, were drawn up before the Mairie, and an orderly was tying to one of the elm trees the horse from which an officer had just dismounted. What might this portend? Master Sardou and a companion slipped out of the room to judge for themselves; their example was immediately followed by every boy in the class; and when the pedagogue finished his sum and turned round, he was alone! No doubt he followed his truants, and soon also heard the amazing news—Napoleon was coming, and Cambronne had come, and had just asked for the Mayor of Cannes!

M. Reybaud happened to be out of town for the day. He had gone forth to see his vineyard, and the spring sap at work in his almond trees; and only after the bells of the big, sombre *paroisse* had rung to *couvre-feu*, did he make his way back into Cannes. As he walked down the hill, he was startled by meeting a *gendarme* with a tricolor cockade. The mayor was convinced of the stability of the government of the Bourbons, and discretion is a real proof of valour, so he settled in his own mind that this offender was tipsy, and, whistling to his dog, he looked hard the other way. But before long he met another tricolor cockade, and then another, and finally, he saw, rising from the sandy *dunes*, behind the chapel of Notre Dame-de-Bon-Voyage, the smoke of a great fire. Cambronne requested him to declare his allegiance to the Emperor Napoleon. M. Reybaud replied that he had, and that he could acknowledge, but one master, His Majesty Louis XVIII.; that, Cannes affording no printing press, it could not be a question of printing any proclamations, loyal or treasonable; that the whole commune could not produce the five hundred rations demanded, and that there were no horses in the district. At that moment a pair of horses did actually arrive in Cannes. The Prince of Monaco, reinstated by the consent of Europe in his estates, was travelling post to Monaco. Him Cambronne's soldiers arrested, and they would probably have seized on his horses had not Napoleon given orders to allow the Prince to proceed. But, before continuing his journey, he was to have an interview with the Emperor, whom he found on the shore, and in rather an irritable mood. '*Où allez-vous?*' asked Napoleon. '*Chez moi*,' was the equally curt reply. '*Dame! et moi aussi*,' retorted the first speaker, and turned his back on the traveller.

By this time the night had fallen.

M. Sardou has told me that the Cannois slept but little that night; Cambronne and Drouot had ridden away, up the Grasse road, with a couple of hundred men, and the whole interest centred round the bivouac on the shore. M. Sardou and M. Barbe both confess how they stole down to the beach to see the show. Of the Old Guard, Napoleon had 400 men, besides 400 grenadiers, 200 Corsican chasseurs, and 100 Polish lancers unmounted. There were also four field-guns, and two mortars from the *Inconstant*. A military chest had been placed to leeward of the camp fire, and on this the Emperor was seated, moody, taciturn, and preoccupied. His chin rested on his breast; he wore his overcoat; and as the flames rose and fell, he would every now and again give an impatient kick with his foot to the blazing brands that rolled towards him. The night, though fine and starry, was chilly. It was also very nearly a fatal one to the Emperor. Out of the Grande Rue, under cover of the darkness, there stole down a native of Cannes who carried an old fowling-piece. He was a butcher, a man of the name of Bertrand, one who, during the ill-starred monarchical rising of 1812, in the South, had had to suffer for his opinions. He detested the smooth-haired Corsican, and at midnight went out to have a shot at the man who, having once already turned the world upside down, had now returned from exile to dispute the throne with the Bourbons. Bertrand rested his gun on a fence, not many yards from the head of which the pale and clear-cut features stood out in the light of the blazing bivouac fire. One moment more and the Emperor's midnight watch would have been his last; one shot, and there might have been no Waterloo, and no St. Helena! But the butcher was arrested by a neighbour, not out of any sympathy with the Buonapartes, but from an impression that were Napoleon to be murdered at midnight, Cannes would be burnt down before midday.

At 2 A.M. the Emperor was in the saddle. M. Reybaud, the mayor, met him at the angle of the Grasse road (where De Bray's shop now stands), '*Où est la route de Grasse?*' asked Napoleon. '*Sire, vous y êtes,*' answered the mayor. '*Quelle heure avez-vous?*' he next asked,

WEST CANNES.

and by the starlight M. Reybaud read the figures on the dial-plate of his watch, and replied '*Deux heures.*' The Emperor drew out his watch, looked at it, repeated the words '*deux heures,*' dropped the watch back into its pocket, gave his horse's bridle a sharp pull, and disappeared from the mayor's sight without another syllable of leave-taking. The ground which rises immediately behind the Grande Rue was then covered with the pine wood of which only two fragments exist, in the *bosquet* of the Villa Rey, and in the clump of trees opposite the gate of the Villa Jessie. The Emperor had placed the military chest in the centre of his little force, of which the Corsican Chasseurs brought up the rear, and in this order they marched up to Grasse, General Bertrand (the same who went with him to St. Helena) riding by his side. Napoleon's mother used often to say of him that ' he had feeling enough to wish that he *had* a heart,' yet to-night, when he rode as silently as if he were indeed what M. de Boufflers called him, ' *the nightmare of the world,*' he must, surely, as the moon showed all the undulating landscape in its sombre monochrome, have asked himself which was the dream— his former glory, his months of abasement in Elba, or this hazardous march under the fast hurrying stars?

Grasse was reached at the dawn. Drouot and Cambronne had already set the printer to work, and thrown off a good many copies of the Emperor's proclamation which, as yet, had only existed in MS. I have seen one of these copies, noteworthy from its arbitrary and magniloquent tone, and also from the fact that the printer of Grasse was too wary to print his own name on the sheet.

Frenchmen were too cautious to commit themselves as yet to any sympathy with the enterprise.

Most cautious and sore perplexed was General Gazan, the commander at Grasse. He had served with Napoleon in Egypt: was he now to have the courage of his opinions, or of his responsibility to Louis XVIII.? He took counsel, as men ought always to do, with his wife, and she advised him to feign absence. Accordingly, when Drouot rang at their door, only Madame Gazan appeared. She was a Swiss, and she assured the Imperial messenger curtly that ' *le Shénèral*' was not in town! The troops under Gazan's orders did not move, but Napoleon, warned by the butcher's attempt on his life in Cannes, marched out of Grasse, and went some distance into the country before he halted for breakfast. Three cypresses, on the brow of a hill overhanging the cascade and the old lazar house, mark the spot where he spent an hour. Our friend M. Frédéric Pérolle, of Grasse, tells me that his father saw the Emperor there, seated on a sort of throne of knapsacks which his guard had arranged for him, and that the depression and irritability of the night seemed all to have vanished. Daylight had brought a return of confidence in his destiny, and in the fortune which had befriended him so often since the days when Madame Letitia lived near him at Antibes, and since he used to be the friend of Ricord, and the frequent guest of the younger Robespierre, at St. Césaire. The whole district was in truth well known to Napoleon, so well known that, looking at the snow-covered mountain range behind St. Césaire, he determined to abandon his guns.

No doubt, when those six pieces had first been landed at Golfe Jouan he had joyed over their possession, and their appearance on the Cours of Cannes had already caused a terrifying report to be carried along the coast, that the Emperor, with artillery, and at the head of an army, was marching upon Toulon. They had been effective in fiction, but in reality it would be impossible to drag them over the snowy roads and round the craggy defiles of limestone that guard the sources of the Siagne. Abandoned therefore they were; the Polish lancers, already encumbered with their saddles, being especially thankful for their disappearance.

Great difficulties and great natural obstacles were in store for this little army, and while Napoleon dined and slept that night under the roof of Madame de Villeneuve-Mouans, at Séranon, France had awoke to the surprise. We know that when the tidings were first taken to Toulon, they must have been very heavy tidings to Masséna, but in Nice a feeling of curiosity existed that was not to be gratified till after nightfall. A friend has told me how he remembers having been taken as a child, by his parents, to a picnic at the Cap St. Jean, and that his betters were much preoccupied that day by the appearance of three brigs, with troops on board, making for the Cap Garoube. That the vessels in question were the *Inconstant* and her convoy they only learnt when, long after dark, the Prince of Monaco drove up to the hotel in the Place St. Dominique, which was then the centre of the fashionable quarter in Nice, and narrated how he had just had an interview with the Emperor.

Little by little the fact of his landing became an

open secret, but there were few, if any, expressions of sympathy. Napoleon was unpopular throughout the south, and he would have to go as far as Digne, where a brother of General Miollis[1] filled the episcopal chair, before he met with any warm supporters of his cause. Only some old soldiers crept stealthily to his ranks, out of Mougins and other villages, glad to hail again the eagles of their old, victorious leader. Yet Napoleon was uneasy, and when on the second day of his march he reached the town of Castellane, on the Verdon, he sent to the Mairie to have two blank passports drawn and given to him. In case of a reverse these were meant to facilitate his own escape, and that of Cambronne, through the Alpine passes into Italy.

[1] Monseigneur Miollis was the saintly and single-hearted prelate from whom Victor Hugo sketched the figure of Monseigneur Bienvenu for his *Misérables*. He was curé of Brignolles, and very poor when Napoleon, at his brother's request, named him to the vacant see of Digne. The letter signifying his elevation was handed to him when working in his garden in a ragged *soutane*. He said that he expected no letters because he never wrote any, and as for this one, of which the postage cost 'trente sous,' he utterly declined to receive it; 'Where,' he asked, 'should I find other thirty sous for my poor?' and it was long before he could be convinced of the change in his worldly circumstances. Though Victor Hugo has made a slightly caricatured portrait of this excellent man, it must not be forgotten that the bishop really rescued from want and crime a miserable convict who had tried to rob him. The real 'Jean Valjean' when reclaimed was sent to serve under General Miollis in Egypt. He was in Digne and on half-pay when Napoleon passed through in March 1815. He then re-enlisted, and fell at Waterloo. The Bishop's chaplain, who only died a few years ago in Grasse, was aware of the details of this story, and took pleasure in telling it. Monseigneur Miollis, who literally gave all his goods to feed the poor, and who traversed his alpine diocese on a donkey, is by no means forgotten in the grave where he lies in front of the high altar of his cathedral at Digne.

On the morning of the 5th of March such Parisians as perused the *Nain Jaune* read a letter which complained of 'having as yet written all in vain with a goose-quill, *mais peut-être serai-je plus heureux avec une plume de cane: j'en essayerai.*' Here was another enigmatical saying, and evidently penned by some one already in the secret. But to the government the matter was still dark, and only at 1 P.M. did Chappe receive the message from the General in Lyons, to whose duty it had fallen to forward Masséna's first telegraphic announcement of the landing. M. de Vitrolles has told us how the king's gouty fingers were unable to tear open the fatal message, and what preparations were immediately commenced to check the march of the invader. Louis certainly showed great *sangfroid*; perhaps he hardly realised at first the immensity of his peril, and, indeed, it was generally thought that Napoleon would go into Italy, and there put himself at the head of the Neapolitan army. But Napoleon had for long been sounding the feelings of the French troops, and what he really intended to do was to put his fortune at the mercy of the regiments collected in Dauphiny. Grenoble lay before him, and on the temper of the large garrison collected there must depend his success or his ruin. Grenoble would make of him Cæsar, or nothing.[1]

[1] This is not the place in which to follow the Emperor's march beyond the limits of the Maritime Alps. An account of his arrival at Grenoble, compiled, as these pages have been, from the lips of witnesses, may be found in the *Edinburgh Review*, vol. cciv., under the heading of the article 'Dauphiny.'

CHAPTER XXII.

OFF THE BEATEN TRACK.

'Il y a toujours profit à sortir des routes battues.'—J. AMPÈRE.

I. NOTRE DAME DE LAGHET.

'E vidi, e piansi il fato amaro.'

To reach Laghet you must turn to the left before entering the village of Turbia. The whole ground is one vast vineyard, an amphitheatre of terraces supporting vines. I counted eighty-two terraces below the road, while above its level thirty-one crept up the face of the steep limestone hills which encircle the village of Turbia. The *turris via* from which it takes its time-honoured name, the great trophy of Augustus, commands a neck, or passage, among these rocky defiles. Down below you can hear the surf breaking on the beach, and on the sighing wind come little veils of mist which envelope you for a few moments, blurr all the landscape, and then scud away to leave you again in sunshine, and near the foot of the tower which an emperor built, and which Marshal Berwick blew up. He must have been a very poor archæologist, for his explosion not only split and dismantled the tower, but it also shivered the inscription which recorded how Cæsar Augustus conquered the tribes. Of the fragments only twelve pieces have been recovered by an age that does set some store on its monuments; ten pieces were sent to the museum of St. Germains, one is at Nice, and the twelfth, which used to exist at Turbia, has disappeared. The trophy stood beside the Imperial highway. Almost immediately after taking leave of that highway, you drop into the ravine of Perdiguière, to follow, for the distance of two kilomètres, the line of the old *Via Julia*. The convent of Laghet stands on a rocky promontory between two glens, and is approached by a bridge of one arch. The whole place has a thoroughly Italian look. The cloisters are bare and gloomy, and echo to your footfall; and to-day, the great gilded church is empty; only the neat garden that slopes to the torrent shows that there are still some inmates in this once famous convent of the barefoot Carmelites, at the shrine of Our Lady of Laghet. The walls are gay with garlands of *ex-votoes*, with silver hearts and wooden crutches, to say nothing of such a terrifying collection of pictures of 'carriage accidents,' that only a just confidence in the cheery, little Breton ponies that had brought us over from Nice, prevented me from feeling nervous for the rest of the day. On Christmas and on Trinity Sunday, and on the feasts of the Virgin, crowds flock to this place; yet I think there must be a little exaggeration in the numbers stated to swell the processions. That fifty-two processions may have occurred in two months is possible, but that two thousand persons were present on fifty-two occasions seems incredible, when one thinks how desolate are some of the districts between Nice and the Italian frontiers.

The wonder-working statue dates from 1662, when a certain Giacinto Casanova, of Nice, thought it would be right to replace a worm-eaten, little, wooden statue of the Virgin, which is now built into the wall behind its robed and crowned successor. The princes of the House of Savoy have always had a singular devotion to Our Lady of Laghet; the silver lamps are their gift, and, as such, they still burn before an altar connected with the saddest hour in Charles-Albert's life, with his last Communion in Italy.

The demands of the Liberal party had forced him to take up first the questions of constitutional reform, and then of war with Austria, both of which had remained in abeyance during the last years of King Charles-Félix. The new king was a sort of Murad the Unlucky. Everything to which he put his hand failed; the very skies made war on him; and tempests and cholera ravaged a country he did his utmost to govern according to progressive ideas.

The '*Statuto*' which he granted at Turin in July 1848 excited an almost delirious joy among his own subjects, and a contagious enthusiasm. Mentone and Roquebrune, revolting from a Prince of Monaco who scoffed at a '*Statuto*,' joined themselves to Piedmont, and the noise of their rejoicings, as they spread into Lombardo-Venetia, increased the discontent against the Austrian rule. Horace Vernet has done a great picture of Charles-Albert, riding his charger, while drenching rain-clouds are seen to sweep across the country and the battle-field he surveys. It is a typical picture, for one campaign broke the strength of Charles-Albert's forces, and the loss of the battle of Novara broke his heroic spirit. When night had fallen on that disastrous scene, the king, who, to use his own words, 'had not found death in the combat,' made a last sacrifice for the good of his country. He abdicated in favour of his son, and then started at once, nominally for Turin. The Austrians, encamped at Novara to intercept communications with Vercelli, had placed an outpost and two guns on the road. About midnight the captain of the post, hearing wheels in the distance, gave orders to load with grape. The gunners were standing motionless at their pieces when a light appeared. The advancing wheels were not those of Piedmontese artillery, but of a travelling carriage, in which a gentleman was found travelling rapidly in the direction of Turin. 'I am the Comte de Barge,' said the traveller, who soon, under the escort of some hussars, found himself in the presence of General Count Thurn. In the anteroom a sergeant of Bersaglieri was confronted with him, but the sergeant replied that he did not know the name in the army of any Comte de Barge. 'Observe him well,' said Count Thurn. The man approached two steps, fixed his eyes on the traveller, and grew pale. 'Ah, *sicuro*, I remember him now: that Comte de Barge fought close to the King.' The sergeant was dismissed, and the traveller invited to take a cup of coffee with the General at headquarters. Charles-Albert accepted the coffee, and remained for a short time engaged in conversation. In it he displayed so much ability and grace that after his departure Count Thurn expressed surprise that a guest so gifted should occupy only the insignificant rank of a colonel in the Piedmontese army. '*That, Sir, is the King,*' replied the Bersagliere. 'Gentlemen,' cried Count Thurn, 'Heaven protects Austria! Had the battery fired on the carriage, it would have been said that, equally implacable and perfidious, we had assassinated Charles-Albert by a dastardly stratagem.'[1] Meantime, four horses were whirling the broken-hearted King to Laghet. The Carmelites, who had not heard of the lost battle, had no reason to suspect anything unusual in the visit of a gentleman to their church. But this one knelt long before the altar, and sighed deeply. He next asked for a lodging in the monastery, and obtained it. The rest is best told in the pathetic words of this inscription:

QUÌ
LA MATTINA DEL 26 MARZO 1849
CARLO ALBERTO,
LASCIANDO I CAMPI FATALI DI NOVARA,
SOSTAVA IGNOTO ESULANTE,
QUÌ
PIAMENTE CONFESSO, E ALLA MENSA DI GESÙ
RINCONFORTAVA LO SPIRITO SOFFRENTE,
RINOVÒ IL SAGRIFIZIO DI AFFETTI E DOLORE,
QUÌ
PERDONÒ LE INGIURIE,
PIANSE LE COMMUNI SCIAGURE
E ABBANDONANDO COLLA PRESENZA L'ITALIA,
NE RACCOMMANDAVA I DESTINI
AL PATROCINIO DELLA
VERGINE MADRE.

He then stole quietly down the ravine to Nice, where a sad meeting took place between himself and its

[1] See the Campaign of Piedmont, translated by the late Lord Ellesmere from an article contributed to the *Revue des Deux-Mondes*, by an officer attached to the head-quarters of Charles-Albert. 1849.

governor. Dejected and weary, the self-made exile explained to his faithful servant that this must be a last farewell. Still under the name of Comte de Barge he crossed the Var, and stood on French soil. M. Tripèt-Skrypetzine, who was then in Cannes, tells me he can remember the popular emotion all along the coast when it became known that Charles-Albert had abdicated, had slept at Antibes, and had sent for its commandant, General de Parron, to tell him of his projected retreat to a spot near Oporto. A still stronger thrill of emotion awoke at midsummer when tidings came from Portugal that the king was dead; just four months after that Communion of *affetti e dolori* at Laghet.

II. THE CASTLE OF BEAUREGARD.

' Where shall we keep the holiday,
And duly greet the entering May ?
Too strait and low our cottage doors,
And all unmeet our carpet floors :
Nor spacious court, nor monarch's hall,
Suffice to hold the festival.

' Up and away ! where haughty woods
Front the liberated floods :
We will climb the broad-backed hills,
Hear the uproar of their joy :
We will mark the leaps and gleams
Of the new-delivered streams,
And the murmuring rivers of sap
Mount in the pipes of the trees :
While cheerful cries of crag and plain
Reply to the thunder of river and main.

. . . . . .

What god is this imperial heat,
Earth's prime secret, sculpture's seat ?

> Does it bear hidden in its heart
> Water-line patterns of all art,
> All figures, organs, hues, and graces?
> Is it Dædalus? is it Love?
> Or walks in mask Almighty Jove?
>
> . . . . .
>
> For thou, O Spring! canst renovate
> All that High God did first create.'—R. W. EMERSON.

This expedition took us not only off the beaten track but over the limits of the department of the Maritime Alps, since about twelve kilomètres beyond Grasse, and near the ruined castles of Tignet, we crossed the boundary line of the Siagne. Yet as the district once belonged, and does still in part belong to some of the great families of Maritime Provence, I will describe here how, for two long summer days, we explored a country which as yet has no railways, and no inns. In two years' time the projected line from Draguignan through this central valley will lay it open to visitors, but except in Montaroux I doubt if at this moment even the most hardened tourist could find a night's lodging. The *logis* at the Mule Noire is most forbidding. Montaroux, for a Provençal village, is unnaturally clean and tidy, but Calian is uninviting, Fayence, in spite of its good pastry, is not to be recommended, and Seillans is quite the most dirty and ramshackle village I ever beheld. We had therefore great luck in finding at our disposal the Castle of Beauregard, which the Comte de Barrême kindly hoped might act as a half-way house for us between Grasse and Draguignan. We left Grasse at 8 A.M., and drove under the wooded crags which carry the ruins and the hamlets of Cabris and St. Césaire. The situation of the latter is so commanding, that it was visible to us all that day, and even on the following day, till we had dropped into the basin of the Argens.

After passing the Siagne, we had to cross the hill which receives, and merits, the name of the Col noir. Dense thickets of ilex give it this sombre hue, and even on a May morning its woods are gloomy, but I wish to mention that here we found the rare *Orchis hircina*, of which the long, tangled beard, the grey-green hues, and the ancient, goat-like smell, are alike extraordinary. As far as Montaroux we had followed what our coachman called the '*strada maestra*,' but at that place we took a district-road to the right, and under a very hot sun, drove through Montaroux, and got our first view of the fine ruin of Calian on the opposite hill. Both these towns were formerly appanages of the family of Grasse, and both were ruined in the autumn of 1792. 'There was then,' says M. Taine in his exhaustive account of the conquest of France by the Jacobin party, 'no village but possessed forty *mauvais sujets* always ready to fill their own pockets. That was precisely the number that fell on the Château of Montaroux.' Those castles were all really the property of the State, but the greedy neighbours, finding public interference in the affairs of the *émigrés* too laggard, declared that castles placed on heights were obnoxious to the inhabitants, and, taking the law into their own hands, they seized everything they could find. Everything disappeared: stores, furniture, books, even the utensils of the cellars and kitchens.

The church of Calian has a low truncated spire,

and, like the castle, is built of a very dark red sandstone. The tones of these buildings, especially in this land of pearly limestones, and the way in which they group themselves against the background of blue hills, make a really charming picture. At this point you find yourself nearly opposite Fréjus; to the left lies the Tanneron range, of which the frowning forest was in the good old times haunted by a dragon; that dark central mass is La Roquebrune, while far away to the right, beyond the chains of Les Maures, and satisfying the sense of breadth in the picture by its vast air-spaces and its faintly tinted outline, rises the great, grey crest of Mont Gibal, that dominates Toulon.

Seen close at hand, how beautiful this Provençal country is in May. That hedge is of yellow jessamine, yet those forest glades where herds of ponies graze might be in Hampshire; those giant boles might be in Sherwood; but the tufts of grape hyacinths, the flocks of goats, the smoke from the huts of the charcoal-burners, and the wild fragrance of the thickets, wi h the subtlety, delicacy, and variety of the mountain outlines, all remind us we are in Provence. And there towers Mont Lachen, with snow on its grim head, and through that deep gorge the Siagnole cleaves its way to join the Siagne, and beyond it is the village of Mons. The Genoese *patois* of the Genoese founders still lingers there, and I hardly know a more lonely, or a more lovely spot than the mill of Mons, seen, as we saw it, by the light of the setting sun which lit up all the oaks of Beauregard, and drew out all the fragrance of its milk-white thorns.

It was now past six o'clock, and we were not sorry to have reached our destination, and, leaving the carriage, to alight under the spreading horse-chestnuts of the terrace. The Castle of Beauregard, built early in the seventeenth century, is of the orthodox Provençal pattern, that is to say, it is a square mass, with four flanking towers, with a staircase up which you might march a battalion of infantry, and a great, black, ruinous kitchen in which you might turn a coach and six horses. Its owner, the Comte de Barrême, seldom, if ever, resides here since the death of his first wife, but when he kindly put his castle at our disposal he desired his factotum, M. Isidor, to do the honours of a place which certainly deserves less neglect. Its situation is beautiful: with its meadows, its deep torrent, and its three thousand acres of oak forest, it might be made a charming country home. But, alas! the trees are fast being cut to make sleepers for the new railway; the Comte de Barrême now lives near Avignon, and it is long since any feet have paced, as ours did that evening, the Lady's Walk, that long, grassy terrace which, for a kilomètre or farther, runs below the forest-clad hill, in the direction of the mill of Mons.

We dined and slept soundly after a drive of twenty-eight kilomètres, and next day we rose early to inspect the castle, and the portrait of the Villeneuve who brought this estate, by marriage, into the family of its present owner. But we had a long day's work before ourselves and our horses, and we felt that we ought not to linger, the more so as the steep road by Bouripaille was pronounced by M. Isidor to be too rough for our carriage. It remained, therefore, for us to retrace part of the way to Calian, which I could not regret, as it gave us a second opportunity of seeing the forest; this time in all the freshness of a May morning. We also

CASTLE OF CALIAN.

found the village of Calian *en fête*; it was the day of the annual fair; garlands hung across the street, there was a man with a *troupe* of performing dogs, many heads looked out of windows, and from far and near carts came pouring into the place. I did not see any dazzling beauties, but some handsome swains, well fitted to do execution among the tender hearts of Calian. How could a tender heart resist a pair of dark eyes, and a voice singing :

> Madeloun, mets ton bonnet,
> Mets ton bonnet,
> Madeloun :
> Allons nous en courir la plaine,
> La plaine, et le vallon.
> Tous deux, nous tenant par les mains,
> Nous irons courir les chemins,
> Tu n'as pas besoin de velours,
> Sur les roses de ta jeunesse,
> Un ruban bleu dans tes cheveux,
> Et te voilà presque duchesse :
> Mets ton bonnet le plus coquet,
> Mets ton bonnet, Madeloun.

We next left Fayence,[1] which once yielded to Lesdiguières, and its ugly modern ruins that have nothing heroic about them, to the right, but near Seillans we got out to visit a beautiful, little, twelfth-century chapel. The ascent of a long *col* occupied many hours, but when we had surmounted it we found ourselves in the

---

[1] The name of 'faïence,' or 'fayence,' for glazed earthenware, is generally derived from the town of Faenza, near Bologna : but Ménage says, '*Il se fait aussi de la Fayence dans la petite ville de Fayence.*' The little town between Grasse and Draguignan existed before the sixth century, and there is a letter of St. Gregory (590) in which the Pope thanks Abbot Etienne of Lérins for some shallow basins and plates which the Abbot had sent him. Query—Were they made at Fayence, or were they early specimens of ware from the potteries of Vallauris ? The clay of Vallauris has been worked since the days of the Roman legions and their early occupation of Maritime Provence.

valley of the Argens, and nearly in sight of Bargemon, as we drove under the romantic crag of the Lover's Leap.

In the village of Bargemon we were able to post a letter for home, because a diligence which plies between Castellane and Toulon calls here daily for the bag. We left the horses to bait for a couple of hours, and walked down, past the church with its fine flamboyant doorway, to the ruins of the old castle, and then, after paying our respects to Moreri's monumental pillar and bust, to the château of the Marquis de Villeneuve-Bargemon. There we had the bad luck to miss the pleasant host and hostess, but the servants brought us tea on the terrace, and the great heat of the day was over by the time that we started again for Draguignan, where we were to dine and sleep at the Hôtel Bertin. The new railway works might be traced near the bridge of the Argens, forming a curious contrast with the silent woods, and with the many mediæval hill-chapels with which this country abounds. On the right bank of the Argens we found the splendid spikes of the *Orchis militaris*, of which the size and vivid hues are as beautiful in their way as was that exquisite *Orchis albida* which we picked in the Lady's Walk at Beauregard.

The Hôtel Bertin at Draguignan is well kept, and that town repays a visit, less because of the tower ascribed to Romée de Villeneuve, than because of its historical position on what was the old, royal road to Aix. This way came Jeanne de Naples, and the cruel Armagnacs; and this way came Charles V., while later still the Leaguers and the Carcistes made central and eastern Provence desolate during the wars of religion.

Though life is still fairly primitive in Draguignan, there is a public library in the town, and some movement in its wide streets. There is also good food in its markets, and quiet for those who seek it; and for us that day there was a train at 11 A.M., which took us to join the main line, near the chapel of Ste. Roseleyne-de-Villeneuve, and at the junction of Les Arcs.

III. A CELTO-LIGURIAN CAMP.

'Mais le système de fortification de ces places de sûreté était quelquefois formidable, et fait le plus grand honneur aux ingénieurs celtes ou gaulois qui en avaient conçu le plan et dirigé l'exécution. . . . L'oppidum constituait ainsi une véritable citadelle, et la limite de la résistance n'était marquée que par celle des approvisionnements. . . . Dans la précipitation de ces émigrations temporaires, la plus grande partie des vases étaient brisés : ainsi s'explique tout naturellement la quantité vraiment prodigieuse de débris de poteries de toute nature dont les murs de l'enceinte étaient criblés, et dont le sol des oppida était littéralement couvert.'—LENTHÉRIC.

THE primitive tribes who fortified these hills with their many camps had to fear enemies who came by way of the seaboard. Who the camp builders were might be read in the famous inscription which Cæsar Augustus placed on his Trophy at Turbia to immortalise his conquest over them all. The repetition of the same list on the triumphal arch at Susa further helps us to conjecture the distribution of these tribes, and to identify them correctly with certain districts. Grasse was anciently the capital of the Deceates. Was it then against these grey lines of stones that the soldiers of F. Flaccus threw themselves when, on his return from Marseilles (B.C. 120), he determined to subdue the

Deceates, and to add their patrimony to the list of his conquered districts?

About these Celto-Ligurian camps which dot the hillsides from the Loup to St. Vallier, I had read M. Sérailler's monograph, and many instructive pages, but I had also read the 'Antiquary' of Sir Walter Scott, and to tell the truth I was a little sceptical about the whole affair, and not a little afraid of finding a guide who was a Dousterswivel, and 'Aiken Drum's lang laidle,' instead of the primitive pottery of the camp builders. It was, therefore, with delight that I accepted M. Frédéric Pérolle's offer to be my guide to a genuine camp of the Celto-Ligures. We had spent the day at Gourdon, and after exploring its church and castle, and wandering over the zigzags which lead up from the valley of the Loup to the little plateau of Gourdon, we started on foot for the camp.

One needed goat's feet for such a walk. The spot lies a little behind Gourdon, and to reach it you must follow a very rough track, which takes you as far as a small tenth-century chapel, a little, early lighthouse of Christianity, standing stranded and solitary among the folds of the hills. To the right of it is the camp. There could be no doubt about it; it was a real camp, a genuine Celtic *oppidum*, with a double *enceinte* of walls built by no common builders, considering that these walls, ten feet in thickness, are formed of cyclopean and unmortised stones. Broken pottery lay about in quantities. It was of two kinds: the more primitive sort, which is coarse and ill baked, had served for hearthstones and ovens, but of the other vessels had been made. I got several fragments which were curved, and had neatly moulded rims, and I noticed that the fine, red clay of which they were made was mixed with mica. This material is not to be got in the neighbourhood, and it must, therefore, have been dug in the Esterels for the special purpose of making domestic utensils.

From the spot where we stood I could see another camp, crowning an eminence nearer the Châteauneuf road. It must have been easy for the two camps to keep up a system of signals both by night and by day, while they both served to protect a broad *corrie*, or valley, covered with the lines of primitive sheepfolds. Here then the natives defended themselves, and preserved under the cover of their forts the herds on which they depended for provisions. The country, which is barren in the extreme, has altered little in nineteen centuries. It is a grey world of stones, looking so solitary and so *uncanny* that it was difficult to believe we were within an hour of the factories of Grasse, and that below us lay the rich bays of Cannes and Antibes. Not even on the west coast of Sutherland have I ever seen a more desolate tract, and the ruined camp well deserves the name given to it by the peasants, '*Leis murassos*,' or the walls!

VILLA NEVADA.

IV. VILLA NEVADA.

'Mes compagnons étaient les morts, quelques oiseaux et le soleil qui se couchait.'—*Mémoires d'outretombe,* vol. ii. p. 277.

'Let us sit upon the ground
And tell sad stories of the deaths of kings.'—RICHARD II., act iii.

THIS history of a '*ville d'eaux*' is unavoidably something of a necrology, and if adversity has long had the credit of making strange bedfellows, what shall be said of the cemetery of a town like Nice, Cannes, or Mentone? These are not the 'graves of a household' of brethren, kinsfolk, and acquaintance, who, as they grew in beauty side by side, filled 'one home with glee,' but the fortuitous concurrence of many strangers, of the weary and the suffering, of wayfarers suddenly arrested here by the hand of death, and owning no tie in common but their accidental visit to this or that portion of the Mediterranean shore.

'Ordered to the south of France' is generally the first scene of the last act of the drama; and if sometimes, thanks to these fair skies, we see Death baulked of his conquest, yet too often we are obliged to note his gradual advance.

The late excellent Archbishop of Canterbury, Dr. Tait, came often to Cannes, but the last time that we were privileged to spend an hour with him at the Terres-Blanches of Pégomas, it was evident that even the sunshine of the Riviera could not long preserve him to the Church of England. Sir Fenwick Williams passed many winters at the Hôtel de Provence, and left charming souvenirs in Cannes of his courtesy and his kindness. Lord Russell lived at the Château Ste.-Anne the winter after the Franco-Prussian war; Mr. Gladstone visited at the Château Scott in 1883, and both statesmen regained strength in an extraordinary manner. But the results are not always so happy. I remember seeing Ernst, the violinist, in the last year of his life at Nice. His lean fingers still at moments caressed his instrument, but on his shoulder one felt that a still leaner hand was resting, and that the plaintive strains of his own *Elégie* would soon sound above his cold remains. Tamburini, on the contrary, though helpless in his wheel-chair, met disease and decay with a laugh; but perhaps the saddest invalid I ever knew was Count Harry Arnim. Lodged in a very dull villa behind the Château Leader in Cannes, half-blind, and wholly devoured by *ennui*, he really was that '*roi qui n'était pas amusable*,' whom family and friends failed to console. To his vaulting ambition and his ulcerated temper the skies and flowers of Cannes presented no soothing charms; he called the place the ' *centre de la nullité humaine*,' and he exchanged it next year for Nice, with, I fear, pretty much the same result, as far as his happiness was concerned.

A Frenchman once said of the three rival watering-places, that men went to Nice to amuse themselves, to Cannes to be married, and to Mentone to die. M. de Loménie certainly ended his life of study at Mentone, and so did the English historian, Mr. Green; but, in spite of the saying, I think that the majority of memories hangs about Cannes. The Villa Montfleuri was inhabited by Prince and Princess Christian of Schleswig-Holstein the winter after the Franco-Prussian war, and it was there that the English Princess endured through many anxious weeks, when the Prince of Wales lay sick well-nigh unto death at Sandringham. But the Villa had some years pre-

AT THE VILLA MONTFLEURI.

viously been occupied by Alexis de Tocqueville. He and his wife ended their lives in that house, within a few feet of each other's beds, and within a few days of each other's release. Prosper Mérimée died in Cannes, in spite of all the care and kindness of his two English friends. Louis Blanc and J. B. Dumas there ceased to trouble, or to learn; Victor Cousin died in a châlet near the level crossing; Bunsen dwelt at the Villa St. Pierre, while Auerbach died at the Pension Mauvarre. His public funeral, which took place in Germany, was followed by crowds of Germans, all too ready next year to participate in that disgraceful anti-Semite movement which made them forget that their favourite novelist had been a Jew. Alexander Munro, the sculptor, had some of his happiest inspirations at Cannes, and his empty studio at La Tourelle is still eloquent of the young artist whose genius budded beside a Highland firth, and faded on this southern sea-margin. Rachel's stay at the Villa Sardou (at Cannet) has been charmingly described by Matthew Arnold:

> Unto a lonely villa in a dell
> Above the fragrant warm Provençal shore,
> The dying Rachel in a chair they bore,
> Up the steep pine-plumed paths of the Esterelle,
>
> And laid her in a stately room, where fell
> The shadow of a marble Muse of yore—
> The rose-crown'd queen of legendary lore,
> Polymnia—full in her death—'T was well!
>
> The fret and misery of our northern towns,
> In this her life's last day, our poor, our pain,
> Our jangle of false wits, our climate's frowns,

> Do for this radiant Greek-soul'd artist cease:
> Sole object of her dying eyes remain
> The beauty and the glorious art of Greece.

I have asked myself, which of the cemeteries of Nice, Cannes, and Mentone is the most beautiful? The last commands the sea and the 'morning land,' as if its silent congregation were but waiting for the signal at which God shall make 'an awful rose of dawn,' and the dead shall arise. That of Nice had a sheltered and strangely sequestered calm; but I think the prize of beauty must be given to God's Acre in Cannes, where the graves lie between the unchanging hills and the ever-changing sea. I love its pine-plumed ravines, and, above all, its horizon, which is quite unique; and often, when, like Chateaubriand, I have seen before my eyes 'the graves and the setting sun,' I have raised them with thankfulness from the soulless body, just committed to its rest, to the half circle of those hills which seem in their strength to recall the promise of old: 'Like as the hills stand round about Jerusalem, so the Lord is about them that fear Him.'

In the public cemetery of Cannes there is both more order and more taste than is often found in France. The Allée des adieux is almost dignified, and the whole place at the Fête des morts looks like a garden, where without a doubt the most touching feature is the mound which covers the vast common grave of the victims of the great inundation of October 1882.

In the Protestant ground, Lord Brougham's granite cross looms, huge and grey, across the flower-beds. In fact, there are here some very beautiful monuments;

for example, the one erected by a mother who now lies between her two sons, and that placed by a girl over her betrothed, whom she had to lay under the sod on the day and at the hour which was to have been that of their wedding. Perhaps the finest is that tall, white plinth which serves to mark the resting place of the late Sir John MacNeill. Its white and serious dignity recalls that manly beauty, so little touched by age, which used to be one of the most welcome and most familiar sights in Cannes.

But the graveyards do not hold all the dead who die, and whose requiems have been said beside this fair-smiling shore. The Villa Oscar-Bermond at Nice, and its little memorial chapel, are still eloquent of the death of the Tzarévitch Nicholas-Alexandrovitch, which took place in Nice in April 1865.

The morning of his fatal seizure was as pearly and auspicious as any day in this land of sea and sun could well be. The air was balmy and light, the great Judas tree shook showers of blossoms on the bank, and the tall date-palm barely felt its crown of leaves stirred by the breeze when the heir of All the Russias fell stricken to the earth. Then began the despair! The messages to the Préfecture; to the Church, where prayer was to be made; to the roadstead, whence the frigates must go out to fetch the royal kinsfolk; to the station, whence telegrams, speeding across Europe, summoned a father, and a sweet young bride. The Tzarévitch lingered long enough to receive her kiss, and then, with the breath of the orange-flowers stealing through the closed *persiennes*, he died, laying down on that day his heritage, the eighth part of the globe.

The story of his death, of his widowed bride, of his lying in state among the flowers, and of the transport of his body to Villefranche, had an extraordinary fascination for the late Duke of Albany. His Royal Highness, while thanking me for the pleasure once derived from my little novel of 'Vèra,' told me that he had, while at Villa Nevada, borrowed a copy of the book that he might read once again the account of the Tzarévitch's death. His face, in speaking of that event, and of the many grave and tender incidents connected with it, showed the keenest sympathy. Ten days later I carried a basket of the Narcissus-of-the-Poets up the little garden-stair of the Villa Nevada, and placed it near the feet of our Queen's youngest son. He himself now lay cold and dead: with his hands crossed in that last supreme repose which is most welcome surely to the suffering and the sensitive. But for the sad and tear-stained faces of his attendants you might have said to yourself that this sudden sorrow was a dream. Not only was the little house, where the blameless idyll of the last five weeks had passed, unchanged, but the very scarlet clove-carnations that he loved glowed under his windows. Dusk and the darkness were gathering. Outside there were the pine-woods; long bars of cloud, ominous and dull, lay against the sunset, while from the slate-grey sea a thin veil of mist crept landwards over the far-stretching town. Inside there was the silence that may be felt, the white face under the hardly whiter flowers, the repose, and the purples of the dead—

> Take the last kiss—the last for ever:
> Yet render thanks amid the gloom.
> He, severed from his home and kindred,
> Is passing onward to the tomb:
> For earthly labours, earthly pleasures,
> And carnal joys *he* cares no more.
> Where are his kinsfolk and acquaintance?
> They stand upon another shore.
> Let us say, around him pressed,
> Grant him, Lord, eternal Rest.[1]

A few days later, all glistening in the sunlight, the funeral cortège wound down the hill from Villa Nevada to the station. The hearse, with its silver shields, had been originally built to convey Nicholas-Alexandrovitch to Villefranche harbour. It had then been followed by the Tzar and his sons on horseback. To-day an English prince was lying in it, the muffled drums beat, the cannon of Ste. Marguerite boomed across the waters, and the rose hedges seemed to open to let him pass. I saw the coffin lifted out. The heir of the English crown, and the amiable prince to whom the crown of France descends by inheritance, handed it over to the Mayor of Cannes. He drew aside the black curtains of the travelling hearse; there was a movement, and a heavy thud, and then rose-wreaths innumerable were piled above each other, and above the early dead.

All inanimate nature looked glad and glorious, but the eyes of men and women were dim with tears when

---

[1] *Stichera of the Last Kiss* (Dr. Neale's translation).

the last gun fired, and when, with a scream, the train moved out of the station bearing its burden of sorrow; the Queen's eldest son was taking his young brother to his last home, to his place among the tombs of the kings.

When Prince Leopold was seven years old he lived in Cannes, at the Château Leader. There he heard of the death of the Prince Consort. The grief of the child was then intense, but he was not very communicative. He only said, 'Let me go home! Take me home, please, to my mother.' On April 2, 1884, that wish was finally granted, and this shore of the southern sea will behold him no more for ever—

> Cha till, cha till, cha till Mac-Criemhainn,
> An cogadh mo'n sith cha till e tuilleadh![1]

V. NOTRE DAME DE GAROUBE.

'Thence we coasted within two leagues of Antibes, which is the utmost town in France.'—EVELYN'S *Memoirs*, vol. i. (1644).

THAT is the name of a tiny chapel on the farthest extremity of the Cap d'Antibes. Built among a wilderness of rocks and of myrtle thickets, this shrine of Our Lady, if not far set 'amid the melancholy main,' is at all events pushed out among the reefs of the roughest piece of sea to be met with for miles. It lies so close to the level of the waters that the light of its trembling

---

[1] For aye, for aye, for aye Maccrimmon,
In war or in peace will never return!

From the *Lament for Maccrimmon*, a Gaelic hero who in these words is said to have predicted his own fate.

lamp can only rarely have been noticed a true '*Stella maris*' by the boatmen of Antibes, and till lately this must have been a lonely spot. The Chapel has now many neighbours—first, the great Hôtel de Cap, then M. Wylie's palatial villa at Eilean-Roc, and the amazing vegetation of Closebrooks, to say nothing of an always increasing crop of houses built on speculation.

There is no part of Provence fairer than this promontory of Antibes. The great headland is as bold as any part of the coast of Assynt; the *pineta* (at the spot chosen for his villa by the late Duke of Albany when youth and hope were strongest) might be at Pisa; the rare Irises in M. Theuret's garden are a flower-show in themselves; the splendid holme oaks of the Villa Ennery are unique in their beauty; and the bit of shore under the terraces of Villa Agard is worthy of Baiæ. All these things are delightful, and have but one drawback, namely, their exposure to all the winds of heaven. The scenery is extraordinary at night, when the moon reigns queen of a hushed or heaving sea, and when from the woods comes the song of the nightingale, or the plaintive note of the little cue owl, which is as the very voice of solitude.

The port of Antibes is always full of pictures. There is the old town with its two tall *vigies*, its miniature fort, its chapel, and its cypresses, with the bastions of Guise, of Rosny, and of the Dauphin pushed out into the stony fields. It is from the Place d'Armes that the best view of the Alps is to be got, when the sky is unclouded, and cut only by the glaciers of the Gélas range, of the Pic de Mercantour, and of the Pic de

Prats. The coast stretches away towards Bordighera, all flushed with light; the delicate tints of the nearer mountains are set off by the white background of the snowy peaks, and by the dark blue of the sea. Every glacier from Lescherène to the Col de Tende seems to assert its cold beauty, the villages beyond the Var look like castles, and here, in the foreground, you pace under the boles of the olives, among the rose hedges, the picturesque wells, and all the happy, luxuriant growth of a Provençal spring.

The town of Antibes, the earliest Greek settlement in Maritime Provence, is a dull, sleepy, little place, where everything is on a miniature scale: the fort, the garrison, the mole, the esplanade, the old citadel, and the older circus, where an inscription tells us that a little Roman boy once 'danced, and pleased, and died.' The town used to suffer from an insufficient supply of water, but in 1785, an ancient acqueduct traced out and restored by the care of Colonel d'Aguillon brought into Antibes the rush of fresh water which now rejoices every householder and wayfarer alike. The work, which cost 72,000 livres, has prepared the future of Antibes as a health resort. As regards the city itself, it must be confessed that the streets are so narrow that to drive a pair of horses through them is a trial to the nerves; and, in truth, the bishopric and the governorship must have been on a small scale also. The crozier and Chapter were in the eighth century removed from Antibes to Grasse, because of the insecure position of this 'the utmost city in France;' but military governors Antibes did long possess, and often of the bravest.

MEISSONIER AT ANTIBES.

Aragi's history enumerates them—Lascaris, Vallette, Forbin, Bouthilier, and the rest; and he makes one realise how harassing to the Antibois in early days were the Moorish settlements of the Great-Fraxinet near St. Tropèz, and of the Little-Fraxinet near St. Jean.

As a fortress Antibes has had just two periods of importance. The first was during the wars of the League, after which Henri IV. commenced those fortifications which are still called 'of Rosny' and 'of the Dauphin,' and that Fort Carré which Vauban was to develop in a later reign. Its second epoch was during the early years of the Revolution. Constant military movements and the campaign on the frontiers of Piedmont then filled it with troops. It was within reach of Toulon, and also of Genoa. Buonaparte, who was a prisoner in the Fort just after the events of the 9th Thermidor, knew the place well, and once settled Madame Letitia near it in a small house. There were till recently persons still alive who remembered seeing her go and come between her house and a little stream where the linen was washed, at the period when Napoleon's friendships with Ricord and with Augustin Robespierre were more interesting than really useful to her ambitious son.

The sunlight of centuries has baked to a most brilliant hue the limestones of which Vauban built the square fort. In fact, artists are always charmed with Antibes. Meissonier's sketches of it are delightful, and, three years ago, M. Zuber's clever brush was employed on the long lines of sea and shore, on the mysteries of interlacing olive boughs, and on the poetic details of a truly Provençal landscape. There is a choice of roads, to say nothing of creeks and caves in which to spend an idle day, and among which to lose one's friends at a picnic. I remember once searching vainly for hours among these bays and headlands between Antibes and Notre Dame de Garoube, for the steam-launch of the *Firefly*. Several parties of people coming from different quarters continued to miss each other; and it was past 4 P.M. before all the 'lost sheep' of that picnic were safely gathered on the yacht's deck.

CHAPTER XXIII.

MENTONE.

'Les perdreaux sont nourris de thym, de marjolaine, et de tout ce qui fait le parfum de nos sachets : j'en dis autant de nos cailles grasses, et des tourterelles, toutes parfaites aussi. Pour les melons, les figues et les muscats, c'est une chose étrange. Mon cher cousin, quelle vie ! . . .

'Hélas ! nous avons cent fois plus froid ici qu'à Paris. Nous sommes exposés à tous les vents. C'est le vent du Midi, c'est la bise : c'est le diable ! Nous ne respirons que de la neige. Nos montagnes sont charmantes dans leur excès d'horreur. Je souhaite tous les jours un peintre pour bien représenter l'étendue de toutes ces épouvantables beautés.'—MDE. DE SÉVIGNÉ.

THE winters in Provence succeed each other, but assuredly do not resemble each other. The oldest inhabitant invariably offers this excuse for bad weather, that *never*, within his memory, was anything so untoward or so unpleasant seen before. But, alas ! every history, like every chronicle, enumerates years of dearth and hardship; tells of great storms and great floods, of failure of crops, and the recurrence of all the ills to which fields are heirs. From their pages I am obliged to conclude that the Provençal climate is, and was, and is likely to remain, one of contrasts and of extremes. The winter of 1865–6, for example, never knew a cold day till March 1. I had gone to church on Christmas Day in a white cloak, between hedges of roses; but when on March 1 the hills were white with snow, one's ideas about the seasons became confused. The winter of 1871–2 was one of floods, of a great display of *Aurora Borealis*, and of a water-spout. The winter of 1874-5 had only one great storm—on the morning of Easter Day. That of 1880-1 had over thirty days of unclouded sunshine; while in the spring of 1882, there were fifty-four days without a drop of rain. On the other hand, in the following October Cannes was flooded, walls fell down, people lost their lives as well as their property, and that was the occasion on which eight corpses were carried up the hill to be buried, at the public expense, in a common grave. The winter which followed that catastrophe was cold and inclement. Not only did snow fall on our heads on the afternoon of January 27, when Lady Wolverton assembled her friends for the first time after Mr. Gladstone's arrival at Château Scott, but a worse surprise was in store for us all. When the shutters were opened on a March morning, behold a world of snow! I happened to be staying in the country, and I shall never forget the sight of the pine woods, and of the hill sides inclosing the fairy valley of Pégomas, which might readily on that morning have been supposed to form a landscape in Sutherland! Lord Houghton, who was expected to meet us at luncheon, found difficulty with a pair of horses in making his way out to Terres-Blanches, and he has been convinced ever since that the climate of the Riviera is rigorous in the extreme. It is too true that when we returned to Cannes, we found the mimosa trees broken, and the palms bent with the weight of snow, to say nothing of the wreaths of half-melted ice (which lay for four days behind every wall), and of the destruction of a year's harvest on the olive and orange trees.

Bad weather is very wretched on the Riviera. The houses are not intended for it. Rain leaks in at half a dozen places at once, and the better your fires the more you suffer from the draughts, which, from door and window and skirting board, from cupboard and cranny, come forth to seek out the weak points of your frame. Invalids should begin by hanging up curtains everywhere, and put their faith rather in the *portières* which exclude cold air than in the fires which create heat. That heat will, in the first place, draw out a dozen draughts, and it will, in the second place, *draw up* the sewer gases from the roughly fitted drains of your villa. No invalid should sleep on the ground floor, or under the roof; in fact, all outside walls are dangerous for him, a saying he will not be disposed to contradict if he has once watched the building of a wall, and seen for himself how flimsy and far from airtight these modern houses are. Wooden floors being rare, he must resign himself to a carpet, and to having that carpet well lined with hay, else he will suffer from the cold of the brick floors, which really seems as if it would draw life away through the soles of the feet. I recommend loose, knitted socks drawn over the shoes, and a fur rug, and a footstool filled with hot water rather than the charcoal *chaufferette* which is used by the *bourgeoisie*. And let me say a word about violent exercise under a hot sun, and the chills following on it, and plead for the use of the *tisanes* which the English despise, but which are invaluable in restoring suspended warmth and checked perspiration. A pinch of lime-flowers, of dried violets, or of guimauve will furnish (in a pint of boiling water) a warm and soothing drink. Camomile tea will be found tonic, and the infusion of a fresh lemon diaphoretic; while orange-flower water is a reliable sedative. Two ounces of it in a wine-glass full of warm water (or beaten up with a raw egg into a *lait de poule*) is a drink to be used in the sleepless exhaustion of great mental distress. The graver cases of cerebral excitement, and the exciting effect of the climate of the Riviera on the nervous system, are too well known to those who, year after year, have to see many tragic examples of the injudicious use of this climate; but I doubt if they are sufficiently realised in England by people who imagine that the influences of sea and sunshine can only be beneficial to them. Nice is generally allowed to have a more exciting air than her neighbours, while that of Mentone is praised as being mild and unirritating. It would seem, therefore, to be counter-indicated in the cases of languor resulting from long and enfeebling illness, while, like its neighbours, it is invaluable in the *early* stages of pulmonary disease. Volumes have been written about all these health resorts to point out their merits, and tables of temperature are submitted to patients who must wonder, after perusing them, how it is they still contrive to catch such very bad colds. But the truth is that the actual situation of the house and room is of more importance than any meteorological table, and the question resolves itself into one of shelter, and above all of precaution. There are spots about Mentone into which the north and the east winds cannot penetrate, and where the reverberation of the sun's rays off the limestone rocks will raise the mercury to a

LA ROQUEBRUNE.

degree unknown either on the Promenade des Anglais or on the Route de Fréjus.

Mentone seems to me to be richest in these sunny nooks; in dry, *wady*-like ravines, where the lemon trees grow, and where a very high and a very fairly equable temperature can be secured. It also possesses variety. Those who find the East Bay airless can betake themselves to the western side, and catch the wind currents that ascend and descend from the valleys; they may also dwell on the shore, and hear the waves drawing the tinkling pebbles down the beach, or make life one long picnic under the pines of the Cap Martin. The situation of La Roquebrune [1] is tempting to those who like a higher level, and it is so beautiful that one regrets (in the train) the old posting road, and the dark-blue iris fringing its crumbling walls. The *flora* of Mentone, rich and varied as it is, consists mainly of the flowers that love the compact and Neocomian limestones. You get the pale Lavatera near the sea, and the Russian snowdrop, and purple stocks, but in the woods you can get delicate coronillas, and the Judas tree, and at an elevation of 3,000 feet, thickets of hepaticas, and clumps of primroses. I remember that of the latter we picked a basketful on the slopes of Mont Braus, and wore them proudly on the 19*th of April* at a most pleasant luncheon party at Mr. J. B. Andrews' villa at La Pigautié. He has some splendid orange trees, and that day the hedge of quinces was beautiful with pink, shell-like blossoms, while the great white arums in the porch were only

[1] I have to thank Signor Corelli for this pretty sketch. The original picture is in the possession of Her Majesty.

exceeded in their beauty by the beds of Ixia, which flowers in Mentone with a luxuriance I have never seen excelled.

But of the lemon trees that fill that garden, and every garden, and every dell and ravine near Mentone, what shall I say? Who can praise enough what Elisée Réclus justly terms '*le divin fruit?*' With what a careless grace are the long, pendulous sprays flung hither and thither; how star-like are the white flowers, with their faint purple pencillings; how delicate, how fragrant, varying, is the scent of the fruit! And which kind shall I praise the most? The *verdani*, chosen for the trade with America; or the *petit cédrat*, with its waxy face; or the lemon called 'of Nice,' which, to my thinking, combines every possible merit? It is the best to squeeze over your oysters, the best for making lemonade, and perhaps the best to cut in slices for the tea table, though for this last purpose the *aspernum* (the lemon without pips) runs it hard. All sorts of forms may be noticed among lemons. There is a pear-shaped kind which grows on a pretty, dark-leaved tree; there is the lemon, forked and horned like a radish, called *merveilleux*, and the lemon with a ring, and eke with two rings, the *bimamelatum*. Some notion of the variety that exists may be gained from the fact that a hundred and thirty-seven varieties of the family *citrus* are enumerated in Risso's catalogue. I was charmed, however, to hear from Professor Dyer that there is no truth in the old, vulgar error which maintained that the '*blood orange*' is a cross between an orange and a pomegranate. No such cross fertilisation ever takes place, and the blood orange is simply a freak of nature, a *scherzo* as the Italian peasants would say. But to return to the lemons. The whole wealth of Mentone lies in this crop, and the crop depends on the mercury not falling below 27° Fahrenheit. On a night that threatens frost, the Mentonese proprietor will sit up with his lemon trees, light large fires, and endeavour in every way to protect them! And not for nothing are these golden drops produced. Lemon trees have to be tended and manured, woollen rags being the manure which they most affect; and the fruit has to be first carefully picked, and then carried down to the town, to the large wholesale warehouses. One such I visited. It belonged to M. Borano, and was near the railway station. I saw 20,000 lemons on the floor, and was told that there were 14,000 in cases in vans at the door. The price obtained varies from fifteen francs per thousand, to sixty francs the thousand: a margin that gives room for hopes and fears, and for a little gentle speculation among the brokers. But Mentone has no other trade. Since its annexation to France it has no longer the mild, political excitement of giving or withdrawing allegiance to the princes of Monaco. Being inclosed by rocks and seas it can never increase to any such prodigious extent as Cannes now threatens to do; and for many years to come I fancy that invalids may lead a fairly rural life among the easy-going Mentonese. They are still rather a primitive people, and the old town has, like the big church, a distinctly Italian type. Yet the dialect is not an Italian one. Mr. J. B. Andrews, who has mastered its idioms, has even prepared a grammar of it, and he has managed to preserve some of the national songs and local legends of the place. Here is a song, of which he has furnished me with both the words and the music, while Madame Nicholas Viale vouches for its being a genuine peasant's song.

OU ROMANI FIORI.
(Ronde mentonnaise.)

These songs, not unnaturally, praise the flowers and fruits of a happy region which has no other wealth; but, like the costumes of the peasantry, old times and their old themes are fast going out of fashion. Look at that wrinkled *maigrana* (grandmother) as she totters home from the baker's; the capeline shakes on her white head, and she wears the bodice and petticoat which her children and grandchildren despise. The little ones who leap around her and her loaf shout '*Lou paing! lou paing!*' (*pain*). They are pretty, for the Mentonese are a comely race, with more of beauty than the mongrel populations of Nice and Cannes. Close behind her comes the honey-pedlar: a most picturesque figure! Her petticoat is pale green, her apron is checked blue and white, but she has a black handkerchief, and a great, red jar of honey is poised upon her jetty curls. She carries her glittering scales, and, like the lemon-carriers and the washerwomen, she walks quickly, and is very erect. At the foot of the steps there meet her two barelegged fisher lads who sell sardines, the whole street echoing with their long-drawn cry of '*Bella sardi—ina!*' They are followed by a Venetian knifegrinder, who is called *Zanni*, and wears a fur cap, and by the man who mends saucepans. I don't think he has many customers, yet his cry of '*Casserô—ole!*' is as lugubrious as if broken hearts were his theme, till he gets jostled aside by the vendor of a cake in which the *frétin* is baked, and which is about as big as a cart-wheel. People buy slices of it; and then a girl sells roses and pinks to some English ladies in their ulsters, and we will follow them, for they are going in the direction of the long, sea wall of the Quai Napoleon, and of M. Henfrey's villa. Lord Hatherton having presented to us the owner of that pretty châlet, we were very kindly shown over it, and one morning Mr. Henfrey also took us out to the olive-ground where the Queen used to sit and write letters in the dappled shade. All her subjects must be grateful to Mentone's bay, which gave her that pleasant holiday. One liked to look at the roses and creepers, at the lemons, and at the arums in the grass, and to feel how much she must have enjoyed them, while by her very appreciation of them all she managed to give great pleasure in Mentone. The only person Her Majesty displeased there was a little, barefoot girl. Little Louisine had come down from the hills to see the Queen of England, and she waited till she attained her object. She beheld the Island Queen, but, oh!—vanity of human wishes!—that august and gracious Lady wore—a black bonnet! Ought she not to have had on a crown at least two storeys high, like the one which belongs to Notre Dame de Laghet? But not a bit of crown did she wear! Only she had blue, *very* blue eyes, and there was a little, just a little comfort in that for Louisine!

The beautiful valleys that, like the sticks of a fan, converge upon Mentone, deliver it from the reproach of being strung upon the dusty highway which you must perforce follow, to the right hand or to the left. Those high roads are, of course, the main features of the place, either across that wonderful torrent of St. Louis into Italy, or, in the contrary direction, when tourists find plenty of jingling pony-carriages to take them to Monte Carlo, or up to Turbia. Still I hope that when the municipality of Mentone grows very rich, it will cause a number of roads to be made; for example, to beautiful Gorbio, up to the old palace of the Lascaris, for it is provoking when the coachman gravely tells you '*Il n'y a plus de route*,' and your acquaintance with any district comes to an abrupt close. Roads for lame and asthmatic patients need not interfere with the feats of more sturdy pedestrians, who can not only explore the hermitage of Gourg-del-Ora, but ascend the countless goat and mule paths with which the country abounds. There will always be happy valleys for them to traverse on foot, and wild mountain defiles for the French troops. We met a company of infantry starting the other day for St. Agnese, a spot at least 3,000 feet above the sea level, where they and their mules were to train for a mountain campaign.

A very good road runs due north from Mentone to Sospello, and thence to Tende, and the Italian frontier. We followed it one day, and greatly enjoyed the expedition. The drive to and from Sospello (by Castillion) requires four and a half hours for the ascent from Mentone, and three for the return journey. You leave

Mentone by the Borrigo valley, and pass on the left, among the lemon groves, the fatal mill where Honoré III. of Monaco ground such bad meal for his subjects, and compelled them to eat it. Monte has to be passed through, and then you leave Castelleraz on the right, before reaching the really Alpine scenery of the Gourg-del-Ora. After a halt there, you begin to ascend by zigzags through the pine woods to the water-shed at Castillion, a strange, Moorish-looking eyrie of a town, which, inclosed inside a wall, is perched on a crag between the two heads of Mont Braus.

From this spot, which used to be one of considerable military importance, you can gain a bird's-eye view of the mountains. In front of you is the valley in which Sospello stands, with roads leading to Nice and to Italy. Behind you is the long valley you have just climbed from Mentone and the sea, while to right and to left the mountains stand in double and triple ranges.

From Castillion we pushed on to Sospello, a town which has vestiges of its old importance, and which, till recently, had a fairly pleasant and fairly cultivated little society of its own. The streets are dark, narrow, and very unsavoury, and here, as in Grasse, you can see how they were capable of being overawed or defended by the tower-like houses of the more powerful inhabitants. A carved stone over a doorway still secures for one house the name of the 'House of the Consuls.' On another the Lamb and Banner of the Templars is displayed; there are the ruins of their stately Commanderie, and of an ancient hostel with great, arcaded stables, such as you see in the background of an Italian picture of the Nativity. The modern inn which is on the south side of the bridge, is quite tolerable, and a diligence plies from it (in six hours) to Nice, by Ventabren and Escarène. Anyone wishing to explore the districts of La Brigue and Tende might sleep here; but the midsummer heats must be intense in this place, which receives all the sunshine, and is sheltered from every wind. Quite the most interesting thing in Sospello is the tower of the church. It is all of a dark, dressed stone, and dates from a very remote period. It must, in fact, have sounded its bells for more than eight centuries, and have risen black above the terrible fires once lit under its shadow, when so many Albigeois were burnt alive in the public square.

CORSICA, SEEN FROM MENTONE.

INDEX.

AGA

AGAY, 9, 25, 27
Aix, 93, 114, 226, 244
Albany, *His Royal Highness the Duke of*, 299, 357
— *His Royal Highness the Duke of York, and of*, 301
Albigeois, 206, 257, 281, 379
Amboise, *conspiracy of*, 109
Andrews, *Mr. J. B.*, 36, 371, 373
Antibes, 20, 21, 22, 23, 101, 108, 114, 181, 187, 190, 191, 193, 326, 364, 366
Antipolis, 7
Argens, *the*, 247, 349
Argentière, *the*, 19
Arluc (*ara lucis*), 32
Auribeau, sur Siagne, 5, 275
Avedic, 132
Aversa, 241
Avignon, 243, 244, 247
— *plague of*, 245

BALBI, 197
Bandol, 275
Bar, Grasse, 89
— *le*, 86, 89
Bargemon, *castle of*, 279, 281, 349
— *church of*, 349
Barras, 89
Baux, *les*, 70, 268, 297
Beaulieu, 18, 193
Beauregard, *castle of*, 279, 342, 346, 347
— *forest of*, 345, 347
Beuil, 196, 197, 295
Biot, 20, 84, 108, 224
Blacas, 277
Blood oranges, 309

CLA

Borrigo, *valley of the*, 375
Bouillède, *la*, 19
Boulouris, 27
Brague, *the*, 19, 21, 23
Brancolar, 324
Brigue, *la*, 17, 41, 48
Briguegasques, 41
Brougham, *Lord*, 4, 323

CABRIS, 89, 95, 96, 342
Cabris, *Marquise de Grasse*, 91-96
Cagnes, 10, 190, 204, 294
Cagnette, the, 19, 204
Calian, 190, 344, 347
Cambronne, *General*, 327, 330, 332
Cannes, 2, 4, 5, 6, 25, 28, 29, 30, 34, 41, 44, 53, 84, 122, 129, 143, 146, 165, 167, 175, 176, 187, 191, 207, 274, 317, 325, 326, 331
Cannet, 40, 84, 122, 165
Cap Garoube, 32, 174, 362-366
Cap Roux, 28, 145
Carnival, *of Nice*, 192
Carnoules, 2, 210
Castellane, 89
— *family of*, 270, 272
Castelleraz, 375
Castillion, 375
Château de Barlas, 193
— Leader, 324, 359
— de St. Michel, 324
— Scott, 353, 365
— de Thorenc, 324
Châteauneuf, 350
Cheiron, *the*, 18
Cimièz, 130, 179, 183, 184
Citrus, *varieties of*, 369
Clausonne, 32, 181, 242, 255

Clus, *de St. Auban*, 87
Clement V., 258
Clement VI., 243, 245
Clement VII., 246
Col de la Crous, *the*, 195
Col di Fremamorte, 199
Colle, *la*, 204
Corelli, Signor, 368
Coursegoules, 102, 229
Cypières, 272

DRAGON, *of the Tanneron*, 347
Draguignan, 76, 247, 342, 347, 348
Drouot, *General*, 322, 333
Durazzo, *Charles of*, 198, 247

EGITNA, 317
— Mons, 317
Enchastraye, 198, 199
Escarène, 376
Esteron, *the*, 46, 196
Esterels, *the*, 8, 9, 15, 25, 26, 27, 187, 230
Estrella, *fairy*, 9, 10
Eza, 18, 47, 60, 193

FARANDOULO, *the*, 33
Fayence, 278, 343, 348
Floods, 245-365
Fort Carré, *the*, 362
Foux, *the*, 19
Fragonard, 88, 188
Fraxinet, *the Garde*, 292, 362
Fréjus, 1, 5, 7, 143, 182
— and-Toulon, *bishops of*, 173
Friuli, *channel of*, 146

GARDANE, 28
Gattières, 207
Gaude, *la*, 67, 206, 207, 208
Gazan, *General*, 333
Gilette, 199
Godeau, *Monseigneur Antoine*, 116, 117, 118
Golfe-Jouan, 25, 204, 326
Gorbio, 272, 374
Gourdon, 86-89, 275
Gourg-del-Ora, 374
Grasse, 2, 62, 82, 83, 86, 88, 89, 90, 93, 95, 97, 99
— *Counts of*, 310, 315
— *Viguerie of*, 19
Grenoble, 327, 328, 336
Grimaud, *bay of*, 4, 25, 292

Grimoald, *Gébelin, de* 292
Grimoald, *death of Gébelin de*, 293
Guébis, *valley of the*, 197
Guillaumes, 197

HENFREY, *châlet of Mr.*, 376
Henri IV., 113, 115, 320, 365
Honoratus, 144-157
Hospitallers, *the Knights*, 56, 108, 256, 264

INNOCENT X., 273
Iron Mask, *the Man in the*, 122
Isnard, *Maximin*, 88, 95, 97, 98, 99, 100
Ixias, 372

JAMES I., *of Aragon*, 277
Jasmin, 30, 345
Jeanne, *Queen*, 8, 9, 27, 186, 197, 236, 250
Jonquils, 83
Jordany, *Monseigneur*, 174, 177

KARR, *Alphonse*, 7, 80

LAGHET, 337, 341
Lascaris, 89, 110, 112, 186, 229, 271, 273, 274
Laval, *plain of*, 5
Lemons, *trade in*, 370
Leprosy, 47
Lérins, *the*, 25, 143, 150, 151, 155, 158-177, 182, 186, 188, 256, 269, 311
— *règles de*, 149
Lesdiguières, 114
Lombards, *of Gourdon*, 89
Louis, *of Tarento*, 241, 244
Loup, *the river*, 19, 86, 223, 224, 227, 252
Lubiane, *the*, 19, 204

MAGNAN, *the*, 19
Malvans, *the*, 19, 204, 209
Mantis, *the praying*, 6, 7
Marcaret, 145, 148
Marchiel, *M. de*, 137-141
Marchiely, *de*, 130
Maritime Alps, *the*, 15, 17, 26, 68
Marseilles, 24, 179, 180, 239
Massena, 121, 188, 190, 191, 200, 201, 323
Massier, *M. Clément*, 43

Matignon, *family of*, 298
Maure, *la*, 32
Maures, *les*, 292, 295, 347
Meissonier, 365
Mentone, 4, 5, 294, 364, 367, 368, 369, 374, 375
Mentonese, *dialect of the*, 36, 37, 373, 374
Merimée, *Prosper*, 4, 214, 356
Mesgrigny, *Monseigneur*, 87, 234
— *M.*, 237
Métayage, 75, 78
Miollis, *General*, 334, 335
— *Monseigneur*, 335
Mirabeau, 54, 59, 91, 93, 95, 97, 120, 188, 190
— *castle of*, 96
— *hôtel*, 88, 90
Mistral, 15
Monaco, 289-300
Mons, 37, 87, 344
Mont Agel, 179
— Braus, 375, 368
— Chevalier, 317
— Gélas, 18, 199
— St. Cassien, 322
— Vinaigre, 28
Monte, 375
Monte-Carlo, 2, 7, 193, 289, 290, 291, 294
Montolivo, *Abbé*, 36, 193
Moors, *the*, 14, 32, 33, 56, 161, 163, 184, 187, 226, 292, 293
Moresque dance, 33
Mouans, 275
Mougins, 87
Mourachone, 19, 67
Murat, *Joachim*, 191, 322

Napoleon, 4, 5, 173, 188, 189, 190, 191, 283, 286, 326, 327, 333, 336
— *quai*, 376
Napoule, 5, 273, 274
— Montgrands of, 278
Narcissus-of-the-poets, 224, 360
Nice, 1, 178, 181, 183, 185, 186, 187, 188, 190, 191, 193, 197, 201, 203, 231, 232, 242, 255, 272, 273, 274, 334
— *county of*, 195, 202
— *port of*, 183
— *treaty of*, 233
Notre Dame d'Avignonnet, 33

Notre Dame de Bon Voyage, 321
— de Garoube, 360, 363
— de Laghet, 337, 376
Olive, *culture of*, 60, 61
— *failure of*, 43
Orange flower, 84
— — *water*, 370

Paillon, 19
Peasant proprietor, 70, 72, 75
Peerages, *of Provence*, 269, 270
Pégomas, 24, 67, 86
Péone, 197
Pérolle, M., 86, 255, 333, 350
Péronne, *treaty of*, 297
Pigautè, *la*, 368
Piol, *the*, 272
Pisani, *bishop*, 120
Plague, *the*, 245, 320
Porphyry, 27
Porto-Ferrajo, 326, 327
Promenade des Anglais, 192, 363
Provence, 13, 14, 15, 16, 17, 24, 27, 32, 33, 35, 41, 44, 55, 89, 107, 110, 115, 119, 210, 211, 229, 241, 247, 250, 253, 275, 281
Provence, *Auberge de*, 273
— Maritime, 13, 111, 243, 251, 254, 271, 274
Puget-Théniers, 42, 196, 197, 255, 263

Quelin, Monseigneur, 262

Réclus, *handbook of Elisée*, 4, 369
Renaissance, *in Provence*, 109, 250
René, *King*, 35, 270
Reyran, *coal mines of*, 27
Riou, 19, 34
Rochetaillée, *la*, 87
Roquebrune, 17, 289, 368
Roubion, 276
Roya, 18, 19, 81

St. Agnese, 374
St. André, 192
St. Anne, *chapel of*, 321
St. Auban, *clus de*, 27
St. Bassus, 82
St. Cassien, Mont, 322
St. Catherine, *of Siena*, 246
St. Césaire, 87, 333

SAI

St. Claude du Cannet, 321, 322
St. Dalmas, 198
St. Etienne, 193
St. Ferréol, *isle of*, 146
St. Honorat, 143
St. Jeannet du Var, 206, 207
St. Lambert, 101, 104, 115
St. Laurent du Var, 205
St. Louis, *bridge of*, 375
— *of France*, 220, 258, 259
St. Loup, 154
Saint-Mars, 123, 141
St. Martin de Lantosque, 199, 201, 202
St.-Martin-lès-Vence, 251, 254
St. Patrick, 155
St.-Paul-du-Var, 25, 203, 221, 269
St. Pons, 132
St. Porcaire, 162, 163
St. Raphael, 7, 79
St. Roseleyne de Villeneuve, 280
St. Tropèz, 3, 301
St. Trophinne, 103
St. Vallier, 87, 239
St. Véran, 101, 103, 104
St. Vincent of the Lérins, 151
Sardou, M., 328, 330
— *villa*, 357
Sault, *Comte de*, 113, 244
Saut du Loup, 18
Séranon, 334
Sévigné, *Mde. de*, 229, 266, 300, 364
Siagne, 10, 19, 26
Snowstorms, 364, 365
Société Foncière Lyonnaise, 1, 80, 320
Sospello, 5, 190, 374, 375
Suffren, *Admiral*, 301, 303, 310
Surian, *Bishop*, 119

TEMPLARS, 56, 186, 207, 240, 251, 264
Tende, 17, 272
— *Beatrice de*, 272
Théoule, 28, 29
Thorenc, 87
Tinée, 34, 198, 199
Tisanes, *use of*, 366
Toulon, 3
Tradelière, *the*, 146
Trayas, 27
Troubadours, 38, 249

ZUB

Turbia, 34, 337, 338
Tzarèvitch, 359

URBAN VI., 246, 247
Urban VIII., 272, 273
Utelle, 199, 255

VALESCURE, 8
Vallauris, 27, 164, 172, 242, 255
Var, *the*, 17, 24, 181, 196, 207, 342
Vauban, 87, 122, 188, 202, 213, 218, 234
Venantius, 143, 145
Vence, 34, 47, 84, 92, 101, 109, 121, 203, 231, 252, 254, 257, 263, 278, 282
Ventabren, 376
Ventimiglia, 17, 24, 185
Vésubie, 192, 197, 199
Via Aurelia, 5, 29, 34
— Domitia, 181
— Julia, 34, 338
Villa Derweis, 325
— Dognin, 324
— Haussmann, 325
— Luynes, 325
— Malvilan, 87
— Massengy, 276
— Montfleuri, 320, 324, 353, 354
— Nevada, 351
— St. Pierre, 354
— Sardou, 355
— la Tourelle, 355
— Vallombrosa, 324
— Victoria, 324
Village, the deserted, 193
Villars, 196
Villefranche, 25, 26, 187, 193
Villeneuve, *family of*, 112, 113, 120, 276–287
— Arnauld *de*, 257, 258
Villeneuve-Loubet, 222, 235
Vitrolles, *M. de*, 336

WATERSPOUT, 365
Water supply, *of Antibes*, 365
— — *of Cannes*, 323
— — *of Nice*, 191
Woolfield, *Mr. W. R.*, 323

YORK, death of the Duke of, 300

ZUBER, sketches by M., 36

www.ingramcontent.com/pod-product-compliance
Lightning Source LLC
Chambersburg PA
CBHW071858230426
43671CB00010B/1387